L

$pent

Your Money Mindset Is the Key To Your Financial Freedom

Stephanie Holmes-Winton

[handwritten inscription]

Copyright © 2011 Stephanie Holmes-Winton
Cover Design Copyright© 2011 Adam Murray
Edited by Sarah Facey/Cynthia McMurray

Printed and bound in Canada at Friesens

Library and Archives Canada Cataloguing in Publication

Holmes-Winton, Stephanie
    $pent : your money-mindset is the key to your financial freedom / Stephanie Holmes-Winton.

ISBN 978-1-927003-04-6

    1. Finance, Personal. 2. Budgets, Personal.
  I. Title. II. Title: Spent.

HG179.H65 2011   332.024   C2011-904405-6

First printing 2011
Second printing 2012

10   9   8   7   6   5   4   3   2

Published in 2011 by Bryler Publications Inc.
Box 1035,
Chester, NS
B0J 1J0   Visit our website at www.brylerpublications.com

Acknowledgements

For every mistake, every misstep and everything that has led me to this moment, I am grateful— whether I liked it or not!

The creation of this book has been a journey and like any journey, I encountered many wonderful people along the way—so many that it would be impossible for me to mention them all here. So, if you were kind enough to comment on my work at one time, or you taught me all the 'ins and outs' of mutual funds over a cup of coffee, or perhaps even taught me what not to do—thank you!

To my cheerleading team at *The Group*, you guys have helped me push every boundary I have; and even those I didn't know I had. I am so glad I've made my Tuesday mornings about you for almost five years now. And in particular, my fellow Money Maven, good friend and sage advisor, Wendy Brookhouse, thank you for sharing your "shiny thing" idea; it has made a wonderful addition to this book. Thank you for allowing me to share it with others.

To every advisor who has taken the initiative to work with clients on both sides of the balance sheet, I promise it's worth it. To everyone who has purchased this book, thank you!

And last but certainly not least, to Cynthia and her team at Bryler Publications. I'm so glad I'm not in this book alone. Your feedback, guidance and experience has been of exponential value to me.

This book is dedicated to the two most important
men in my life; my husband Ric,
and my son, Brandon.

Their patience, understanding and support
are the only reason I can stretch to meet
my full potential and do crazy things,
like write two books
in two years!

I love you both very much.

Table of Contents

Introduction

"Every adversity, every failure, every heartache carries with it the seed of an equal or greater benefit."
~ Napoleon Hill

This certainly isn't the first book written about money and as sure as I draw breath, it won't be the last. My goal was to take a different approach to a book on personal finance. I've picked up so many books over my time in the financial services industry, each of them promising that all you need is to read that book, follow the instructions, and all will be right with the world. I won't make you that promise.

I will say, however, that this book is a great guide, a wonderful starting point and a great resource to refer back to so you can keep on track. This book will not replace the financial professionals in your life, nor do I intend it to. In these pages you will find practical ideas that can compliment your financial plan (or motivate you to get one) and help you maximize your financial behaviour so you can get the life you want from the money you already have.

People often ask me where my insights on money and its use come from. They often assume I must have a degree in finance, or perhaps even psychology. At the risk of bursting my own bubble, I have neither. The next assumption is that I must at least have a CFP (Certified Financial Planner, the most common financial designation), which I don't.

I have good reason for my aversion to actually completing my CFP. I have taken quite a few of the CFP courses and passed with flying colours. There is nothing wrong with the course, and I believe it is an important designation. Even though I don't think there is anything wrong with the CFP I was working on (the material I had access to was pre-2011), there was something missing—debt and cashflow management. These topics were included in the text to some degree, and yes, a CFP does learn the math behind typical debt products but there was no useful information that could lead me to believe that someone with a CFP was capable of building a financial plan that included paying down debt at maximum efficiency. Especially not with a clear knowledge of today's debt products and client-spending recommendations. This is not to say that an individual with a CFP hasn't learned this information on their own, but it is to say that one cannot draw the conclusion that a person with the letters C F P behind their name, is somehow stamped with a secure knowledge of debt and cashflow management. I am known by my clients, colleagues and the financial industry to have expertise in debt and cashflow management. Until the CFP aligns with that skill set, or there is a separate certification I can acquire to set apart this very important and valid knowledge, I feel it is misleading to the public to flash CFP credits. When, and if that day comes, I will pursue my CFP with the same passion and dedication I had to write this book.

If you asked me a decade ago if my upbringing came with a vast financial education, I would have replied with a resounding "NO". I grew up the oldest of two daughters, my mother a teacher and my father a draftsman, in a middle-class neighbourhood in Dartmouth, Nova Scotia (across the harbour from Halifax). I don't remember wanting for anything in my early years. I do remember noticing my father always had the latest gadget, including but not limited to, a gigantic satellite dish atop our house. We had a decent home on a lovely and safe street where it was even safe to play in the woods. We had bicycles, a great swing set and a basement playroom full of toys. Life was just fine.

I do remember the occasional scrap between my parents, usually over large purchases like my Dad's blue Camaro back in the early 80's or when the very first computer came home. Like many parents, mine took the traditionally accepted approach to teaching us about money. They gave us an allowance for which we needed to complete chores to ensure we'd receive our funds. They made us save some of our allowance along with any gifts of money received by relatives. These were lessons most parents then, and now, would agree are valid. Basically, from my viewpoint as a child, everything seemed pretty normal and pretty darn good. I didn't get everything I wanted, but I felt safe and secure and I didn't worry.

Major Crisis #1

Fast forward to my teen years. By age 13, my parent's marriage was off the rails and the financial rock I thought we must have been living on began to show massive cracks. After some serious turmoil, my mother left my father in the middle of the night with my little sister and me in tow. It was one of the scariest nights I can remember. In that same night, I was secretly struck by the most overwhelming sense of relief; I told no one. This secret came from a place of being ashamed to feel free at the thought of a broken but peaceful home. It seemed that everyone expected me to be traumatized by the end of a volatile period in my young life, but I wasn't. I wasn't sad my parents were divorcing; I was just relieved the palpable sadness was over. Before it got better, it got just a little bit worse. With nowhere to go, we stayed one night—thankfully, only one night—in a shelter for women and children. My mother, sister and I huddled up on three cots in the corner of a small room. I don't think any of us slept much that night. It's the first time I can remember being afraid of what was to come next; afraid and relieved, it was a weird construct of feelings. Up to that night, my biggest fear was getting a bad mark on a math test—that was a pretty huge fear in my world, actually. I can't remember much else from our very brief time in that place except the sounds at night. The noise was soul shattering. On the rare occasion that I let my mind wander back, I can still hear it. It was sad and hollow, like many people weeping in unison behind closed doors. The thought of it still sends a cold shiver up my spine. I am thankful that shelters like that one exist, but I wouldn't wish the experience of having to stay at one on my worst enemy.

The next day, we went to stay with family friends for a few weeks, even spending Christmas with them. Eventually, my mother was able to get together enough money to put a deposit down on a rental house. For the first time since we left in the night, we were alone.

Lesson #1

When we moved into our new abode, my mother found out there was a cost to having never had a power bill in her own name (the old bill had been in both of my parent's names but never just hers). In order to get an account with our power company in Nova Scotia at the time, you needed to make a fairly large deposit; a deposit my mother simply didn't have. I remember my mother being so sad, and so worried about what to do when the bill with the deposit came in. As if by some cosmic miracle, just in the nick of time, her very first child tax credit cheque came in (she'd never qualified before because of the level of income in her previous two-income household). It was just enough.

This taught me a few things. I learned it was okay to be scared and that I could handle seeing my Mum scared. We weren't made of porcelain and we didn't break. I also learned that doing the best thing for the long-term (I totally believe then and now that her decision to leave was the right one), can often be terrifying, but if you know you've made the right choice, you just have to hang on through the anxiety and things will work out.

My mother left the marriage with nothing but debt. After a few years managing on her own, she was able to put together enough of a down payment to buy a small semi-detached home where she still resides today. It was such an accomplishment for her to have purchased her own home and I was so proud of her, I was so proud of us.

Gift #1

During the process of purchasing her first home on her own, my mother let me in on a lot of the details. I knew how much the house cost. I knew how much the monthly payment was versus the rent she had been paying. I learned about property tax and maintenance. I found out how much money my mother made. I don't think she intended to tell me that but it was eye-opening. At age 15, many parents may feel that sharing such delicate financial details with children can be too much of a burden, but I disagree. She showed me both sides of the balance sheet. She displayed effective financial decisions while showing me past consequences of not-so-effective decisions. My mother gave me the greatest gift; the gift of perspective. You see, there are far too many brilliant students who graduate from amazing programs with a wonderful education yet they don't have a clue what a reasonable interest rate is, or what kind of life a certain amount of income can purchase them. It's like wrapping a child in bubble wrap only to push them over a cliff. I truly believe older children need to be made more aware of real-life family finances.

> Many people fear that talking to their children about money will somehow inflict damage on them. Some parents fear their children will "blab" all of their personal financial information to everyone. But once children are 12 years or older, not helping them understand money can leave them unarmed to deal with their own money when the day comes. The act of giving an allowance or teaching a child to save or donate money is valuable. However, an allowance does not prepare a child to understand the consequences of taking out a student loan or signing a mortgage.

By 1996, I graduated an average/good student from high school. I had concentrated quite a bit of my studies on sciences with the lifelong goal of becoming a veterinarian. I didn't have the desire to spend four years getting a BSc, so I went straight to a practical course where I could pursue a career working with animals. I didn't end up taking out a student loan. The GIC my parents bought me back in the early 80's (the days of 18 percent GIC rates) and the whole life policy, which I cashed out, was enough to cover all of my tuition, books and some of my living expenses.

I paid the rest of my living expenses with the child support my father paid me directly during school, along with a couple of really good-paying summer jobs. I was never allowed access to the full funds from my savings or the accumulated money from my summer jobs. My mother kept the lump sums in her savings account on my behalf and I simply got a monthly deposit into my account.

Major Crisis #2

One month I did run out of money; some bad decision making on my part. I called my mother in a panic, asking for money to "get me through". She told me she'd take care of it and I was to go to the Acadia Lines bus terminal the next day.

Lesson #2

The next day, I presented myself at the depot expecting to pick up an envelope but my mother had other plans. She had sent me a box. As you might have guessed, there was no money in the box. There were, however, two loaves of bread, a jar of peanut butter, a few rolls of toilet paper and a note that read something like:

Dear Stephanie,

I love you too much to teach you that when you spend more money than you have that you can just ask for some more. In this package you'll find enough supplies to ensure you are neither hungry nor dirty by the time you get your next deposit.
I love you,

TTFN
Mum

Gift #2

I was quite pissed off, but secretly very grateful. I graduated debt free.

In 1998, I graduated with honours from the Agricultural College with a diploma from the Animal Sciences program. At 19, I had essentially completed my post-secondary education. During my search for employment, the best job offer came from a farm corporation out West. So, I packed up my belongings, my dog and my cat, and flew out to Alberta. I took a job I got over the phone and moved into a place, sight unseen, that my new boss had picked out for me. In Alberta, I moved around a lot, taking many jobs where I got a ton of life experience. During my time out there, I learned to change the clutches on an automatic transmission and I was even suspended in a tractor bucket high enough to shove insulation into barn eaves. I learned to mend fences, ride horses, and managed multiple half-assed attempts at roping a plastic steer head mounted on a bale of hay.

Major Crisis #3

After three-and-a-half years doing hard manual labour on farms all over Southern Alberta, I became ill in early 2001. I was admitted to the local hospital where I was told I would need to take several weeks away from the farm to recover. When I explained that I worked for a farm where there was no disability coverage, the doctor gave me two choices; I could work or I could live. I chose to live.

I had been diagnosed with mono, and at the age of 22, that is a bigger deal than it is for a teenager. What I really needed was time off, but when I phoned my boss to make an attempt to work something out, he fired me.

In a flood of tears, I called my mother to let her know that not only had I lost my job since I wasn't able to work, but I had no disability coverage. I got rid of every possession I owned, except my new puppy, Reese, the clothes on my back and my 1996 Dodge Neon. A friend I had gone to college with, who was also living out West, happened to be heading home around the same time, so I talked him into driving home with me. In March of 2001, I, along with my dog and my old Neon, arrived back in Nova Scotia.

Lesson #3

Losing everything was both traumatic and cathartic. I was safe and warm back home with my mother and while I didn't know exactly what I was going to do, I felt secure in the fact that losing just about everything might be the best thing that ever happened to me. I could suddenly see that getting sick and having to let go of so much meant there was room to be more, do more and grow more. It hit me that this apparent trauma would allow me to explore who I really wanted to be. Once again, trauma and relief became intertwined in my life. During the days I had to spend resting, I remember thinking how much I'd like to run a business. I racked my brain thinking of what kind of business. I'll admit the list seemed pretty limited at the time.

Gift #3

After sticking to the doctor's orders and taking just under eight weeks to get my strength back, I was chomping at the bit to get back to work. I was entertaining the idea of going back to school and becoming that vet I so longed to be back in elementary school, when I literally stumbled into my first sales job.

My initial introduction to sales was selling cutlery direct to the consumer by doing in-home demonstrations. It was good stuff, not cheap—I still use it in my home today. After a few months of learning how not to be afraid of the discomfort that is the sales process, I was getting pretty good at it, but I was a little bored. While I did agree it was a great, quality product, I didn't feel my purpose on earth was to sell cutlery. I didn't feel I was really doing anything with my life, but I did know I liked sales. I liked helping people, and what's more, I was good at it.

A family friend who worked for a large national financial services firm as a Financial Advisor took some time to see my cutlery demo. When I was finished, not only did she make a purchase, she offered to introduce me to her manager.

Remember I told you I had come home from Alberta with nothing. I ended up borrowing money from my sister just to make my car payment that month and I even had to ask for some change to cover pantyhose and bridge tolls just to get to the interview. Hardly the picture of financial competence myself, I was pretty skeptical when I showed up to meet the manager. Surprisingly, that manager turned out to be wonderful and made me feel excited about the possibilities; in fact, he and I are still in touch today.

Before I knew what was happening I was whisked into a meeting room to fill out the required personality test. My references were checked and there were a lot of questions for me about what I wanted from life. It was strange to be interviewed about what I wanted. I couldn't recall applying for work and being asked what I wanted before. In the end, they liked me; they really liked me!

During my first year as an advisor, products like insurance, mutual funds and GIC's were the sole focus of my business; after all, that was the only thing I was really trained to do. I felt (and still do) that those products were sound choices to implement in support of a good financial plan. I grew frustrated, however, with the sheer lack of planning that was going on in the industry itself. The most difficult pill for me to swallow was that so many people I worked with expressed an interest in being given advice on debt and spending.

Okay people, don't start freaking out, but yes, that is how a good number of advisors come to be. Regular people with the right personality and temperament are recruited by many financial service companies to become Financial Advisors. I hate to tell you this, but being selected to be a Financial Advisor—and the likelihood you'll do well—is more about how self-motivated you are and how well you interact with others than it is about knowledge of finance. To the finance companies' credits, it is much easier to teach someone about financial products and theories than to take someone with a financial background and teach them to have a particular attitude or personality. Now, they just don't put some sort of badge on newbie advisors and send them out into the world to help people manage their life savings. There are licensing exams and training is required before a juvenile advisor hits the road. Don't get me wrong, there are advisors whose education in finance or business is an asset. I'm just saying it isn't the major factor in the probability of one's success as an advisor, and it isn't a must when finance companies recruit. Your current advisor could have been a teacher, a police officer or even an Animal Science Technician before they were your advisor. This isn't a bad or good thing; it just is.

Thinking I could really help people, I bounded into the manager's office, looking to find out more about what course I could take to learn to really help people manage cashflow and debt.

I was nearly laughed out of the office. I was told I wasn't best served working with people who had "those" kind of problems.

But the more I worked, the more I found that even people with good incomes, and some retirement savings, could still be struggling with debt. What my manager called "highly desirable" clients, which they wanted me to seek out, often had "those" kinds of issues. I found that making good income and having assets was not evidence that you didn't have debt. Most people needed help to manage debt and spending in order to build more wealth and retire in true comfort.

The issue was more that managers, like many (including most other advisors), assume that if a client makes a good income and has assets accumulated in retirement accounts, that they MUST not have debt or spending issues. But I've often found that debt can be just as much a problem for those with high incomes, even if they've put money into investments. I routinely have people who come to me with $300,000 plus in retirement savings but they are struggling to get their debt down. They aren't behind, they aren't in "bad shape", but they are one crisis away from being in big trouble. If you only looked at the asset side of their equation, which most financial pros do, then the greatest opportunity to help the client can get missed.

So there was demand. I could feel it in my bones and the situation that has unfolded since then has only confirmed that my intuition was correct. When I tried to be the solution to the problem, to be the supply to fill that demand, I was told there was no training or solution I could provide to them. I was dealing with perfectly wonderful people who had great potential to meet their financial goals, if only I could find a way to teach them how to harness their cashflow and pay down debt efficiently. These were educated, well-intended people who I was told weren't worth my time. The only hurdle between these people and financial independence was how they used their money, not how much money they had.

You'll figure out as you read on that I'm not so good at taking no for an answer. So, I set out to figure out what I had to do to be the change I wanted to see in my industry.

After much thought and just over three years with that particular company, I resigned in search of more independence and ownership so that I could be that change I so desperately wanted to see. While I did learn a lot in that first job, it was simply time to move on. It may have been a good place to start; but for me, it was ultimately not the right place to mature in my career.

After getting married in September of 2004, I found myself a fully independent advisor for the first time. With a whole new world of possibilities at my feet, my journey really began. This book is about everything I have learned between that moment and now. I'll share with you what I've discovered about financial behaviour, managing spending and mastering debt repayment. I'll show you the secrets to gaining control over spending and how to redirect funds to get you what you really want. Most importantly, this book is about how you can take what I've learned from not only my own mistakes and success, but from those of the thousands of people I've worked with over these first ten years.

This book is a catalyst, not a cure. So take a deep breath and choose to take the first step in reclaiming your financial power.

CHAPTER 1

Your Money Is Where Your Mind Is

"Wealth is not a matter of intelligence it's a matter of inspiration."

~Jim Rohn

Working with people and their money has taught me a lot, but I think the most important lesson I've learned is that no matter what our education level or income, most of the financial decisions we make are a direct result of our personalities. We make decisions based on our natural instincts. The problem is that our natural instincts are designed to keep us alive in the face of mortal danger, not make us smart with money. A fair amount of finance can be counter-intuitive to our human nature. We can often make financial decisions based on fear rather than fact. We bob when we should weave because we think that's what we should do. We don't even bother to check if weaving would serve us better. A study between December 31, 1989 and December 31, 2009, looked at investor behaviour and found that over two decades, the average person who invested in equities earned 3.17 percent per year, while the S&P 500 index returned 8.2 percent per year on average.[1]

---

[1] Dalbar 2010 QAIB - Investors Can Manage Psyche to Capture Alpha released April 2011.

Some would jump to the conclusion that overpriced or even poor investments were to blame. The report determined the disparity was attributable to investors buying stocks during manias and selling them during times of panic (I have seen this myself). People make financial decisions in search of relief or control, but they often "cut off their nose to spite their face" so to speak. Also, the report noted, "Investors with certain personality types, such as confident alpha males, are often more prone to making emotional investment decisions."

Fight or flight is not a suitable instinct for investing, borrowing or saving. The sensation that anything that we aren't sure about should either be avoided at all cost or defeated, keeps us from properly assessing the true benefits or risks inherent to any number of financial decisions. People will sell an investment they previously said they'd be willing to hold for a decade after only two years immediately following a sharp reduction in the market, fearing there is more to come. Rarely, will that person slow down enough to evaluate how that investment has weathered past economic storms. They don't consider whether or not their actual goals have changed, or they fail to remind themselves they are still 25 years from retirement. Once they've made the call and sold that "bad" investment, all they remember about their investment experience is losing money, even if the market ended up recovering. We do the same with debt. We tend to put it into a context that makes us feel better. This is why people often feel "safer" with a fixed rate mortgage and multiple credit cards with double digit interest rates, even though that is clearly not to their financial benefit.

I like to refer to our financial personalities as our Money Mindsets. How is your Money Mindset affecting you?

The Money Mindsets

In this chapter, you'll learn about the seven Money Mindsets;

more importantly, you'll find your own. I have been able to distinctly isolate seven different financial personality types while working face-to-face with hundreds of people to change their spending and saving behaviours.

Taking the Money Mindset quiz will identify the mindset that most closely matches your financial decision-making tendencies, including spending, saving, and investing. It's not unusual to find glimpses of yourself in parts of each Mindset definition, but your primary Mindset identified by the quiz is most likely to highlight your dominant financial behaviour.

None of these Mindsets are particularly good or bad; they just are. Different levels of financial agility (which we'll discuss in the next chapter) can be present in all the Mindsets. Your Mindset simply represents your most intuitive feelings and personality traits as they relate to the way you use your money. The point of this measure is not to put you in a box where you are a saver, and therefore good, verses a spender who is bad. Rather, I want to help you find out what drives your money behaviour so you can use this knowledge to get the life you deserve.

Together, your Mindset and your financial agility score will help you use this book to achieve the financial harmony all of us deserve in our lives. Be brutality honest as you answer the questions. Don't give the answer you think you should record; that will only lead to inappropriate advice.

So go on, discover yourself a little…

Money Mindset Quiz

Read the questions on the following pages and put a check mark next to the answers that most closely match your feeling about each.

You can also take the quiz online at: www.themoneyfinder.ca. There, you will find additional resources and can share the Money Mindset quiz with others.

When you meet with a Financial Advisor,
banker or planner of any kind:

1. You try to figure out what they are up to. You don't trust "financial types". You figure they are all out for their own best interests and have little regard for yours.

2. You are proud of your ability to save but not interested in discussions that involve taking any degree of risk.

3. You spend half of the appointment explaining why you haven't really started to save for retirement (all good and true reasons, of course).

4. You tell them of your grand plans, describing in detail your dreams and goals. You are excited about the idea of investing to grow your wealth!

5. You ask all the questions. You just met this person! There is no way you are telling them your every financial detail in a first appointment.

6. You are happy to talk about your assets, particularly your ability to manage them yourself. You are quite comfortable with listening to a second opinion, but you don't want to go into detail about your personal finances. If they stick to investments and small talk, you are comfortable.

7. You immediately trust them. After all, you don't understand this money stuff and you'd much rather someone else deal with it. You figure they are the professional, they must know what they are doing.

If you felt you made a financial
mistake you would:

1. You don't make financial mistakes.

2. Make sure never to make that mistake again. It's stressful to even think about the mistake. You become a financial Fort Knox. No more risk. Ever!

3.   There was a good reason for the mistake. It's not the end of the world, so you don't get too worked up about it. You needed to buy that car you weren't sure you could afford and it's not your fault you lost your job and had to skip those payments. You couldn't really help it, so was it even a mistake?

4.   Try to learn from the mistake, but you don't let it slow down your mission to achieve your goals. If it became an issue in future financial endeavours, you'd have a clever back story and could likely deal with any bumps in the road.

5.   Tell no one. Pick up the pieces and get over it. Even if someone was talking about having made the same mistake, you would never admit to having made it yourself. You never confide in anyone you don't have to.

6.   Sue whomever you felt was responsible for the mistake into the next century. You are not stupid, so the only way you could have made a mistake was because you were tricked into it.

7.   Feel foolish and stupid, but also vindicated that you, indeed, should not be the one making your own financial decisions.

When making investment decisions:

1.   You carefully examine your choices. You take no one's advice. You might look at a suggestion, but it's just that; a suggestion. The final decision is always yours, and you know it. You hate fees and are comfortable making your own investment choices. You prefer an order taker when you buy investments compared to someone who offers advice.

2.   You do invest, or at least you call it investing, even if it is really glorified savings in retirement accounts. Guarantees are important to you. You don't like surprises or risk and you'll sacrifice today to avoid needing to take risk tomorrow in order to achieve growth.

3.   You don't really invest. You've got a pension and a group investment at work, so you don't really feel the need to make investment deci-

sions. You'll get around to investing when you've got more free cash-flow but for now, you don't really worry about investing.

4. You shoot for the moon. You are all about the risk, baby! You want to know what rich people do and you want to do that, too! You prefer investments you can touch, like income properties or commercial buildings, but if you have to go retail, you want to make some serious coin in doing so.

5. You try to make independent decisions, even if it means taking one professional's advice and placing the investments with another. You like to keep your investments separated and you don't like to discuss your accounts with anyone. You'll ask peers or family for their opinion on certain things, but you will never divulge what you have decided to do with your money.

6. You invest big sums because you make big money. Even if you are carrying debt, you still like to make larger investments. Usually, if there is a tax advantage, you are far more motivated to invest. You aren't too aggressive, but you definitely aren't safe. You are proud of your portfolio.

7. Do what you are told. You just don't know what you don't know and you feel that if you are buying your investments through any sort of professional, then you won't have to worry about things.

You think credit cards are:

1. Great tools. You understand you need to use them to build credit and while you are at it, you'll take some points, too. You don't like to carry a balance on them, but you have no fear of using them.

2. Horrible. You don't even like to have them, let alone use them. You may use them from time-to-time for items you must purchase with credit cards, like plane tickets, but you pay them off online the second you've completed the purchase.

3. Wonderful. If it weren't for your credit cards, you would have to make very different decisions. You only use them for good reason and pay

the bill off as you can. While you prefer not to carry debt on your cards, you feel if the means justify the end, then it's okay.

4. For using. You'll pay them off when you are making the big bucks, but in the meantime, you use them when you feel it's a good idea.

5. To be kept to yourself. You may use a credit card, but you prefer not to in public. You don't want anyone looking at what kind of card you have or deciding who you are based on the fact that you are paying with credit.

6. For flashing. A platinum card for you. Credit cards are a status symbol. They say a lot about who you are and how successful you've become. You are on a mission to attain the most prestigious card you can get your hands on.

7. For someone else to worry about. You may well use a credit card, but you either have an automatic payment come out so you don't have to worry or think about it or your other half deals with paying it. The only thing you do is use it.

If a friend asked you for financial
advice you would:

1. Happily tell them about all the things they should be aware of. You'd warn them about financial professionals and fees. You'd tell them about the market and discuss some of your greatest picks.

2. You'd warn them of the dangers associated with risk of any kind and encourage them to be as frugal as possible. If you had a horror story, you'd share it. You'd encourage them to save and keep track of their spending.

3. You'd ask them why they were asking you then you'd console them on whatever the issue was by telling them things are never as bad as they seem. If it was an opportunity rather than an issue they wanted to discuss, you'd remind them that life is too short to invest more of their hard-earned dollars. If they are on track, do they really need to

think about opportunities, or could fun be a better use of their funds?

4. You'd encourage them to follow their dreams and push the limits. While your advice might not contain a lot of concrete actions, you'd be very encouraging.

5. You would listen to them and make a few suggestions, but you would stop short of sharing any of your actual experiences. If they kept bugging you, you'd send them to your bank for more information.

6. You'd tell them about the firm you deal with and how great the service is. If there was any prestige involved in who you were dealing with, you'd be sure to bring that up, too.

7. Look at them like they'd lost their mind. You aren't a good person to give financial advice and you'd say so.

When making a vehicle purchase:

1. You evaluate every detail carefully. You shop online, compare prices and interrogate the sales people. You are not happy until they are not happy.

2. You hate buying a car! They are depreciating assets and you hate being in debt on them more than anything. You saved for this car, but if you can, you'll spend even less than you saved.

3. You think to yourself, "Hey you only live once!", and go for the car that makes you and your family the happiest. You'll make your finances work around it.

4. You know you are going to be doing really well in the next few years so you lease a nicer car then you would have been willing to buy. You are sure by the time the lease comes due you'll be able to afford buy an even nicer car.

5. You go everywhere and check out even the cars you know you can't afford. That's none of the sales person's business. When you are good and ready, you'll make your decision and not a minute before.

6. You choose the item that aligns with the image of success you have built for yourself. You believe that if you are doing well, it should be easy for others to tell.

7. You don't look at the price if at all. If you can avoid being involved in the decision you'll defer to your spouse. If you don't have a spouse, you rely on the sales person to help you make the best choice.

When buying a home:

1. You research the realtor you work with first (if you even work with one). When you do get to looking at homes, you examine every detail of the property itself including utility cost to run the home, property taxes and the like. No detail is unimportant to you. You staunchly negotiate your price and you'll walk from an uncooperative seller.

2. You save, and you save, and you save. You will NOT buy a house without a sizable down payment. You worry more about the mortgage and how fast you can pay it off than the features of your house. If you have to work harder to pay it down faster, or hold off on renovations, you are game.

3. You pick the house that feels right and check the price tag after. Your home is an investment and you believe that it's all about the kids, the convenience and the contentment of your family, so you make the best choice for them and work out the details as they come.

4. You go after your dream home. You find out what you qualify for and you go to your limit. You may have to borrow some of the down payment but you'll be ahead of the game as the value of the home rises so you'll benefit in the end.

5. You just want a house that does what a house is supposed to do. You don't care about how fancy it is, all you want is a roof over your head and a floor under your feet. You don't want to stand out as someone who is showing off. You'd rather have a life than a nice house.

6. You look for the nicest house on the block. You can afford it and you'll settle for nothing less than the best. You want a manicured lawn and

curb appeal that says, "I have arrived!"

7.   You care about where your home is located, and how many bedrooms and baths there are in it, but financial details are not your area of expertise so you'll go along with anything within the budget set by your spouse, or your bank.

When choosing a mortgage:

1.   You make your decision based on the facts. You look at the mathematical difference between mortgages, focusing on the rates in particular. You are nobody's fool and you will not pay more than you have to.

2.   You are a fixed rate only kind of person. You are not willing to deal with fluctuating mortgage payments. There are enough unpredictable financial episodes in life; you don't need to deal with one more. You do care how long it takes to pay your home off and do your best to reduce it at all costs.

3.   You take whatever you qualify for. As long as you can make the payment, it's all good. You don't get bogged down in the details. The lower the payment, the better. You don't worry about the time it will take to pay it off, your concern is how much it costs today.

4.   You take a mortgage out a little higher than you really think you qualify for, but you were approved, so you must be able to afford it. This home is an investment, after all. You are not worried about the rate as you wouldn't have been given a mortgage you couldn't afford.

5.   You like the idea of fixed but you might go for a variable rate mortgage. You don't want to deal with multiple people, though, so it's one broker or one bank for you. The less people messing with your finances, the better.

6.   Mortgage smortgage . . . You make a lot of money, way more than you need to pay any kind of mortgage on your home. Rate doesn't really matter as long as it's within normal ranges. How long it will take you to pay it off doesn't matter either. You make enough to wipe it

out when you feel like it.

7. You don't even look closely at the mortgage document, let alone read it or even pay attention to the rate. You're not the best person to make those decisions, so you defer them to the banker, mortgage broker or your spouse. Fixed vs. variable? Does it matter?

Expenses related to food:

1. Are controlled. You may not actually be the one in at your house who buys the groceries, but there is a budget and it had better not be ignored on your watch. You do eat out, but only when you have to. Your spouse or family members know you expect them to keep eating out to a minimum.

2. Are budgeted. You'll buy groceries with cash if you can. You don't eat out very often, it is far too expensive so you avoid it whenever possible.

3. Off limits. Food is important. You want to feed your family good food and you will not compromise when it comes to their health.

4. Are all about enjoyment! Your grocery bill is smaller than the norm because your dining out costs are generous. You love to enjoy the good life and you frequently dine out.

5. Are low. You don't spend a lot of money on food; just enough to get the basics.

6. Just are. You don't know have a clue how much they are and it doesn't really matter. You make good money and you expect to eat well so you don't pay much attention to the total cost.

7. Are not just food. These days the local grocer has half a department store in the middle of it and you take full advantage of all the time and money it saves you to shop there.

Expenses related to items like kids activities and sports are:

1. Negotiable. If your child wants to do something, they'd better prove you won't be wasting your money if you fund it. They need to really want to do it and they need to commit to doing that activity for a period of time. You may even attach chore conditions to the cost of that particular activity.

2. Limited. While you feel it is important that your children are active and engaged, you don't believe in putting your family at financial jeopardy for their activities. So, in order to enroll your child in anything you first make sure you can afford it then you decide how important it is. Your children are not allowed to have so many activities that they can barely catch their breath, so you limit the number of sports or hobbies they take up at once.

3. Non-negotiable. Kids' sports and activities are a must. If it takes you longer to save for retirement, or if your debt takes longer to get paid off, the kids will not suffer for it.

4. Very important. Your children are your life and they come first. If they are willing to work hard at a sport, or if you want to put them in an activity, you just do it. Your kids may never reach their full potential if their wings are clipped early in life.

5. Acceptable. If you have the funds left over to cover what your kids want to do, then you are okay with them doing it. You don't want your kids in the yacht club necessarily, but you are generally supportive of their interests, as long as you don't have to re-mortgage the house to afford them.

6. Part of their social standing. Your children must be involved in something if they are ever to amount to anything. You want them to be successful and you feel it is important they be well rounded. You have plenty of money to fund their pursuits and prefer they take up something admirable.

7. A reason for you to chauffeur. You feel that your children's extracurricular pursuits are just part of being a parent. You worry more about how to get them there on time and less about paying for it.

Now, tally your points below:

All of your 1's = 7pts
All of your 2's = 6pts
All of your 3's = 5pts
All of your 4's = 4pts
All of your 5's = 3pts
All of your 6's = 2pts
All of your 7's = 1pt

Your Total _____

Quiz Key:

7-28 — The Polly Anna
29-35 — The Masquerader
36-42 — The Undercover Agent
43-49 — The Dreamer
50-56 — The Justifier
57-63 — The Bunker
64-70 — The Brick Wall

Now that you have found your Mindset, turn to the next chapter to read the description. Keep in mind, many of us could be a mixture of more than one Mindset. Right now, we are just looking for the most dominant Mindset related to your specific financial behaviours.

CHAPTER 2

The Mindsets

The Dreamer

You've been taught or learned that anything is possible; and rightfully so, because anything is possible. This belief that you can do anything is one of the greatest things about you. Everyone loves that you are so driven to lead the life you believe you can have.

You are likely an entrepreneur. If you do happen to still be an employee, you're a natural fit in sales where entrepreneurial spirit is always drawing you to a world where the possibilities are endless. The Dreamer as an employee is often running a home-based business on the side, or has plans of making a break for it and striking out on their own. The Dreamer as a business owner is just as keen on chasing that feeling of achievement and success. You daydream about the life you'll have when you get there. You see your goals in vivid Technicolor.

You like books like *The Secret* and *Think and Grow Rich*. Tony Robbins, or any other motivational speaker who tells you to 'just go for it', is your cup of tea. You thrive on exploring your own abilities and pushing yourself to achieve new levels of success. You are generally a reader, or a listener; both audio and tradi-tional books are your thing. You spend a good deal of time and money attending seminars on building your net worth, creating new streams of income or perhaps a how-to seminar on manag-ing investments in real estate or the stock market.

You are a risk taker. You know it takes a nickel to make a dime and you have no qualms with investing in yourself and/or your business. You always believe you'll get back from every investment in yourself, and feel your return will be at least as much as you put into it. You just know you will get what you want if you keep at it.

You have an appetite for risk and you are willing to take them with your career, hard assets, like real estate, or liquid assets, like mutual funds or stocks. You believe that taking a risk is required to achieve great success in life. However, when evaluating an opportunity, it's not uncommon for you to only evaluate the upside. Being a Dreamer, you are just so convinced that the downside won't happen to you that you often try to grab every opportunity all at once and you would feel a real sense of loss if you were to let something pass you by.

Your spending habits are not always atrocious, but for all your ambition, you often overspend. You feel it is a good long-term investment to maintain an image of success. If not now, once upon a time you did subscribe to the phrase "fake it till you make it", which is oh so popular in the financial services world. You sometimes feel that what you can afford might be inconsistent with the image you are trying to project. Perhaps a well-meaning manager or colleague once recommended that you buy something you couldn't afford in order to put the pressure on you to earn enough to cover the payments; you totally went for that advice.

As an investor, you are more likely keen to invest in your business or the bricks and mortar of commercial or residential rental properties than you are to choose mutual funds, stocks or the like. Investments you can touch are much more exciting to you. It's not that you necessarily dislike the more liquid investments held in the market, but you just don't feel like you can control them or get your hands around them.

What you don't realize is that you only have limited control over your preferred hands-on investments. This added sense of control over these more tactile assets may also lead you to remove cash more frequently from them to fund the next big thing. Sometimes, a third party, like an advisor that comes with those retail investments, can be good for you. They may slow you down long enough to think before you cash out to invest in your next "big" idea.

You have a hard time saving. It's not that you don't believe in saving, but you just haven't gotten around to putting much away just yet. Whenever you try to save, something else in your life—usually an opportunity or an image-boosting item of some sort—crops up and directs your attention and your money elsewhere. You figure you'll save eventually, when the big bucks really start rolling in. Net worth and liquidity are two very different things and you concern yourself with the former.

You believe you will become a major success at some point, so you'll pay for all of the spending you are doing today, tomorrow, when the money rolls in. You will also talk yourself into believing that almost any expense is an investment in your future. In many cases, your ambition is thwarted by your inability to save, so you can't actually fund many of your own dreams. Infinite success is what a Dreamer can create for themselves with more disciplined savings; the sky really is the limit!

You may have gone without as a child, or conversely, you may have been raised by successful entrepreneurial parent(s). Either way, something jarred you hard enough to make you believe in yourself and drive you to succeed.

Your friends would characterize you as a free spirit and are certain you can achieve just about anything. Those who know you well believe in you, too, and feel that you are going places. They look up to you, ask for your advice and marvel in your seemingly flawless approach to grabbing your life by the horns. They wouldn't be surprised to read about you in the paper someday —if they don't already—or see you on the tube. You are known by those closest to you as someone who thinks outside of the box.

You can be an easy mark, and you will often buy just about anything that appeals to you emotionally; although you will never admit to that. It is much easier to sell you an overpriced sales coaching program, or Get Rich With Real Estate seminar than it is to get you to save for your taxes. You will go far despite the sometimes self-destructive nature of your financial habits. Be aware, however, that some of your Dreamer habits could unknowingly place a governor on your potential.

Untethered or runaway business growth or the rapid gathering of non-liquid assets like real estate properties is just the type of thing that can actually topple your house of cards. It's not that you shouldn't build wealth, or invest in assets; you, the Dreamer, just have to be very careful not to bite off more than you can effectively chew all at once.

You are impatient with success. You want to have a great idea today and be well-off tomorrow. You believe you will succeed — and you are probably right — you just wish your big break would hurry up and get here. Of all the Money Mindsets, you may have the most overwhelming potential for tremendous financial stability. If you can only wait long enough for your ship to come in, you'll be in the position to truly enjoy it. Keep investing in that Dreamer Mindset of yours. You are passionate and driven.

The Justifier

Just to be clear, we all buy things for emotional reasons — yes gentlemen, even you! Just because your purchases happen to come with an eight-cylinder hemi instead of four-inch heels, doesn't make them any less emotional. Emotions drive so much of our behaviour and money is strongly connected to how we feel about a lot of things. We all buy with our emotions and then justify the purchase with logic and reason after the fact.

The Justifier is the queen or king of rationalizing their spending. As a Justifier, you can come up with a reason for buying just about anything. You would wear it every day of every spring, at least that's what you told yourself when you bought that $400 aquamarine trench coat. It's been three years and that thing is still hanging lifeless in your closet, only donned a half dozen times. Or maybe, it's that V8 pick-up you needed. You swore you'd be doing so many home improvement projects that baby would just pay for itself. If you buy something you don't really need, you can come up with a very convincing back story on the necessity of the item in seconds.

To be a Justifier, you almost always have to have been raised by one. This ability to reason your way out of just about any corner is a learned behaviour; in my experience anyway. (If I said this to a Justifier they would usually deny that fact and then circle the conversation around to explain why the Justifier parent had to be a Justifier.) This level of finding the silver lining in just about any decision is a true skill and luckily for you, it can be used to your advantage; as you'll see later on as we explore your strengths and how to harness them.

As a Justifier, you have a void somewhere in your life and you believe that a nice lifestyle will eventually make you feel better. It's not that you have a bad life or any major problems, but there is some level of anxiety you live with for whatever reason and it makes you feel in control to buy things. There is something about having something new, or even seeing the face of a loved one when you buy something for them, that soothes you. Mind you, the warm feeling is short lived and that's when you start to justify your actions.

You will often encourage others around you to overspend as well so you won't feel so badly about your own spending habits. You are the one who cheers on your girlfriend's purchase of a pair of expensive shoes with a "go on girl, you deserve it!". Or you egg on your buddy to have just one more beer, to play just one more hand or do just one more renovation. You don't mean to encourage anyone to spend beyond their means, but you subconsciously crave permission to spend yourself, so watching others spend their money freely helps you feel more comfortable when you spend.

Your spending habits, while not necessarily sending you into excessive debt, are likely stifling your cashflow's ability to fund an adequate retirement. Again, this helps you justify. You tell yourself, "I can't be that bad, I'm not in huge debt". Whenever you let yourself go there and start thinking about your overall finances, you just remind yourself that life is short and you are the "living for today" type of person. Besides, you have some relative you can use as an example who died too young, never getting to use their hard-earned savings.

You are the sort of person who would spend money you didn't really have on a minivan or SUV instead of a car in your price range when you have only one child. When questioned on your logic, you'd say yes, you only have the one child but you might have more, and you do have a dog, and you do a lot of camping and your child has a lot of friends. Or perhaps, you think ahead about the fact that your now three-year-old might just be obsessed with playing hockey one day and you'll need room for his or her gear; kids start in sports early these days, after all. You are one of the more likely of the Mindsets to replace a car before it is fully paid off. You have a million reasons why it's a good idea, but you rarely take a good look at the financial reality of that choice.

You can be a good saver. You understand the importance of having an emergency fund and totally subscribe to the idea of automated deposits to a high interest savings account. You may even be saving monthly as you read this. As a Justifier, your biggest risk with savings is not that you won't or don't put money away, it's that your skill of talking yourself into purchases is too often used to drain your savings for a "good reason".

The Justifier, as an investor, likes to think of every purchase as an investment or a must-have. It's not a hard asset versus liquid asset choice for you. You can see the value of every interaction in life and you often extract that value and equate it to an investment. You are more likely to invest in a course, an experience, or trip than a mutual fund or rental property. In one way, this is a good thing about you; the downside is that you don't always take the time to plan how you'll afford these "investments", or how to discern whether you'll get value out of them.

When you do invest in your future, you are most comfortable

with things that don't require you to make constant trade decisions. You have likely managed funds of some sort. You are neither overly involved with your investments nor overly passive.
For you, finding the money is the hurdle, not necessarily choosing the investment.

Your friends would characterize you as generous and supportive. They feel like you are always going to be there for them.
As a Justifier, you always make them feel better. You almost
never judge people for their mistakes and everyone loves that
about you. Your ability to rationalize doesn't only come in handy
when attempting to validate an unnecessary purchase. When a
friend has a need to feel better about something that has happened to them, whether by their own doing or by chance, you
are there to comfort them. You make people feel good about their
body, house, car or even their marriage, as long as you think
that's where they want to be. You truly love your friends and you
feel they should never be sad.

You are helpful and kind, but you secretly feel badly about
your finances. When those guilty feelings creep up, you squish
them with your clever reasoning skills. You know you could do
a better job, but you are not so sure you want to give up this habit
that makes you feel so good. Justifying anything, especially the
way you use money, has become a part of you. You have no idea
how to deal with your life when you don't look at everything
through your current filter.

You feel like you are balanced and you will continue to believe that until you burn out, or run out of money and/or energy
that is. You are a good person and you feel you are more than capable of managing your money and your life. However, all the
stuff in the world won't ease what is really bothering you, whatever that may be. You are protective and supportive.

The Brick Wall

Oh my dear Brick Wall . . . you are one smart cookie! You are
also the most stubborn of all the Mindsets. You are convinced

you should get to make any choice you want, after all, it's a free country, damn it. You should make any choice you want and you should get to custom select the consequences. You want what you want, and you prefer to be able to control everything. You feel you are very controlled, disciplined and expect those traits of everyone else. You may not be aware of it, but you can be very vocal with your expectations of others and as a result, you could be perceived as very critical when people don't instantly meet those high expectations.

You make decisions based on logic and reasoning and you carefully weigh your options and review details at every turn. You feel you do not make decisions emotionally. No, not you; those pesky feeling things you've heard rumours about, don't get in your way. You believe if you let your guard down and allow your emotions to show that someone could and would take advantage of you.

Often, the Brick Wall will seek out careers in which they are able to be in control. They make great military officers, school principals, or supervisors. The Brick Wall tends to be a good leader, but sometimes they rule with an iron fist and have trouble listening to others. Not that their ways are without merit.

As a Brick Wall, you don't believe in letting people waste your time and you feel you do not waste other's time. You are a 'no-fooling-around', 'straight-from-the-hip' kind of individual; you sugar-coat nothing!

As a spender, you feel very in control. You don't mess around; you research what you want, look it up six ways from Sunday online and go straight out and buy it. By the time you get to the store or car lot, you know more about your desired purchase than the sales guy. You feel confident that you stay within your means, but you may not always confirm that with the same degree of research you put into purchasing items. You are very cautious with big purchases; you ask a lot of questions and go to many sources before making a decision. Anyone who has sold you a car or home theatre system would remember you for sure. All this is not to say that you are in perfect financial shape, although you would likely argue with that.

You're rarely bad with money when times are good, but in the face of a financial crisis, you retreat heavily into denial. You will outright refuse to make necessary changes to get through a tough time. You will stay in a house you can't afford after a divorce, you will not pull a child from private school when you can no longer afford it, you don't want to appear weak or affected by anything that goes on around you.

As a saver, you are pretty darn good at socking it away; once, of course, after you have completed a comprehensive and exhaustive search of every savings account on the face of the earth. If your spouse is not a Brick Wall like yourself, you monitor their spending and worry about their bad habits. You may even be tempted to squirrel away money for a rainy day on their behalf as you may not trust their financial prowess when it comes to acting in their own best interest.

You can be a very savvy investor, but you can be a horrible client. It's not that you lack intelligence or are uninvolved with the investing process, you just don't trust anyone's judgment but your own. You may not realize just how intimidating you can be to a financial professional who has the good fortune of working with your portfolio. Don't get me wrong, you don't always mean to be intimidating, you just aren't always aware of how effective you are at it. You really do know your stuff and you invest in nothing you don't understand.

You need to be careful, however, that the degree to which you scrutinize every investment choice doesn't become a sophisticated form of procrastination, as it can easily result in missed opportunities caused by the time lost doing your in-depth research. Remember, not making a decision is a decision in itself.

Another issue with the Brick Wall is that you often won't make financial changes, even for your own good, if those changes are not your idea. It isn't unlike you to seek out professional advice. The problem, however, is that because you like to be in charge of all financial conversations, it is not uncommon that the professional's advice often goes unheeded.

Your friends would say you are strong and independent, and if they thought you weren't listening, they'd add in stubborn and pigheaded. Many of your friends respect you for your intelligence and determination but wouldn't want to confide in you about areas of their life where they feel they fall short for fear they'd be judged. If you have employees or are in a position of authority, you may feel you have the respect of your team, but chances are that what appears to be respect is heavily tainted fear. People are afraid of what you will do or what you will say; those who respect you will go beyond that and take initiative, putting their whole self into working for or with you.

As the Brick Wall, you want much for yourself and your family and you will not go without. You do care, and you mean well, but you sometimes can't see that being so nearsighted could be very harmful to your financial future. You are analytical and traditional.

The Polly Anna

You are blissfully unaware when it comes to your finances; and that's just fine with you. You have a lovely and pleasant disposition and everyone who knows you thinks the world of you. You are a delight to be around and you don't see the bad in anyone, or any purchase for that matter. You are never any trouble for anyone, preferring never to rock the boat. You are the easiest going of all the Mindsets, as almost nothing can get under your skin.

If you have a spouse, you abdicate your financial responsibilities to them as frequently as possible. If you are single, you do what you have to and keep your bills paid, but you make a conscious effort not to think about your money. If you are in charge of your finances, you find it overwhelming and stressful. You look at it as little as possible, taking the attitude, "out of sight, out of mind". As soon as you find yourself in a new relationship, the minute they move in, you'll hand over every scrap of paper or decision related to your finances. You don't always feel confident in your own financial knowledge, so you feel it best to defer to those who you feel have more experience with money.

You are just as likely to overspend on others as you are on yourself. You can't help but offer to cover lunch with a friend; after all, it's just a few extra dollars for their sandwich and drink. If there is a concert you really want to attend, you'll often buy the tickets for everyone and won't be too intent on getting everyone to pay you back.

If you or your spouse make a healthy income, it's not unusual for you to turn gift buying into a sport. The minute you feel financially secure, you spend quite freely, sure that whoever has a hold of your financial reins is keeping a close eye and would tell you if there were any need to worry. You can sometimes use this tendency to put others first in order to make yourself a martyr. You give until your cup is empty and then emotionally turn on those closest to you because they have taken what you gave.

Sometimes, you even have enough to keep debts paid off in full but you are afraid of doing so, feeling safer to carry debt and know the cash is on hand, even if it costs you 18 percent interest for the privilege. There is something about paying a bill in its entirety that frightens you. If you happen to be looking at your account, you prefer to see those dollars as part of your balance rather than have them go out to a bill, even if that feeling costs you a fortune.

As a saver, you also delegate. If you are married to a saver, or a financial professional has convinced you to commit to regular automated savings—that is difficult for you to access on a moment's notice—then you have savings. Otherwise, you are more of a pay cheque-to-pay cheque kind of person. If no one else has influenced you to save regularly, you just don't. It's not that you don't believe it's important, you just don't like dealing with anything to do with money and the stress of exploring your savings options nearly causes you to break out in hives.

If questioned about your spending, even if it were terribly out of control, you may giggle or almost try to flirt your way out of the conversation as a defence mechanism. As a Polly Anna, it is possible that someone, a parent or former partner or spouse, has controlled you with money before. You can take out your past negative experiences with money by developing some seriously expensive passive-aggressive spending habits. You are no dummy, but sometimes you feel that life runs smoother if you downplay the level at which you could understand your money.

As an investor, you are scary. Again, it's not that you don't agree that investing for your future is important, you just don't participate. If someone were to eavesdrop on your conversations with your banker or financial planner, or even your spouse, they'd hear you continuously say, "Well, I trust you . . . whatever you think, you know what's best". These are horrifying phrases. While that makes you really easy to deal with, it also means that when you aren't happy with the consequences—even temporary ones— you abdicate the blame to the same person you gave your decision making power to. So, if that advisor/planner/banker made a sound recommendation but you happened to get caught up in some severe volatility (be it personal or market related), even if it is temporary, you will assign 100 percent of the responsibility to them.

You find it stressful to even think about investments. The whole process is overwhelming and unappealing to you and you will agree to whatever you need to, just to get away from it. This is something that not only puts your own financial future at risk, but it can cause professionals or others to inadvertently act on investment choices or directions from you even though you don't really understand or feel comfortable with those decisions.

If you go through a relationship breakdown, the finances often come as a surprise to you, even though you wove the wool that you pulled over your own eyes. In fact, it is not uncommon for your financial situation to be an overall mystery if you are married to any of the other Mindsets (with the exception of the Bunker), which can set you up to be taken advantage of.

Your friends would describe you as sweet and selfless and a doormat, even if they knew you were listening, because they know you wouldn't say a thing to defend yourself. They would say you are a loyal friend, a considerate co-worker and an adoring wife/mother/girlfriend/daughter. Your good friends worry about you and they know you are easy prey for someone who wants to take you for a ride. People love you, care about you and want to protect you.

You wish there was no money and that we all just had what we needed. You wish your family never has to worry about money. You even shudder at the thought of any of your children learning their life and money lessons the hard way. You love life and in every way you are living it to the fullest. You subscribe to the "live for today" theory and expect that tomorrow will take care of itself. You are kind, considerate and hopeful.

The Masquerader

You are a very smart individual and chances are you are very well educated. If you don't have some background in finance, like a degree in finance, accounting, or mathematics, anyone who knows you would certainly think you did. You may even have a career in the financial services industry; in particular, you might be a high-earning banker, advisor or financial company representative.

You may also be a physician, dentist, psychologist, or other highly esteemed professional. You worked hard in school; in fact, you work hard at everything. You work hard; and you play hard. Your image leaves nothing to be desired; you have the life that everyone who knows you expects you to have. If you play a sport, you are one of the standouts on the team. If you attend a corporate social event, you are wearing the most expensive suit in the room. If you are off for a boys/girls weekend, you are the big spender.

You made a deal with this world—you would work hard at school and build a great career; in return, you expect not to have to worry about money. You feel you are expected to live a certain lifestyle and you do not disappoint. From the outside, your life looks perfect. You have two kids and a white picket fence. You drive the right car, live in the right neighbourhood and rub shoulders with all the right people. Your friends want to be you and you know it.

People make assumptions about you. They assume that with your background, or obvious intelligence, that you must know what you are doing with your personal finances. The Masquerader, however, is just that—a Masquerader. If the people who admire your life got a look at your balance sheet, they'd see they were wrong to make the assumption that your intelligence automatically spills over into your ability to handle money. This doesn't mean you are bad, it just means you are a walking contradiction.

One of the definitions of the word image is: "to reflect a vivid representation of what is real". But for many, image is more about creating a character that is then projected to those around you. The Masquerader is a prime example. As a Masquerader, you think of your image as something to shape, and live up to; what you put forward as a public face. You would be less than pleased if your image was an actual reflection of your real financial decision making skills.

As a spender, you are every high-end sales person's dream customer. You love brand names, quality products and scarcity when you make a purchase. You don't look at the bill at a restaurant when it comes to the table, you just slap the plastic down. You love to attend charity auctions and fancy functions where your fineries will not go unnoticed. You don't pay attention to anything when it comes to spending. You do have good cashflow and as long as the money doesn't run out and you have no emergencies, you'll be able to continue to spend in a fog, paying little attention to your totals.

The Masquerader gets a rush from spending. If you are self-employed or a business owner, you might actually seek out the pressure that comes with making massive purchases you can't quite afford. You are a nightmare with a fluctuating income. You feel on top of the world when you are surrounded by what you feel is "The Good Life", which to you, means "The Good Stuff".

Of all the Mindsets, you have the biggest struggle with 'stuffitis'; especially with major purchases. Your stuffitis often flares up with the big stuff because you feel you need to go over the top, especially with major purchases, like your car.

As a saver . . . simply put, you are not a saver; at least, not if you can help it. You figure your cashflow could cover most reasonable emergencies until it doesn't. Probably the only reason you might save is if you are married to a saver. You believe it better to have access to a line of credit on the very off chance you'll need it rather than stashing cash away for a rainy day. You don't totally dismiss the importance of savings; you feel that, in particular, those with lower or more volatile income streams than yours, could strongly benefit from saving regularly—but not you.

As an investor, you prefer hard assets that others can see, especially things like buildings on which you can place your name—in big letters, if possible. These types of assets are much preferable to more liquid assets that only you and your institution can see. You may have a healthy portfolio, but it could be outweighed by your debt. You are not a particularly difficult client. It can sometimes be a challenge to get you nailed down to make deposits and you will rarely fess up about your debt to anyone who also manages your assets. You are careful to make sure no one is able to see all of your debts and assets side by side unless absolutely necessary. If an advisor calls you on your cashflow, you will try to avoid the discussion, steering them back toward the investments or into your business, if possible.

You are more likely than some of the other Mindsets to invest money and then in short order, take that money back out. This increases your risk of losing money on investments like mutual funds, stocks or other market-based funds because they can be volatile over a short period of time. Experiencing a short-term loss like that could turn you off these types of investments, driving you more headlong into real estate, or business investments. It is also not uncommon, however, for you to dip into those assets as well, looking for cash when you find yourself in a corner. You have great potential for financial success if you stop taking out early returns or dipping into your capital to fund your spending habits.

On occasion, the combination of your spending, savings and investing behaviours intersect and you find your cashflow strapped. This can cause extreme pressure, which is intensified by a feeling of obligation to keep the facade afloat. At some point, it will become more than you can bear. Your ego and other people's expectations have worked in concert to hold you back. You'll never reach your full financial potential with only the tools you obtained during your education.

Your friends would describe you as confident and intelligent, some would even say cocky. They look up to you and use your lifestyle as an example when counselling their children about the life a good education can afford. Those around you, who are less successful in their careers, wish they'd worked as hard as you did. Some are envious of your life, which is A-okay by you. People think you've got your act together and admire your success.

You are the least likely of the Mindsets to talk with your children about money, since living the facade is much easier than explaining it. You figure if you give them whatever they want, you'll never have to go into the details with them. You tend to guide them toward a career of a similar status and pay grade as your own. You love your kids and perceive any lack of abundance in their lives as unacceptable.

Your greatest fear is judgment and you'll do whatever it takes to keep from feeling judged. You are well-educated, brilliant and you are just fine with the common assumption that you must be good with your money. Your carefully crafted exterior is the first to come tumbling down in the face of a declining economy. You are cunning and focused.

The Undercover Agent

The CIA should have snapped you up when they had the chance. You are the most stealth-like with your financial habits of all the Mindsets. In fact, your spouse would have to hire a forensic accounting team to figure out what you are really doing with the money.

You are the most likely of the Mindsets to hide money, savings or spending. It's not that you are necessarily intentionally trying to be deceitful, but you just feel money is very private and you prefer to keep it that way. You are a fan of separate accounts for both you and your spouse. You have your list of expenses you are responsible for paying and your spouse is expected to pay the remaining ones. You feel it's up to each of you individually to manage your cashflow. You owe no one an explanation when it comes to where your money goes. Once you've paid your share, you feel that if you want to light your money on fire and do the dance of the seven scarves around it, it is no one's business but your own.

As a spender, you are very inconspicuous. You often live a middle-of-the-road lifestyle and where your money is going, isn't often as obvious as a fancy car or a big house. You are more likely to spend your money on experiences rather than tangible things. When you do buy anything, small or big ticket items, if you are questioned about how much it cost, you might even round down the price a little.

You like to do everything and be everywhere and you have expensive taste for certain items, particularly consumables like a good wine, and frequent meals out. You've been known in the past to "surprise" loved ones with exclusive vacations on short notice. Your spending habits are okay but there isn't a lot of evidence lying around your house to prove it. When the mood strikes you, you just act. Anyone that knows you wouldn't say you spent a lot of money because your spending is so spread out. It would be hard to notice unless they followed you around with a calculator. If you tracked your spending for a month though, you might find you spend more on discretionary items such as coffee, clothing and lunch out than you do on your mortgage payment.

Female Undercover Agents, in particular, will go as far as hiding a purchase in the back of the closet and removing the tags.

Then they slowly weasel it into their clothing collection, hoping no one will notice. When you make a larger purchase, you'll finance it on your own, avoiding joint applications and possible accompanying joint decisions at all cost. Your spouse likely doesn't even know what credit cards you have, let alone if there is a balance on any of them. I've even seen Undercover Agents send "secret" bills to a P.O. Box rather than their home address where it could be seen.

As a saver, you are equally secretive. If you are a saver, you will go as far as opening up different savings accounts at different institutions, not wanting even the bank to get a clear picture of your total savings. Undercover Agents can be good savers, but they are not always the most efficient ones. You are remiss to share that you have a secret stash of cash even in emergency circumstances, believing it's best you always have access to that money, no matter what. As a single person, your spending and saving patterns affect no one but you, however, in a committed relationship, keeping secrets can be very costly and your partner could take your behaviour as distrust in them, possibly even putting your relationship in jeopardy.

When you invest, you tend to be very difficult to advise because you aren't forthcoming and even when you do seek advice, you may be given unsuitable recommendations based on the incomplete information you provided. Anyone who gives any kind of financial advice for a living should rely on full disclosure, otherwise they could unintentionally tell you to zig when you should zag. The Undercover Agent is most likely to seek out the services of an advisor who will allow them to simply tell them exactly what kind of account they would like to open and what they would like to invest inside it. This is because, as an Undercover Agent, too many questions about your entire financial picture spook you and you feel uneasy having to share details, even with the most well-respected professional.

If you are an Undercover Agent who is over spending, you'll likely be withdrawing money from those secret accounts just as fast as you save or invest in them. If this is your M. O., you'll be even more hesitant to share the details of your cashflow, debt and savings with any professionals you deal with.

For the most part, as the Undercover Agent, your friends describe you as extremely social and the 'life-of-the-party'. They don't see you as secretive at all. Even though you are very social and everyone knows you, it takes you a long time to form a deep relationship with anyone, even longer to trust them; if you ever do. You are probably not even aware of how guarded you are.

The Undercover Agent wants a great life. If this is your Money Mindset, you likely believe that because you work hard, you deserve the lifestyle you are living. Every now and then, you do look at the total debt you have and continue to accumulate, and sometimes, you even stop to contemplate the fact you might not be at the place in your life you expected you'd be by now. You tell yourself that you don't have a fancy car, or a big house, "It's not like I'm living above my means", which isn't necessarily true. Just because your spending is harder to see, doesn't mean it's under control.

The Undercover Agent who doesn't put money away for the future would say they don't invest because there is a chance they could lose money, but realistically, they never stop to think they are losing every dollar they spend when it is not put into savings. It's just an excuse.

For those that do decide to save, the problem is that since the Undercover Agent is so good at hiding their spending, they can never accurately account for it either, which means predicting their actual income needs later on will be a guess at best. Ultimately, this could leave them without enough money socked away when it counts. If this should happen, the Undercover Agent will likely just blame the government or big business for the fact they have to live on less.

You are mysterious and independent and this is how you approach your finances.

The Bunker

You are a shelter in a storm, the rock-solid foundation your family is built on. You are very careful with money, to the point where you will recycle the tags from your bread bags for later use. You may be a child or a grandchild of the depression and the fear of loss runs deep in your veins. Sometimes you feel your frugality is a badge of honour. You don't realize it, but you often alienate people with your constant focus on how little you manage to spend.

Your greatest fear is to lose everything, having to worry about money. What you don't realize is that you live your greatest fear everyday because all you do is worry about money, no matter how much you have managed to gather in order to protect yourself. You consistently take a conservative approach to everything you do. You don't value things as much as security. Your home is nice and well maintained, big enough for your family, but nothing is overdone. The cars you and your family drive are reliable, affordable and you drive them years longer than most. You take care of your things; waste not, want not is a motto you live by.

Even the thought of spending frivolously causes your heart to race. You think five-dollar lattes are for people with holes in their heads and that eating out is for birthdays and anniversaries. You have great respect for your money and don't take a single dollar for granted. When you do make a purchase, it is always something that is of good quality because to you, frugal doesn't mean cheap. After all, you don't want to pay for things twice if you can avoid it, so those purchases you feel are necessary, are worth the investment.

You like saving for the things you purchase, although sometimes you save and save. . . and save, and don't ever purchase what you intended. You are not the favourite customer on the local car lot, although you come in with plenty of cash to put down, and usually to buy a car outright. You are not swayed by fancy features and options. You don't do the up-sell. You are the least emotional about your purchases of all the Mindsets. Cars are for getting you from point A to point B, houses are to keep you warm and safe, clothes are to keep you covered and food is to nourish you.

Your steadfast commitment to living within or even below your means may have an adverse affect on your children. There is a rebellious teenager in all of us that doesn't always grow out of the strongest feelings of deprivation. For example, if your parents made you do all your chores, have your breakfast, do the dishes and get dressed in your Sunday best before allowing you access to your Christmas presents, you may vow never to put your children through that. In other words, if your children see how you behave with money as 100 percent sacrifice and zero percent fun, those well-intended behaviours of yours might send the pendulum of your children's financial behaviour in precisely the wrong direction.

The Bunker practically invented saving. It's what they do best. Generally speaking, the Bunker is the world's best saver, however, there are circumstances, like being married to another Mindset with opposite behaviours or not earning enough to really save, that can put a crimp in your saving intentions. In those cases, your life is deprivation 24/7 and you don't even get the payoff from the security of having savings. Normally, The Bunker is very much the grasshopper to the general population's ant; slowly and consistently squirreling away every spare penny.

Your intense need to feel safe can sometimes put you in financial harm's way, especially when fear is used to sell you products or services. For example, you love to buy the extras when they make you feel safe. If you feel you can buy something to keep anything bad from happening, like extra warranty on electronics, you'll pony up the additional funds. When it comes to financial products in particular, you will often go with something familiar, even if it costs you more in the long run. Your need for security can cause you to lull yourself into making choices that aren't in your best long-term interest. When it comes to investing, your fear can get in the way of your intellect.

While you do invest, you don't tend to take much risk, even long-term investments. When you do take any risk and your investments go down even a small amount, you jump the gun and immediately put it all back into cash. Rather than taking the time to research investments, you probably revert to whatever you've done in the past. In reality, this is not an issue, as long as you are willing to put more into long-term investments to make up for the lower growth rate you might have to endure as a result.

You sometimes feel deprived, but you shove that feeling down by reminding yourself of your fear. You feel too guilty to enjoy anything you purchase anyway, so what's the point? You always have your mortgage locked in for example, because you feel that is the safest route. You will rarely investigate other options, because you believe 'the devil you know' is better than even mathematical proof of any other valid strategies.

Your friends and family would say you are very careful, even timid. While they find you incredibly reliable, they worry you are not happy. Everyone feels they can count on you. You are great at controlling your spending—a little too great.

You are cautious and trustworthy.

If you don't agree with your results, another way to score yourself is to look at the most common choice you made with your quiz answers.

More 1's = The Brick Wall
More 2's = The Bunker
More 3's = The Justifier
More 4's = The Dreamer
More 5's = The Undercover Agent
More 6's = The Masquerader
More 7's = The Polly Anna

CHAPTER 3

How NOT Fine We All Are

*"Inaction breeds doubt and fear.
Action breeds confidence and courage".*

~ Dale Carnegie

"We were fine . . . and then . . ."

These are probably some of the most famous last words I've heard and they've been uttered by nearly every person I've ever seen in financial trouble. So many of us think that fine is the opposite of 'in crisis'; but it's not. ***Financial stability is not a destination; it is an active state of being.*** It is a daily practice. You don't get to financial stability and sit there; you work to stay in a place of economic agility day-by-day. A place from which you can take time to make the right decisions when standing at any crossroad in your life. You might as well accept it right now . . . we are never fine. We are either in an active state with our finances or a passive state, but we are not fine. We are in crisis or we are not in crisis, but we are not okay. I can tell you every person who tried to explain their sheer financial ruin to me who lead with, "We were fine", was obviously not fine. They were not in crisis the moment before they were in crisis and they passively managed their money at that time. But they were not fine.

How "Fine" is your Mindset?

The Justifier: You are an expert at beginning sentences with, "We were fine . . . and then". For your Mindset, the problem always comes out of nowhere.

The Bunker: You are always on the quest to be "fine", but likely have trouble ever accepting you are there.

The Dreamer: You don't need to be fine. You believe things will always work themselves out, so worrying about being fine or not is a waste of your time and energy.

The Brick Wall: You wouldn't believe me anyway. If you think you're fine, no one can tell you any different. If you don't think you're fine, you aren't going to admit it until you figure out how to fix it. Even then, you will only speak about your "non-fineness" once you are completely stable again.

The Undercover Agent: You don't want to divulge enough details with any one person to discover if you are fine or not.

The Masquerader: If you are not fine, you are likely the most aware of it, but that is the whole point for you anyway. It matters not if you are fine, it matters that you appear fine.

The Polly Anna: You don't even want to know if you are fine or not. You trust someone else will see to that.

So, if you've picked up this book because you were fine, or you think you are fine but you'll take a peek just in case, remember, you are not fine—none of us are. Rather than worry about whether you think you are doing okay from a financial perspective, answer this question:

How prepared am I for a crisis or an opportunity?

The reason both are important is because the financial consequences of either can be quite similar. The cost of not being able to make a purchase can be equal to the impact of being stuck in a corner, unable to respond to one of life's curve balls. In other words, living in a place of economic agility is as much about seizing opportunity as it is about being ready for an emergency. I find most people don't think of it that way. They think of needing savings to cope when they are exposed to a crisis, like a car breaking down, an unexpected illness, a leaking roof or an emergency trip to care for an ailing relative. We rarely think about the fact that there is a cost associated with having to pass on opportunities of a lifetime; all because we weren't ready.

Example Crisis:

The transmission in your car throws a spastic fit 30 days and 1000 km after the warranty runs out and a new one will cost you $4000. You have no other choice but to put it on your credit card at 19 percent interest because you didn't put money away as a savings cushion in anticipation of crisis.

Example Opportunity:

The stock market is down 40 percent of its height. You see the stock price of a company that you know well and have great faith in its ability to recover. That particular stock is down 35 percent. Unfortunately, you don't have a stash of cash to invest in it.

If either of these situations presented themselves
would you be ready?

What if the gain or cost was greater?

In your working life, have you ever been forced
to make a decision for financial reasons where you truly
would have wished for better options?

I have never met anyone who, after working for any length of time, could say money never dictated a decision they would have made differently if they'd been able to do so. If you are the first, please put this book down.

Active vs. Passive Financial Behaviour

Most of us are either actively managing our money or we are passively handling it. There is nothing more important than paying attention to your money. You can't change something you aren't paying attention to. You can't get the best life from your finances if you can't tell where your cash is going. Great things can happen by accident, but the greatest things tend to be on purpose. If you happen to have a few happy accidents on top of being great on purpose, that's wonderful. But you just don't want to rely on happy accidents.

Displaying active financial behaviour doesn't mean you need to know everything about money. It doesn't mean you have to write down every penny you spend, or obsess over every intricate detail of your bank statement. Being present in your own financial decisions is not about spending hours of your day researching funds or checking your bank balance online each time you leave the house. Being present with your finances means you make sure you understand what you are doing and that you are committed to keeping on top of it.

Examples: Passive Financial Behaviour

- You use your debit card for most purchases
- Your bank statements are still in their envelopes
- You never read the information on the funds you invest in. You figure the advisor or banker you deal with must know what they are talking about.
- You are not sure what your company retirement savings plan is invested in, but you're sure its fine

Examples: Active Financial Behaviour

- You check your monthly bank and credit card statements as they come, looking for inaccuracies
- You use pre-determined amounts of cash for all your variable spending
- You are very clear about what you are investing in and you know how to retrieve information on your funds
- You understand the lending products you use and feel confident you are using the most cost-effective products you have access to

You may look at both lists under each type of financial behaviour and feel you have a little of both in you. That's okay; there is no right or wrong. Where you are now, just is. It's only once you know better that you must hold yourself accountable to do better. For now, just take the time to figure out how active or passive you are with your money.

Take a few minutes to think about how you manage the following aspects of your finances, putting a 'P' beside items you feel you are more passive with. Alternatively, jot an 'A' beside those items you feel you manage actively. Again, you are not wrong or bad for having some P's, the most important part of this exercise is to get a feel for where you are now.

- Statements for bank accounts, investments, pension plans, group benefits, insurance policies, etc.
- Making investment choices
- Day-to-day spending e.g.: groceries, gasoline, clothing, entertainment, etc.
- Borrowing money and use of any credit purchases (including store cards and no-payment, no-interest plans)
- Paying monthly bills
- Major purchase decisions, like buying a car or a new home
- Minor purchases like electronics, furniture, appliances etc.
- Rental or income properties
- Home renovation or maintenance
- Your retirement or financial plan

4 pts for every A
-2 pts for every P

My Money Management Score: _____

Money Management Key

40-36 – Extremely engaged in all aspects of your finances
35-28 – Very engaged in most aspects of your finances
27-10 – Somewhat engaged in some aspects of your finances
9-0 – Very passive in most aspects of your finances
Less than 0 – You have no clue what is going on with your finances

We'll use this score later on to uncover just how "fine" you really are. Then we'll explore the personality traits that come along with your Money Mindset and how they can be used to your advantage when it comes to money, which will ultimately lead you to the most practical and useful advice for your particular situation. Remember, these are not right or wrong answers;

this is simply your baseline. As you move forward, you will realize that for you, there are some areas of your finances that are better managed passively. You will also find there are many areas where being passive is almost always too expensive.

Mindset tips

The Justifier: You are extremely passive with your money management. At first, you may feel uncomfortable with the thought of taking control, but this book will help you reduce the anxiety you feel when you consider your finances and how you are handling them.

Your score: If your baseline was very low, you could be setting yourself up for failure. The combination of your charismatic ability to reason, combined with little attention to your finances can be toxic.

The Bunker: You are a far more active money manager, almost to the point where you don't allow yourself or your family to enjoy your hard-earned dollars. You may find this book can help you learn how to let go a little but still feel safe and on track.

Your Score: There is no need to worry about a high score unless you are feeling stressed over the fact that you are holding onto your money too tightly. If you had a low score, then you are likely a full on stress ball, consumed with worry and guilt about your finances but too afraid to look at them. Believe it or not, a Bunker Mindset can still be a passive money manager. The easiest way not to feel stressed about money is to ignore it . . . right?

The Dreamer: You are very passive with your day-to-day money, but far more active in the management of financial decisions (even if you do it through your rose-coloured glasses). This book will help you learn how to balance your active and passive behaviours so you can still feel free to "dream", but within a space that allows you to reach your goals.

Your score: You could go either way but the higher your score, the more likely you are to be consistent with your success. Paying attention to day-to-day spending will be the key to your financial freedom.

The Brick Wall: You are the most active money manager of all the Mindsets. In fact, you are not passive when it comes to any financial matters. This book can teach you how to let go and still feel in control, especially when it comes to trusting your spouse with money.

Your score: If you are not the highest score possible, I'd be surprised. As long as it doesn't cause you stress, a high score for you is just perfect. Should you have a middle or lower score I would expect you are extremely stressed. Making your money management style more active will benefit you.

The Undercover Agent: You are a very passive manager of your day-to-day expenses and more active on the big things, like buying a home or investing. This book will show you how to let go of some of your trust issues around money and see the true benefits of opening up about your finances.

Your score: You are more likely to be middle of the pack, although a high score would be better. If you have a lower score, you may feel like you "make good money but can't figure out where it all goes".

The Masquerader: You are passive on all counts of spending. You can use the tips in this book to learn how to set limits and still have a life.

Your score: You are doing well to have a mid-level score. If your score is low, you probably play hard but you fall hard, too. Managing both day-to-day and major purchases is the key to getting and sustaining true wealth.

The Polly Anna: You are so passive with finances that you are happiest when you have absolutely no clue what is going on. This book will help you better understand your financial behaviour and realize that knowing what is going on is not as scary as you may have thought and can actually make you feel empowered and safe.

Your score: You are the most likely to have a negative score. You really need to work on your money management. Baby steps are fine, but you need to consistently take on a more active role in your household finances.

When you are not prepared for the unexpected, you can often get forced into a corner where the only choice you have wouldn't have been your first choice. This feeling of being trapped by your life circumstances and then feeling forced to make less than ideal choices, is incredibly draining. How many people—yourself included—never do what they want with their life because they feel they can't afford to take the risk. I have found in my decade working with clients and their money that this can often lead to a cascade of less than optimal decisions. The first step of harnessing your financial power is to be an active participant in the decisions you make. It might take a little extra time up front. It might even be uncomfortable, but I promise discomfort is where growth comes from and you need to sit with that anxious feeling and force yourself to face your money. Every step you take to grab a hold of your financial power will feel less unpleasant. In the meantime, you will have to accept that meaningful change can cause the urge to squirm. Just hold on and sit still anyway.

What if?

There are enough insurance and investment commercials about the risks of not dealing with your "what ifs" to bore one to death; so I won't make you watch any of those. Just for kicks, let's play the "what if" game with your real life. Please rate your ability to react to the following crises and opportunities by circling the response that is closest to your current situation. At the end, add up your points and write in your score. We will then apply your results to your own Mindset.

1. *What if you lost your job tomorrow and didn't find another one for 10 months? When you find another job, your salary is 80 percent of what you used to make.*

   a) I have enough savings to get me through without changing my lifestyle or reducing my monthly savings/investment contributions. I would take the time to find the right job.

   b) I have enough to get me through if I cut my expenses back, and I know how to do that. I would have to stop investments/savings until I went back to work.

   c) I don't have much savings, but I've got access to a low rate line of credit. If I cut back spending, and suspended my monthly savings/investing I could get through the 10 months.

   d) I have no savings and very little access to open credit right now. If I lost my job over a 10-month period, short of cashing out long-term funds like RRSP's, I don't know what I would do.

e)   I'd freak out. I have no savings, long or short-term. If I lost my job for that period of time, I would be in real trouble.

2. *What if your young child was very ill and ended up in the hospital full-time for two months?*

a)   I could take my vacation time and sick time then, beyond that, I could afford the time without pay for the remainder of the two months by using a small portion of my savings.

b)   I would take my vacation and sick time, but then I'd have to use up all the savings I had if I funded the rest of the two months myself.

c)   I would take my vacation and sick time since I have no savings. I'd have to go into my line of credit to survive the additional time off required.

d)   I'm self-employed. I have no vacation or sick time to take, so I would have to do a combination of dipping into savings and going into debt.

e)   I could take the vacation and sick time I've got left for this year, but with no savings and no access to low interest credit, I'd have to work as much as possible over this time.

3. *What if you could max out your retirement savings accounts where your investment could grow? And when you withdrew the money to live on, it would attract neither tax nor have an impact on government benefits?*

a)   I've already maxed out my retirement savings accounts with investments. I am not holding cash, high interest savings or guaranteed interest bearing investments in my retirement savings accounts.

b) I have some money in a retirement savings account but I'm not maxed out. I am not holding cash, high interest savings or guaranteed interest bearing investments in my retirement savings accounts.

c) I don't have a lump sum to max it out but I am able to invest in a retirement savings account regularly. I would not hold cash, high interest savings or guaranteed interest bearing investments in my retirement savings accounts.

d) In order to max out my retirement savings accounts, I'd have to take money from my line of credit.

e) I have no way to come up with the cash I would need to invest in a retirement savings account, let alone be able to max it out.

4. *What if a cottage you've had your eye on for years goes up for sale well below fair-market value? Having a cottage is one of your major financial goals.*

a) Perfect! I have the cash to buy a small cottage property outright. As long as my family is going to use it, I'd snap up that deal.

b) Great! I've been saving up to make a large down payment on a cottage. I could make an offer tomorrow if I wanted.

c) I have some money aside that I could use to put toward a small down payment on a cottage, but I'd have to finance most of it.

d) I could afford the payments and maintenance, but I'd have to take the entire down payment from a line of credit against my home.

e) Are you crazy? I can't get rid of the debt I've got now! Not only do I not have a down payment, I have no way to get one and I don't have the cash-flow to support the additional costs.

10 pts for every a)
6 pts for every b)
4 pts for every c)
2 pts for every d)
-2 pts for every e)

My Financial Agility Score: _____

Financial Agility Key

40-32 - Extremely agile
31-16 – Moderately agile
15-0 – Low agility
Less than 0 – Couldn't deal with the price of carrots going up 1 percent

Mindset tips

The Justifier: If your financial agility was very low, you need to make saving and debt management a major goal—no coming up with reasons why you can't do it right now! The biggest issue to your financial agility is the fact that you can convince yourself it's not something you need to worry about. High financial agility doesn't get you off the hook but it gives you more options to start with. Any Mindset with low agility is worrisome. It means you can't handle any unexpected expenses. For the Justifier, extreme agility is only good if your spending is well controlled. Otherwise, you are only a few really convincing arguments away from reducing your agility. Being aware of your spending can really be key to keeping or increasing your financial agility.

The Bunker: Low agility for you is likely the result of a life change such as losing a job, divorce or some other unforeseen event for which you were unprepared, but the money you had saved for such an event is now running out. Being married or partnered with one of the other Mindsets can also be the cause of low agility. Low agility in your Mindset could be a case of not wanting to have access to credit. It is important to have a choice between credit and liquidating savings at certain times. Your Mindset is easily dominated. A high agility is great, but you may struggle to take full advantage of it.

The Dreamer: You might be middle of the road here. Not in a wide open space necessarily, but not backed into a corner either. Your greatest challenge is to keep your back out of the corner; never stretching so thin that you can't maneuver. Being more patient to better organize your debt, savings and investments will serve you well in future goals.

The Brick Wall: You are likely have a very high agility score and use it to your full advantage most of the time, except when you don't listen to ideas that are not your own. There may be products or concepts out there to better your finances, but you have to have an open mind in order to take advantage of them. You can still research your brains out if you wish, just be a little more open to suggestions and you could improve your results.

The Undercover Agent: With low agility, you are at grave risk of letting your small expenses sink your financial ship. You should strive to achieve a moderate agility level to be truly able to stay in control of your finances and enjoy all that they have to offer.

The Masquerader: You think your agility is high until you go to make a major purchase and have to move things all over the place to make the numbers work. Look closely at your score and think back to how much of a hassle your last big purchase was. If your agility number isn't consistent with the effort to borrow, it might be off.

The Polly Anna: If you knew enough to complete this quiz without having to look up some of the financial terms, I'm proud of you! If you were brave enough to check out all the details, the results may have scared you no matter which way they swung. The fear of being painted into a corner or being in a wide-open financial space is equally terrifying for you.

Again, these numbers don't mean you are doing things right or wrong; they just help you see where you are.

OSS + Debit Card = Trouble

Ostrich Spending Syndrome (OSS) puts anyone who uses a debit card regularly at risk. One of the most common reasons for passive management of day-to-day money is the fact we often can't see what we are spending when we spend it. We do see what we paid, but we don't see what we spent relative to what we have. It may be that many of us are suffering from OSS. While there is no cure for this modern-day disorder, there are some very effective treatments.

> *The Ostrich, (Struthio camelus), is a large flightless bird native to Africa. It is distinctive in its appearance, with a long neck and legs and the ability to run at maximum speeds of about 70 km/h (45 mph), the top land speed of any bird.*

Ostriches are fabled to bury their heads in the sand when frightened; in reality, they do no such thing. However—here is where you'll see my animal sciences is actually useful for a career in finance—I spent some time with ostriches as well as turkeys (who I have observed doing some similar behaviours) during my time at the NSAC. I once visited an ostrich farm and when the farmer entered their pen, they ran into the corner and laid down, turning their heads making sure not to look at him. I could just picture one saying to the other "Okay, I know he saw us run over here but if we lie really still and don't look at him, he'll never find us. Ready. . . freeze!"

> *Turkey Meleagris (disambiguation): Our domestic turkey is a descendent of what is commonly known as the Wild Turkey, which is native to the forests of North America. There are several extinct species dating from as far back as 23 million years ago.*

I did have far more experience with the much smaller and less dangerous turkey. When my classmates and I would enter the turkey pens at school to move them or handle them for health checks, they would all rush to one corner of their enclosure. Then they would stand with their heads jammed right into the corner. As soon as they couldn't see us, they seemed to immediately relax, as if they are thinking, "Phew. Well, I'm glad they're gone". Seriously, ten turkeys all standing very still in the corner apparently convinced if they didn't look at us, we weren't there. When I would reach for one, no matter how slowly I moved or gentle I tried to be, as soon as I got a hold of them, they'd let out a huge squawk, as if it were a total shock I was so near. I actually like turkeys best of all the fowl I've ever handled. For what they lacked in intelligence, they made up for by being quiet, gentle and easy to hang on to.

Even though ostriches don't really put their heads in the sand, I still like my term OSS; it seems so much nicer than saying, "Hey. Don't be a turkey!"

Back to my point . . .

OSS is the spending behaviour we all practice when we purchase items using electronic methods of payment—debit or credit cards or unplanned cash withdrawals—that allow us to be unaware of our total spending at the time we make the purchase. I must confess, I truly worry more about the contribution of debit cards to overspending even more than credit cards because of the extraordinarily false sense of security debit cards provide. Over the years, I've found that people will often feel that when they use a debit card they are at least spending money they already have. However, if you have any amount of consumer debt, like credit cards or lines of credit, I think unconscious spending of money that is indeed already in your account, is no different than breaking out the Amex. Think of it this way; if you spend an extra $100 this month that could have paid down your debt, how is that any different than having put the $100 on your credit card?

Answer: it isn't.

First of all, even having a balance on a credit card, line of credit or store card is often evidence of some event, series of events or even a pattern of regular overspending. Add to that, not controlling what you spend while you are making the purchase decision, and those balances usually have no choice but to grow. In my experience, that which caused you to run out of money before you ran out of month, could be exacerbated by the use of electronic payment methods. You simply just can't see what you are doing while you are doing it. Now, let me be clear— cash isn't better. Limited, agreed upon amounts of cash taken on pre-determined intervals is better, but multiple ATM runs to keep your pockets full is no better than electronic spending.

Spending using your debit card doesn't stop you from growing debt. You just think of it as spending money you already have, but if you have even a few hundred dollars of consumer debt, you are just kidding yourself. Not paying attention to spending decisions does nothing to get you ahead, no matter how comfortable your current financial situation is. Far too many people overspend using this popular plastic and end up either making lower payments on their borrowings or living in overdraft. Either way, this particular payment medium can cause a loss of control over your monetary behaviour.

Example of OSS in motion

Read through this seven day example. Don't use a calculator and don't try to add it up as you go. Simply read it through quickly and make a quick guess when you get to the end of Sunday as to the bank balance at the end of the week.

It is important that you do read this through quickly, not stopping too long to think. After all, that is how these expenses played out and we don't tend to stop and do the math in real life, so don't do it here.

Monday: You have $3004 in your chequing account.

- You go to the grocery store on your way home from work as you forgot a necessary ingredient for the supper you planned. While you're there, you find a few extra items you could use through the week and grab a snack at the checkout. You spend $44.98.
- Three bills come out of your account automatically totalling $587.

Tuesday: You don't check your balance but you do some quick mental math and think you have about $2300 left.

- You go for lunch with a colleague and spend $20.15.
- You get a latte on the way home. You had a hard day and you are pooped. You need the caffeine to pick you up. The barista tells you about their new scone and asks if you'd like one of those with your order. Exhausted and starving you say yes; you spend $7.78.
- As you pick up the kids from the sitter, you realize that you didn't take anything out for dinner. You hit the local pizza shop and grab a couple of pies for a grand total of $24.88.
- Your spouse comes home and informs you their tire was punctured by a nail that day and they had to stop by the garage. Figuring you have plenty of money left from payday, they don't mention that they used the debit card for $44.57 worth of purchases.
- Your car payment of $340 comes out along with an insurance payment for $119.

Wednesday: Payday was only six days ago and you paid all of your bills online right away so you think you had $2300 give or take on Tuesday. Quickly reflecting back on yesterday, you estimate you spent $45. You think your balance is still pretty close to $2250.

- You pick up some pain reliever at the drugstore for your

child's earache; you spend $9.

- Your child comes home with a book order from school, a permission slip for a class trip, along with a bill for $38 for the whole lot. You write a cheque.
- Your life insurance comes out of your account, another $58.

Thursday: You don't even bother to think about your bank balance today. You don't think you'll be spending any money anyway. You remember only one transaction from yesterday and it was under $10 at the drugstore.

- You take out $40 at the bank machine to get coffee with a co-worker and put some money into the office lotto pool.
- Your spouse takes $60 out of the bank so they have some cash in their pocket for the week.
- Your mortgage payment of $1100 comes out of your account.

Friday: You and your spouse didn't have a chance to mention your cash withdrawals from the day before, but it's no big deal, so you don't worry about it. You remember the mortgage had come out and estimate that you still have $1200 left in your account. It's only another 6 days to payday and you think all the major bills are paid.

- It snowed last night so you didn't have time to eat breakfast and shovel. You stop at the drive-through and pick breakfast up for $4.67.
- You have a busy weekend coming up, so you stop to do your grocery shopping on your way home from work. With a family of four, your grocery bill is typically about $200/wk. This week, you needed to buy a few cleaners and toiletries as well. Dinner will be late, too, so you grab a snack for yourself. Your son is growing out of his PJ's and you spot some on sale for $7.99, so you pick up four pairs. This week is a little higher than usual at a grand

total of $276.

- It's the weekend after all, so you pick up a bottle of wine to share with your spouse at dinner for $21.99.
- Your spouse's lease payment of $456 comes out.
- Your home insurance payment of $64 comes out.

Saturday: It's a crazy day. You have two kids going in two different directions for their activities. Your spouse takes one and you run in the opposite direction with the other.

- Both of you have to take each child somewhere for lunch as there is no time to run home to eat. You spend $19.87 and your spouse $22.32.
- Your spouse takes $20 cash back knowing there will be a cost for parking at the next stop.
- The child who is with you came home Friday with a leaky boot so you stop to pick up a new pair for $39.16.

Sunday: It is a lazy day. Everyone sleeps in for a change. You and your spouse are pooped from the week and don't spend your Sunday morning discussing your individual purchases over the week.

- You rent a few movies for the family and pick up a few treats to go along with them for $18.14.
- Your spouse runs an errand and thoughtfully returns with a latte for you. You know they spent at least $5.

Quick! Don't go back over it. Just write down your first guess at this couple's bank balance at the end of the week shown above:
$_____

One more measure for your baseline is your mental math. It's not just your ability to add and subtract, it's more about how distracting other factors are for you.

Mental Math Key

10 pts if your answer was less than $200 off—Excellent mental math

6 pts if your answer was more than $200 off—Very good mental math

4 pts if your answer was more than $400 off—Adequate mental math (but in the overdraft)

2 pts if your answer is more than $600 off—Poor mental math

My Mental Math Score: _____

Answer: They are in the overdraft by -$436.51

Mindset tips

The Justifier: Anything short of excellent mental math could be getting you in trouble. Your ability to justify costs is magnified by your inability to see them.

The Bunker: You likely have pretty good mental math, but then again, you are more diligent than that couple. If you had trouble with it though, it shows that even you can benefit from seeing when and where your money is going.

The Dreamer: You likely have adequate to poor mental math. Electronic payment is really dangerous for your more frequent transactions for that reason.

The Brick Wall: I bet if anyone did well it was you. You probably also spending part of the time reading this thinking how differently you would have run that week!

The Undercover Agent: This might have been a real "ah ha" moment for you, as you likely bleed money in the same way this couple did. Just like them, you would greatly benefit from control over your spending rather than trying to use mental math.

The Masquerader: You may not even care what your score is, but if you aren't putting away huge portions of those big bucks you make, if your finances are not what you wish they could be then maybe your mental math is probably part of the problem.

The Polly Anna: This was a great exercise for you. I hope it helped you see that it's normal to find money overwhelming or to have it run away with you. But, I also hope you know you can do something about it. You don't have to have great mental math to learn to control your spending and feel great about your money.

Even though I wrote the above scenario, I had trouble coming up with a close answer reading it through and guessing. Just think about it; if it is hard to do without carefully adding one transaction to the next without using a calculator, how can you expect to keep track in real life? Even when it's all laid out in front of you in this book, the flow of life and money commingle. Just imagine adding in the life this couple would be leading in the space between these transactions. This example is based on a real couple with young children and one week of their transactions. No wonder it is so easy to get off track.

These are not stupid people, nor did they fail at math in school. While this might be more the life of a young couple with children who have a smaller income, I often see a very similar pattern among those with much higher incomes as well. Also, of the many seniors I've worked with, even those who have well-funded retirements, I see the same habits and similar results. They may not be living in overdraft, but this same unconscious spending pattern results in far more money going out than they can usually account for when showing me their monthly expenses. The many forms of easy payment we all have access to these days is like adding rocket fuel to an already blazing fire. It's a walking coma of spending behaviour; people just swipe it and forget it.

Now, not all automation is bad; having a mortgage payment, credit card or car payment come out automatically is a good thing. Automated transactions for these more typically fixed and reoccurring transactions is helpful to us as we live our busy lives. Can you imagine standing in a line at the bank to pay your mortgage every month in cash? Even with modern day banker's hours, you'd never get home! Automation is a gift when it comes to saving, investing and paying down debt. There, automation shines.

I've had many conversations about the use of debit cards with so many people and what I've discovered is a theme consistent with a plethora of financial decisions that can be misguided by the fact it feels better. It feels better to tell yourself you are spending from money you have in the bank. It's not uncommon for many of us to have expensive decision making tendencies and they can affect everything from day-to-day spending to buying a new car. It's not that we are dummies; sometimes it's even not that we don't know the facts. It seems that when faced with a decision, anything that makes us feel more secure, safe, normal, happy or even just less uncomfortable, can too easily sway us. I think it's no accident that there are all kinds of financial products, payment methods and general money matters designed to make it easier and more comfortable to act against our own best interest; which is great. It's great because when I started to realize this, I experimented with ways to give the client that same feeling of safety while helping them act in their own best interest.

That same little twinge inside us that makes us freak out and sell our investments at a major loss, seems to weigh in when we make purchase decisions, too, and can have equally devastating results.

The good news is that you can take what you learn in this book about your own money personality and use it to your advantage. If we all start heading toward selecting financial tools and making purchasing decisions that lead us to our best end result, the market will come to meet us.

It's time to take the blinders off. Unconscious spending rarely leads you to your desired result. If you are spending in a daze, no matter how much money you have, you are certainly NOT fine.

CHAPTER 4

Spending 101

*"Beware small expenses; a small leak
can sink a great ship."*

~ Benjamin Franklin

Many of us throw around the word "afford" as if it came with an absolute meaning, or exact limits. But we all place different values on different things or experiences in our lives. So whether you can afford something is often not so cut and dry; both math and motivation become part of the equation. Some people confuse the ability to make payment at the time of purchase of an item or experience as proof they can afford it. Being in denial about your cash flow and racking up your credit cards in order to buy things that represent the lifestyle you wish to achieve some day is an expensive way to put the cart before the horse. This doesn't mean I get to decide for you which carts or horses are important to you. What I suggest is that you consider using realistic and true goals that match your current circumstances in order to motivate small change, micro-goals, if you will, to accomplish the life you actually want. This is not an all or nothing approach; it is an 'only things that matter' approach. Too many of us allow the funds that would amount to progress toward our goals, leak out to pay for things we just don't want that badly.

Conversely, many personal finance gurus will attempt to tell you exactly what you should and shouldn't value and therefore how you should use your money. Advice like: "You shouldn't have two cars", "Give up your coffee in the morning", "Don't go on any family trips until your debt is paid off", may not work for you. These opinions can sometimes cause the desired effect for the short term but not necessarily make it sustainable. Anytime someone gives you advice that doesn't align with your personal life values or your Money Mindset, the probability that you'll manage to make change and continue to progress toward your goals diminishes.

The Justifier: Your behaviour when it comes to your finances is incongruent to your goals. Don't try to explain away a behaviour that is contrary to your long-term goals. If your goal is to pay down some of your consumer debt, you need to make that the focus. Do not allow your cleverly crafted excuses to steer you off track.

The Dreamer: For someone who wants long-term success, you are often not someone who understands that long-term success is unlikely to happen overnight. You say your personal and professional goals are the most important things to you (except for family perhaps), but you'll often sabotage those goals by using borrowed funds to buy yourself the success you haven't quite earned.

The Brick Wall: For a smart person, you can sometimes do things that don't make sense. You are more concerned with being right than achieving your goal. Happiness is almost secondary to your desire to do everything in your own way. You want to know enough about your finances to be sure you are making the best decisions, but you are leery of opening your mind enough to listen when knowledge is being shared with you. Don't worry, no one is keeping score. If you win a million arguments in your own head and you don't reach your life's goals, you'll be the only one affected. Learning to trust yourself a little more can help you listen to others and accept their advice with an open mind.

The Polly Anna: You have to spend some time thinking about what you really want from your life so you'll know if your behaviours are congruent or incongruent with your goals. It's okay to stand up for yourself. With every decision you make, you'll become more confident.

The Masquerader: You are the definition of incongruent. You want to be financially impenetrable, but you put yourself and your family at grave financial risk with your obsession to make sure everyone thinks you are financially secure. You need to figure out what YOU really want. Then, and only then, can you truly start to align your life with your goals. Without this alignment, you may find it hard to be consistently financially independent.

The Undercover Agent: You work hard to hide your goals from others. Continue to do this long enough, and even you won't be sure what it is you truly want. Making incongruent financial choices is common for your Mindset. You say you don't spend a lot of money, yet you don't have much left over from your decent salary at the end of any given month. You need to really take some time to think about your actual life goals. If you focus on those goals, you may find you are brave enough to open up a bit, especially if it increases the likelihood you'll live the life you want.

The Bunker: Your most incongruent behaviour is your very nature. You strive NOT to worry about money. However, because you can become quite fixated on feeling financially safe, you can often manifest your own fear into reality.

Family Financial History

Spending behaviour is shaped by what we see, hear and are told about money while we are growing up. Society, our parents, other family members and financial experiences early on leave marks on us and influence our behaviour, at least to some degree. We all make choices, of course, and the way we were raised doesn't guarantee anyone a particular financial outcome. However, reflecting on our early experiences with money can be helpful.

Perceived Deprivation

"We can't afford it." If this was a phrase you consistently heard as a child, whether you realize it or not, it has likely left its mark on how you think about and treat money. Perhaps, you even lived through days where things were too tight to afford food. As an adult, you will unconsciously want a lot to make up for those things you were deprived of during your early years. Contrarily, you may hold on to every penny with all your might to keep yourself safe.

When I speak to people who are struggling with major financial issues, I often ask how their parents talked about money in front of them.

Without fail, those who had parents who kept their families — whether out of necessity or in order to model frugality — in constant deprivation mode, tend to attach a lot of guilt to spending.

Whether they are overspenders or a super-saver, those early experiences tend to teach them spending money is bad or wrong. Feeling deprived or unsafe because of money when we are young, can cause us to either channel that shame into extreme saving patterns or extreme spending patterns.

The Bunker: Your Mindset may be the result of being raised in an environment that at least seemed depriving to you. Whether it was real or imagined, as the Bunker, you may be trying to avoid that feeling by saving, possibly to an extent that makes you or your family feel deprived.

The Brick Wall: If you were raised with little means, you are careful with money now, but you may blame your parents, a professional or a company of some kind as the reason for this deprivation. You, too, want to make sure you never relive that feeling of deprivation.

Sometimes, someone with this type of financial history will consciously, or even unconsciously, overspend. This destructive spending behaviour however, will eventually result in the very circumstance they are trying to avoid. Even though they may have built a life where they don't need to experience this deprivation again, their uncontrollable overspending will take them to the edge of near debt. History always has a way of repeating itself. This is a hard habit to break using logic and reason; especially since financial behaviour is often not logical or reasonable.

The Dreamer: Being born into a family of lesser means, can be the fuel to a Dreamer's fire. This experience can cause them to define success as the ownership of many luxuries. The desire to achieve this success can lead a Dreamer to put their expenses before their financial horse so to speak.

The Justifier: You may feel you didn't deserve to go through what you did as a child. These feelings may cause you to protect your own children by never allowing them to feel deprived of anything.

The Undercover Agent: You may have been raised to think that having money makes you a bad person and that money or wealth is something to be ashamed of.

The Masquerader: If you were born from nothing, you are never going back! Part of protecting yourself from the past may be the need to prove to others that you've "made it".

The Polly Anna: This kind of upbringing is where The Polly Anna learned that dealing with money was stressful. In a home where money is bad news, The Polly Anna learns that avoiding all matters financial is the safest thing to do.

Misdirection

I've spoken to college students who admit in front of a parent that they find it frustrating and stressful when they say they can't afford something and then proceed to buy the item or commit to the cost despite their inability to reasonably afford it. They have further said that when they call home and ask for more spending money, they secretly wish their parent will say no. It's a very interesting dynamic to observe, but I know exactly what these young adults are feeling. It's confusing. It makes them feel insecure and unsure and wonder whether they might be putting undue stress on their families; or, possibly, if the original objection to the cost was simply to say no for the sake of saying no. Either way, it leaves a mark.

How we speak about, and the manner in which we handle money in front of our children, forever affects their financial feelings. How we deal with money as adults is directly related to how we saw our parents speak about and deal with money when we were children.

Children are not mind readers. They can only model behaviours they can see. If you are saying one thing and doing another, the child is left feeling bewildered and anxious. So, if you save in secret, for example, and then pull out the plastic for everything in public, the only behaviour your child sees in this scenario is you pulling out the plastic.

The following Mindsets are all very keen to keep their real finances hidden. If you are one of these, you'll have more trouble opening up about money, even though you know it would be worth doing.

> **The Brick Wall**
> **The Masquerader**
> **The Undercover Agent**
> **The Bunker**

Meal Ticket

Many people believe that when we are young, if we just work hard and get good grades, go to the right school etc., we won't have to worry about money later on in life. If this is the message you heard as a child or one you are sending your children now, it may not have the desired effect. In fact, you could be inadvertently teaching your children that success means you can get to a place where you can ignore money. Unfortunately, money is always finite and the ways to spend it are infinite. Earning a good living is no guarantee; it only determines the size of your pay cheque, not what you do with it.

Everyone has to pay attention to money and how they spend it, no matter how much you have. Money is a limited resource. We have access to far more ways to spend money than there are ways to earn it. It will never matter how much you make if you never keep enough of it on hand to do the things you say you really want to do in life, like spending more time with loved ones. Abuse of your money will always hold you back—I don't normally speak in absolutes, but overspending deserves an absolute.

When working with these Mindsets, I find they can be more concerned about their visual achievements or financial status than what is actually happening with their money. Wanting either of these things is not bad, but if you are one of these Mindsets, you should always work to be clear that what you seek is actually more important to you than how others perceive you.

> **The Dreamer**
> **The Masquerader**
> **The Brick Wall**

Spoiled Rotten

As children, some of us were told that nothing was too much. It's a completely different childhood experience, leading to a completely different reasoning pattern, which can end in harmful spending behaviour. We all need to be a little bit deprived from time-to-time. We need to want things we cannot have. We need to know what it feels like to wait for something or even to accept that sometimes an item is not wanted badly enough to pay the price. All of this comes with maturity, and when a child is given no limits, they often have to live with negative effects later in life.

When I work with these Mindsets, I often hear them say things about their childhood that leads me to believe they may have left the nest without flying lessons.

> **The Dreamer**
> **The Undercover Agent**
> **The Polly Anna**
> **The Justifier**

So, when I ask people how their parents talked about money, and they answer that they wanted for nothing as a child, I know I am dealing with a slightly different creature involving slightly different motives for their financial choices. I have no doubt their parents did worry about money; they either overspent and their children never saw the debt or they watched every cent they spent, but never let the children in on how they managed the family finances. Either way, their parents worried about money despite the image they portrayed to their children.

As Sir Issac Newton said, "To every action, there is always an equal and opposite reaction." This theory doesn't just apply to physics. No matter how hard our parents tried to protect us or model good money behaviours; and no matter what we try to show and tell our kids, it's always going to leave a mark of some sort. What you need to ask yourself is, "Am I leaving the mark I'd like to leave?" Regardless of the direction, extremes and money don't mix well.

Think back to what you learned about money as a child:

- What message did your parents send by the way they talked about money in front of you?

_____

_____

_____

_____

- What message did your parents send by the way they behaved around money in front of you?

_____

_____

_____

_____

- What category do you most identify with when you read the above examples of financial family history?

_____

_____

_____

_____

- At what age do you remember first worrying about money?

_____

_____

_____

_____

- How would you define your family's financial situation when you were growing up? Did you feel you were poor, safe but had very few luxuries, comfortable, or even well off?

_____

_____

_____

_____

- What message do you think you are sending your children about money by the way you talk about it in front of them?

_____

_____

_____

_____

- What message do you think you are sending your children about money by the way you behave with it in front of them?

_____

_____

_____

_____

Money Leaves Nothing Untouched

No matter how you feel about money, how in control you are or where you struggle with it, money touches nearly every part of our lives. From the time we get up, to the time we rest our heads on our pillows at night, money sneaks into nearly every part of our day.

Here is an example of a day in the life of the average person:

Monday
6:00 am —wake up and head to the gym (costs money)
7:30am — head to work (to earn money)
12:00pm — lunch, either packed or out (still costs money)
4:00pm — go home (the house costs money)
5:00pm — take son to hockey practice (costs lots of money)
6:30pm — dinner (costs money)
8:00pm — watch TV (costs money)

If you really think about it, there isn't much we do, touch, see, experience, use or achieve in a day that isn't touched in some way by money. The heart of your financial situation is your cashflow. From the coffee you buy on the way to work, to the home you drive back to at the end of the day, it all connects back to your cashflow. Money is the lifeblood of your personal finances. How and where you make money flow affects every aspect of your life.

No matter how much money you make, if you don't control spending, you can never fund savings or investments. I often say that a good income is no guarantee of financial security, or financial knowledge for that matter. Sometimes, those with higher incomes just happen to have a much bigger shovel with which to dig their debt hole. Income is only one measure of potential wealth. In fact, income is merely potential wealth. How much you make is not the real predictor of wealth; how much you DON'T spend determines your true wealth.

First, let's get through some of the 'self-talk' many of us use—and I say "us" because you'd better believe I do it, too—when we think about just how much we spend. I didn't learn about money by being perfect, in fact, the most valuable lessons I am sharing with you resulted from my biggest mistakes.

Money is not about MATH

Most budget systems we have access to—be it software or a workbook—don't work well long term. I find that budgets, much like diets, just don't work, as they tend to be so structured it is difficult to manage your life around them. Remember back in Chapter 3, where we went through OSS? How would the family in that example have lived within a budget if they didn't know where they were at any given time?

Would they have logged into their online banking at the beginning of every day? Perhaps they could have called each other to report transactions? Or they could record all of their automatic transactions and additional transactions at the end of each day with receipts. While I'd propose all of these actions might work, I think we need to expect more than "it can work" when looking at lasting behaviour change. Rather, you need to ask yourself, "Is it reasonable that this will work? Can I stick to this day in and day out?"

For most, the answer to any solution that hinges on continuous checking in would be a resounding no. It's no secret that most fad diets are called fad because they don't last. Our culture is slowly but surely discovering that fundamental lifestyle changes are the way to go. Adding new behaviours over time, in such a way that we can easily adapt and sustain them, is where life-altering change begins. Much like eating well has less to do with your stomach and more to do with your brain and what it tells you to do, your finances have less to do with money and more to do with your thinking patterns.

When you set out to manage or change a behaviour, you can't work against yourself and expect to win—that's almost guaranteed failure. When you force yourself to do things in a way that leaves you feeling conflicted, you end up 'white knuckling it' and eventually the death grip you have on your new behaviour will let go. I've discovered that great results are not only more likely, but more lasting, when you identify your natural tendencies. We can then find ways to make meaningful, lasting change by smoothly integrating new compatible behaviours. Compatible behaviours are those you can maintain because they are not pushing you so far against your own grain that you are no longer able to hang on.

Mindset Tips

The Justifier: Mental math is not your friend. Understanding that money is not about math can be very helpful on your journey to financial freedom.

The Dreamer: You can easily distort both the cost of something as well as its value in your life. When life places a major purchase choice in front of you, it would serve you well to talk to someone close to you who is more objective, like a spending confidante you can bounce big buying decisions off of. This person could be your spouse, your friend or a business colleague you can trust. You need a reliable sounding board to keep from overdoing it in the spending, or as you like to call it, "investing" department.

The Brick Wall: You still think this is about money because you can't figure out how people can make the choices they do, even after they know the cost. While your math is sound, your ability to question yourself may be lacking. Hold yourself to those same exacting standards by which you measure others and give yourself a taste of what you dish out to salespeople. Make sure you are living up to your own expectations.

The Polly Anna: Math is not the issue for you since you are never trying to do the math— up until now. If you have to write everything down, open every bank statement or log onto your bank account every day to desensitize yourself to the fear of your own finances, just do it!

The Masquerader: Although you have math skills, it may not have occurred to you that you even have an issue. Paying attention and filtering your goals to make sure they are about your happiness will help keep you from getting distracted.

The Undercover Agent: You were still hoping the infamous magic elves were skimming funds from your accounts. Deep down you know that if the money is gone at the end of the month, you were the one who spent it, but you may feel frustrated about what you can do to rectify the situation. It doesn't feel like you've been buying all that much. Don't worry, your mind can play financial tricks on you and help is on the way. Just keep reading!

The Bunker: You aren't worried about math. Calculators come to you for answers and you know what you spend. For you, the mind tricks affect you more when you are trying to assess things that you perceive to be risky, which could be just about anything you don't already have experience with.

My own example:

I love lattes. To me, they are a food group in themselves. Literally. I have a goal of how much protein I need each day and I discovered my latte contains enough protein to be counted. From someone writing a book about how to manage spending, this confession may seem rather odd. I promise you the reason I'm not a walking contradiction is the same reason you'll actually be able to stick to my tips.

Traditional approach:

A five dollar coffee is unreasonable and it doesn't make sense to divert precious dollars to such a ridiculous indulgence. By cutting out my average five lattes a week, I could save up to $1300 a year. That is serious savings, right? In fact, if I put those latte dollars toward something useful and invested them from now until I reach age 65 (earning an average of 8 percent growth), I could end up with more than $250,000 to top up my retirement income. These dollars here and there add up to some serious dough. If you look at the math, and you were giving me money advice, it would make sense to recommend cutting out lattes.

Here's the problem with this approach. By giving someone like me this advice, you've woken my inner teenager. I can't even really hear this advice through the overwhelming feeling of, "Oh, so you think you are going to tell me what to do with my money? I worked hard for that and I'll do what I please with it". Even, if on the surface, I were to agree to permanently cut out something I really enjoy, over time, I would end up feeling differently, slowing drifting back to my original pattern.

If you were my advisor, and you talked to me for any length of time, you'd discover that asking me to cut out my lattes is an incompatible behaviour change. This doesn't mean that I should just keep on, keeping on, paying no attention to my bottom line. It just means that you took something that clearly mattered to me and you placed your value on it. The value you may have assigned to my latte is incompatible with the value I place on it. It would be very difficult for me to make this change long term, and I can tell you that if this was the advice someone gave me about controlling expenses, I'd resent them and eventually use those feelings as my excuse to return to the behaviour.

Cutting out my lattes = Incompatible with my values

My approach:

What you might try (as my advisor) is not preaching to me about how $5 lattes are a waste of my money. I would suggest that by trying to get me to forgo something I enjoy today in exchange for a reward that is so far away I can't even imagine it clearly, you are likely to fail and so am I. Even if I do take the original traditional advice, my inner teenager will eventually rebel and I'll end up right back where I started, except I'll feel worse knowing what I should be doing.

Let's take a look at both my values and my natural behaviour patterns.

Q: Why do I like my lattes so much?

A: Because they make me feel full. I can savour a latte for hours, reheating it as need be. I never waste a drop. I've been known to put an unfinished one in the fridge overnight and reheat it in the morning. My favourite café, *Starbucks*, allows me to frequently spend as much time in their establishment as I like on any given day, at any one of their locations. In fact, I've written at least a third of this book in their stores and developed most of the concept there. I can have a latte to hold me through to a healthy meal when I get home. I know exactly how many calories, grams of sugar, protein and fat I'm getting. I love the taste, smell, and sound of the café, as well as the variety of flavours available.

I can have meetings in any café location and the staff there recognizes me and many of them know my drink (I might have a leg up, being really short with long red hair and freckles does make me a little easier to remember). And because I can use this café as an office, as well as my latte as nourishment, I place a different value on it than someone else might. There are other things I'd rather give up or reduce, but I'm keeping my lattes.

Q: When do I get a latte?

A: Normally, between meetings or between or as part of a meal. Usually, I have one a day, four days a week and one on the weekend.

Q: How do I pay for my latte?

A: Back in the day, before I became so obsessed with cashflow and debt, I would use my debit card to buy just about everything, and I'm sure I had more than five a week because I was never paying attention. Today, I use cash to pay for them.

These days, I have a different approach with things that I value, like lattes. Valuing something doesn't mean I can ignore what I can afford, but it does mean I don't cut out things based on other people's values. Rather than saying I have to cut them out, I tell myself that I have to decide if I value a latte enough to choose it over something else. I work within a limited amount of funds (I use cash for a personal coffee run, I use my business expense account if the coffee is consumed during a meeting) for my discretionary spending, but I don't make things off limits. I simply make choices as I go along, knowing I've made it difficult to exceed my spending limit.

I looked at my natural behaviours and the pace of my life and made a conscious choice to set up my spending in a way that I can't overspend by accident. I knew that if I tried to keep count of the number of times I frequented my favourite coffee spot in a week, I'd lose track. I knew if I cut them out, I'd give in. I also knew if I tried to tell myself that it was a waste of money, I'd rebel. If I tried to control my behaviour while still using my debit card, my mental math would fail to tally properly.

So here is what I told myself to do:
About seven years ago, I sat down with my husband to review where exactly our money was going and we agreed that

from that day on, we would take a cash allowance for our discretionary spending. As I said, rather than deciding what was and wasn't taboo, we simply agreed as to how much we would spend, allowing us to set our own priorities within those weekly dollars. (I will go into more detail on this set up later on in the chapter).

My husband thinks my latte habit is silly and I think he spends too much on movies, music and books, which take up room around the house. Once we agreed on how we'd run our discretionary spending, however, we didn't have that resentful feeling about the choices the other made. We knew it was fair and square and we knew we owed no explanation to the other about where our spending money was used. This little revelation was the first step in what ultimately led to the development and growth of my business in a completely different direction. It also did something else for me. It helped the totally out of control debit card haze I had been wandering around in. My lattes were even more enjoyable when I understood that I could truly afford them.

Using cash so I can choose within a pre-determined amount how much I'd like to spend on lattes = Compatible long-term behaviour and values I can keep up.

Peer Pressure for Grown Ups

Let's deal with an issue that started on the playground, yet sadly, in many cases, still influences which car you drive today — peer pressure. Many people will read a book like this one, gather some great ideas and then boom, bang . . . nothing! Let me be clear, when you change the way you spend, you may also change the way in which you interact with others who are around you when you spend. I don't mean you are going to run around lecturing others about their poor spending habits. By the way, should you feel the need to do so, save your breath; no one likes it. I mean that in social settings, you might find yourself under intense pressure to hide your new financial behaviour. You may even want to bail on your shiny new habits the second you feel that explaining your changed behaviour might make it sound like you are in financial trouble or worse, that you are poor.

As we've grown into adulthood, we have indeed attached a good deal of value to what we can see when we look at others, and ourselves. I don't just mean physical looks, I mean physical or visible actions. The cars we buy, the neighbourhoods we live in or the places we lunch. In my experience, one of the greatest challenges to the way we spend is how to answer the objections or deal with comments your friends or family may lob at you.

I have to tell you that whenever someone asks me what I do, as soon as I say the name of my company, *"The Money Finder"*, their ears perk up. Normally, as the conversation continues, people have this almost unconscious and automatic need to share something about their financial situation. It generally goes one of two ways; either they share about their struggles with money or they comment on how poor other people are at managing their spending habits. Both of these responses tell me something. The former tells me this person is one of the many who feel like they could be doing better and would welcome ideas to make change. The latter tells me more; it's a defensive response. It tells me the person sharing with me either feels insecure about their own finances or they feel they are of superior intellect or they have another advantage over "those people".

Sometimes, the people that cite the poor financial prowess of others may feel they are identifying with me, that this must be the way I feel. By putting forward the idea that money is good or bad, black or white, and they belong on the right side of those options, they often draw the conclusion that people who use money are good or bad depending on their outcome. Asking this person a few more questions usually tells me one of two things; either the person really does have financial issues of their own that they are insecure about or they think that only bad people make bad financial decisions—which they conclude is because those people aren't as smart as they are.

This looking down our noses at other's financial outcomes is a major problem that thwarts the efforts of people who are wrestling with their own money, fighting to gain control. When we put out the message that making less than ideal financial decisions means you are stupid, bad or undisciplined, it does nothing to increase your drive to change. It could, however, encourage even more behaviour that appears stupid, bad or undisciplined.

Everyone is susceptible to peer pressure, no matter how old, but I find these Mindsets are even more susceptible.

> **The Justifier**
> **The Dreamer**
> **The Polly Anna**
> **The Masquerader**
> **The Undercover Agent**

Please sweat the small stuff

You know that saying 'don't sweat the small stuff' That might be good to tell yourself when you are worrying about something you can't control, like how someone else feels about you. It probably isn't a good use of your time to spend hours trying to figure out how to make someone like you. Worrying about whether or not someone likes you is as likely to produce a positive outcome as attempting to will the Canadian Revenue Agency to reduce your income tax rate by telepathic message. Neither exercise is worth your effort or the energy involved. However, when it comes to spending, the small stuff adds up to big stuff and you do have to sweat it.

There are those who don't need to worry about spending.

They meet ALL seven of the following criteria:

1. You are in your 60's.
     OR
     If you are under 60, you are independently wealthy

and have assets that would be almost impossible to deplete in your lifetime.

2   You can survive comfortably on absolutely guaranteed pensions. Market fluctuations do not matter to you.

3. You have no debt of any kind.

4. You have enough assets that you could withstand a 2008-like market correction up to three times between now and age 90.

5. You are insured to the hilt. Nothing unexpected could deplete your assets.

6. You do not have any children, dependent or adult.

7. You know your spending habits and expenses inside and outside.

If ANY of these seven are missing, the opportunity for the unexpected to deplete your security is always present. I don't say this to scare you, but I don't think most people can be prepared for all eventualities. What I do think is that unless your life is 100 percent guaranteed, whether you make $30,000/yr, $70,000/yr or even $1,000,000/yr, your life will be well served if you pay attention to your spending.

Unless you can tick all of those seven above boxes, you need to control your spending to some degree, so please keep reading. Congratulations to those who can check every box. I am perplexed as to why you would purchase this book, but I hope you like it anyway. And by all means, with all your secure wealth, please pick up a copy or two for people in your life who can't check all those boxes.

"We don't spend a lot of money"

This is a common phrase that often follows, "We were fine . . . and then". And, like the former, it's generally not true. When someone says to me, "We just don't spend a lot of money", I have two questions for them. Why don't you answer them, too?

1. *How much do you spend a month?*

    Most people who feel they don't spend a lot, don't tend to know exactly what they spend either. This tells me that for them, it might be more that they don't perceive they get a lot of value from what they do spend or that they don't feel they are surrounded by things they wish they could spend money on. They don't feel they are getting anywhere or making progress for what they are spending. When you look at your spending like that, you, too, would say you don't spend a lot either, but that doesn't make it so. Think of it this way: if you know that your household income is about $5500/month net in your bank account, and you don't have more than a few hundred dollars in the bank by the time the next check comes in, you are spending pretty close to the $5500 aren't you?

2. *How much is a lot?*

    Again, most people think that spending a lot must mean you are surrounded by stuff, or at least a lifestyle where you perceive great value. Spending a lot must involve some degree of luxury or indulgence. The fact of the matter is that it's entirely possible your absolute bare-bones expenses could exceed your income; that means you spend a lot! Spending, and what value you place on how much your life costs you, is relative. It's subjective and for everyone, it means something different. Consider this; if you are telling yourself, "I just don't spend that much money" but in the same moment you know you are not where you want to be financially, perhaps you are not being realistic.

You don't have to have an extravagant lifestyle or be going on an exotic vacation every year, or be draped in designer duds to end up spending a lot more than you mean to, or can afford. The filter through which you determine how much spending is too much might just be out of focus. So promise yourself, at least until you finish this book, that you'll drop the thought.

Do you know where all your money goes?

First things first: **what you can't measure, you cannot control.** Chances are that if you spend unconsciously, you are spending money on things you don't really value simply because you spend automatically. I guarantee most of you will be shocked when you get a good look at your totals. Your world would be rocked if you really knew how much you spend every year on things that don't truly matter to you. This is why you need to think about every expense at a deeper level. I am not asking you to do anything crazy like turn the heat down until your whole family has to eat dinner in their snowsuits, but far too many of us see far too many things as sacred when they really shouldn't be.

Here's the deal: our brains don't realize there are no more dinosaurs, some of the decisions we make are based on instincts that still behave as if T-Rex is around the corner. We are plotting our lives based on what some consider fairly irrational instincts that are more caveman than Einstein. We need to back the truth truck up on accepted behaviours when it comes to money and shake up how we do things. We should slow down decisions where we tend to get in the most trouble and speed up choices where we procrastinate until the moment of opportunity has passed or worse, years have passed.

There are subtle nuances of money and how it actually affects our lives versus how we want it to affect our lives. Money touches too much for us to merely continue our instinctual behaviours without dealing with this most basic comprehension of our underlying financial beliefs. For many of us, we need help focusing on how we really want to use our money, so we get the results of a lifetime from it. It's time for you to direct your financial future instead of just reacting to life as it happens. I realize this is easier said than done, but it's still worth doing.

So, turn the page . . .

CHAPTER 5

Active vs. Working Cashflow

"The secret of getting ahead,
is getting started"

~ Mark Twain

The hardest thing about managing spending is the fact that with certain expenses, the act of spending happens so frequently and sometimes, unpredictably. Life is non-linear. We can't just decide where we'd like to go from here and expect nothing to shift our path; it's not realistic. For a long time, I found this completely frustrating. I'd feverishly work away at budgets for people, trying to guess what kind of twists and turns would interfere with my diligent efforts to provide my clients with absolutes. Point A to point B planning doesn't work when it comes to spending. So, after a while, I realized that approach was just not going to work. No matter how much math I did, I just couldn't look into a crystal ball and see what lay ahead.

So, I decided to go about solving the problem in a different manner.

I decided that if I couldn't predict the future, I would have to come up with ways my clients could make better decisions in the moment. I told myself, "If I can't control the environment, then I'll have to come up with ways in which my clients can control themselves within that environment". It had to be something that wasn't too complicated and didn't involve a lot of steps or entail too much mental math. I needed ways to slow down or halt the behaviour of those who came to me asking for advice on how to improve their finances, while at the same time, foster new desirable and beneficial behaviours within them.

So, what was a gal to do? I'll give you a hint, you got a little taste of it in Chapter 4 with my self-experiment.

I couldn't follow people around or lock their money away from them. I couldn't force them to apply my values to their lives or decide for them what they should spend their money on, or embarrass them into financial submission. I had to find a way people could create perpetual financial change they could ultimately manage between reviews, even from the other side of the country. I needed something I could get them started on but they could keep going. They needed the skills and guidance I could provide them, but also a behaviour change they could manage, control and shape. That was the key.

So, here is where that took me, and let me tell you, it took me a while. I created two types of cashflow: working cashflow and active cashflow. The first step in controlling spending is sorting out those things you can control. Making a plan that a client of mine can't fund is useless. Tracking spending after you've spent the dough doesn't work either. It is a good investigative tool for me when designing a client spending plan, but it's a poor change management tool. Looking to take control of your finances?

Get Started: Segregate your money
into working and active cashflow.

Working cashflow

Working cashflow is the financial engine of the household. It is the money that gets you somewhere; it pays the necessary bills, it pays down your debt and it saves for your future. Working cashflow is made up of things that are generally lower on the emotional scale. Working cashflow is the broccoli of money. We all know putting more funds toward this category is good for us long-term, but it's usually not as tempting as spending our hard-earned dollars on the candy that looks (and tastes) so much yummier.

Items that would be included in Working cashflow would be:

- *All debt repayments*
- *Interest costs on debts (including leveraged investments, like borrowing to invest in funds or property)*
- *Utilities*
- *Retirement Investments*
- *Company Pensions*
- *Employee or personal health, dental and disability benefits*
- *Child care*
- *Property Taxes*
- *Home Maintenance*
- *Vehicle Maintenance*
- *Vehicle Leases or Loans (although this can be a very emotional financial decision)*
- *Short-term savings*
- *Medical and Dental Costs*
- *School Costs (excluding fundraising or school trips)*

To be clear, debts that already exist could indeed have been related to active cashflow and therefore far more emotional or not necessary, but once they exist, the related costs are part of your working cashflow. Later in this book, we'll discuss ways to reduce the debt related to emotional expenses. But during the initial stages of identifying cashflow types, servicing existing debt is simply a given and therefore part of working cashflow.

These types of expenses are also more likely to be fixed, at least somewhat, and therefore more predictable or more easily planned for. For example, most people don't replace their roof long before they need to because it is fun, or exciting. They wait until they must replace it and then they get a few quotes and figure out where to take the money from and then replace the roof.

Now, a broken refrigerator is a different story. You have to replace a fridge, you can't make your own ice box even if you save up and plan for it. This is why you need short-term savings and one of the things I like people to use their working cashflow for is saving for the things we just can't plan for.

Active cashflow

This is where your greatest ability to live the life you want is found. Active cashflow is, to some degree, the gummy bear to the working cashflow's broccoli. It's the fun—or at least the more fun—stuff, the life stuff, the day-to-day stuff. This is where so many of us allow our day-to-day spending to bleed into debt, even if it really doesn't seem like we "spend a lot of money".

It's not that all items of this cashflow category are not good for you, it's that you can, to some extent, make a variety of choices. These expenses require some degree of control for most folks to maximize the money they already have. Unless you are independently wealthy—and I mean so wealthy you couldn't go broke if you tried—controlling this sector of your finances can be an evolutionary exercise in the money journey that has major implications on your life.

Examples of items that would be included in Active cashflow are:

- *Clothing, shoes and all accessories*
- *Groceries*
- *Eating out*
- *Coffee and other treats*
- *All entertainment, like movies, books, magazines etc.*
- *Sports activities (yes, even for the kids)*
- *Toys and play equipment*
- *Vacations and day trips*
- *Cell phones (unless owned and paid for by your work or your business)*
- *Basically, all technology except your home phone (excluding computers absolutely required for work)*
- *Home renovations*
- *Recreational vehicles*
- *Children's safety equipment like car seats, strollers, cribs*
- *Basically, everything, which you either don't need, or you do need but can in some way negotiate or choose how much you are willing to pay for it*

Some of the items are necessary. For example, you can't go without food, however, you could never drink coffee again and I promise your likelihood of death by caffeine withdrawal is probably pretty low. For many people, these expenses range from black and white absolute needs and absolute wants to other items that are in somewhat of a grey area. These so-called grey areas are usually occupied by expenses that you know you don't need, but life without any access to them, doesn't seem worth living.

Now, I am not one of those personal finance gurus who's going to say, "You can't have anything until you can afford everything you want". I'm not going to tell you that you must cut out a near lifelong brand label habit or lecture you about that vacation you took last year that you couldn't really afford. I believe that lecturing you about what you should have, or could have done is a serious waste of my time and energy, not to mention a serious waste of the precious and limited pages I've allotted for in this book. Insinuating, or even outright telling you that you're stupid for past financial choices, or making you give up the best parts of your day, week, month or year, isn't going to convince you to change a thing; and I know it. Deep down, you know it, too, so don't panic, you are not stupid and I am not going to ask you to give up anything.

Managing Active vs. Working cashflows

These two types of cashflow are a near given for just about everyone. There are things we must pay for to stay warm, clothed, safe and fed; and there are other things we buy that create our life. Both types of cashflow are key to a fulfilling life and the good news is we are free to allocate our funds to what we believe is the best place for them. The problem comes when we can't get far enough away from our own financial landscape to look at the decisions in order to see the ultimate outcome. Are your lunches out costing you a happy retirement? Are you spending money on vacations each year that could have gone against your mortgage, lowering your debt and freeing you to make more fulfilling career choices? Is your money going to anything you don't value enough to warrant the expense?

Only you can answer those questions, but the answers are not found in a social norm, a formula or a certain standard. The answers are found in the 'end' you are trying to achieve. What's more, you can learn skills and behaviour changes that will work with your Money Mindset so the changes don't have to feel so cumbersome. What I see is not people spending too much, or being irresponsible. What I see is people wandering through life not knowing how the decision they make today affects them two days, or two decades from now. We all have spending habits incompatible with the future, or even the current life we say we are trying to achieve, because for the most part, we haven't had access to the tools we need to figure it out.

Your working cashflow of today is all about math and your active cashflow is all about choices. What tends to happen for many is that they let today's choice write the story of tomorrow's math without looking around the corner to see if that's what they really want. Consider the two statements below:

1. *You gain options when you exert more control over your active cashflow.*
2. *Mismanagement or unconscious spending of active cashflow almost always leads to its reduction and therefore less choice in the future.*

Take a minute and think about these statements. How counter intuitive are they? For most of us, our Money Mindset would cloud these two statements, never allowing us to come to either conclusion. How can living life for today leave me with less choice? How does being free lead me down a road to being trapped? How does being constrained and controlled lead me to freedom? More importantly, what if there is a happy medium between the two?

For many people, the behaviour they exhibit does not support what they say and believe to be their biggest goals in life.

Let me assure you, however, there is indeed a sweet spot between what we want and what we need for every one of us. There is a place between living for today and having a life tomorrow that, with the proper tools, is truly a sweet spot in more ways than one. Keep reading and discover how to find your financial sweet spot.

> Your current spending might look like this:
>
> - *About 75 percent of your income is taken up by working cashflow expenditures*
> - *Leaving you with 25 percent of your income, which you have some degree of control over*

Here is a breakdown based on a real case I worked on recently. Later on in the book, I will show you how I help people redirect cashflow. When cashflow is controlled, priorities are clearer and you are more likely to reach your goals and spend consciously.

These are the initial numbers provided by the client based on a budget sheet I had them fill out. This particular couple has a good income and their expenses seemed under control, however, what you can't see from this chart, is that they have no savings; nothing is going into short-term savings or long-term investments.

Let's call this couple the Smiths. Before I meet with a new client, I often ask them to provide their household budget. Have a look at the chart and note the discrepancies from their initial expense sheet (I've rounded the figures off for the purposes of this example).

Housing
Mortgage (taxes, principle and interest) $1500
Utilities (heat, hydro, etc) $500
Phone/cell/internet/cable $300
Insurance (home) $70
Maintenance $100

Transportation
Gas/Fuel $300
Insurance (car) $150
Loan/Lease Payments $1100
Maintenance and Repairs $50
Parking $60

Daily Living
Groceries $700
Clothing $100

Healthcare Expenses
Eye/Dental $20
Prescription $10

Investments
Retirement Contributions $150

Debts
Loan Payments $200
Line of Credit (interest only) $150
Credit Card (minimum payment) $300

Personal Insurance
Life insurance $80

Discretionary Spending
Fitness $80
Travel/Vacation $300
Pets $60
Entertainment $150
Eating out $200
Subscriptions $20
Gifts (all averaged out) $150
Charities $100

TOTAL $6900
TOTAL INCOME $9600
Surplus per month $2700

In theory, these numbers mean that of their $9600/mo income, there should be $2700 a month either sitting in their bank account or going out to some form of expense or savings. In fact, according to the initial data provided by the Smiths, they should have about $32,400 (in an average year) just sitting around. However, that is not what was happening in real life (which is often what I find to be the case).

A look at the Smith's financial reality came from their actual spending patterns gathered by using specialized software. The clients followed the instructions and downloaded all transactions over a specified period of time (usually 6 months). The downloaded data provided a very different story. Their working cash-flow items didn't change from their estimate to their actual amount but their active cashflow painted a very different picture. There were serious discrepancies between the couple's estimates and their reality. This has everything to do with the type of cashflow the different expenses fall under. No one accidentally overpays their mortgage, they might pre-pay, yes, but no one overpays in an over-worked, over-tired spending haze. Now, add these spending realities to the fact there is no room made for savings or investments and then what picture do we have?

The Smiths are not stupid people, I would argue they aren't overly indulgent, they are simply spending unconsciously. Their reward for which is a lack of financial agility. While these two were not in crisis when they came to see me, they did feel stuck. Figures like their mortgage, car payments and insurance costs (again, working cashflow) were accurate but take a look at some of the other categories (bolded). Would you say they were okay?

Housing
Mortgage (taxes, principle and interest) $1500
Utilities (heat, hydro, etc) $500
Phone/cell/internet/cable $300
Insurance (home) $70
Maintenance $600

Transportation
Gas/Fuel $300
Insurance (car) $150
Loan/Lease Payments $1100

Maintenance and Repairs $50
Parking $60

Daily Living
Groceries $1600
Clothing $500
Healthcare Expenses
Eye/Dental $20
Prescription $10

Investments
Retirement Contributions $150

Debts
Loan Payments $200
Line of Credit (interest only) $150
Credit Card (minimum payment) $300

Personal Insurance
Life insurance $80

Discretionary Spending
Fitness $80
Travel/Vacation $600
Pets $60
Entertainment $600
Eating out $500
Subscriptions $20
Gifts (all averaged out) $350
Charities $100
Childcare (they'd forgotten to fill it in) $1200

NEW TOTAL EXPENSES $11,150
TOTAL INCOME $9600

Monthly Deficit -$1550

Not only did that clear up why there was no leftover money, but it showed me why they were growing debts in the form of a line of credit and credit card. I can't stress to you how common this scenario is. Basically, if you find you don't have hundreds or thousands of dollars floating from one month to the next as it accumulates, then you are spending it all somewhere. You may be spending even more if your debt is growing. The Smiths weren't really doing anything too excessive as they saw it. They had a nice home and two new cars, but they didn't feel as if they were surrounded by over $11,000 worth of expenses each month. But little things were adding up. They'd stop at the local home improvement store almost every weekend, easily racking up $150 here and $200 there.

Both parents would often buy lunch rather than pack one even though the house was well stocked with groceries. They routinely bought fresh fruit and vegetables but would often end up tossing them as they couldn't use them before they went bad. They didn't plan their meals for the week, so they'd buy what looked good and figured they'd come up with a way to use it before it went bad. After a long day at work and two tired kids, they would end up ordering pizza or stopping to pick something up on the way home. Both parents worked a lot and placed a high priority on "quality" time on the weekends. That meant a lot of day trips, which almost always included two meals out. They had a membership at a local bulk buying store and that was really driving up their grocery costs because they would pick up three times more stuff than they had on their list every time they set foot in that particular store.

So, as you can see, little stuff isn't quite so miniscule. It's a big part of total cost. In the last chapter when I told you to please sweat the small stuff, this is exactly what I was getting at. This couple is wonderful, well educated, high income earning, but the speed at which life is moving is really driving them not to pay attention to their spending. Their small leaks were on track to doing some serious damage to their financial ship.

What would your working vs. active cashflow look like? Before you finish this book you should take the time to figure it out. Look at least six months back into your spending. There are a number of free cashflow management tools online that you can use to capture this data rather than sift through months of bank statements or ask your financial advisor if they provide such a tool to their clients. Some do, some don't, but it might save you time if they already have something on hand you can use.

Use the chart on the next page to get started.

My Working cashflow

Mortgage _____

Credit Card1 _____

Credit Card2 _____

Loan _____

Property tax _____

Home Main _____

Vehicle Loans_____

Vehicle Main _____

School Fees _____

Utilities _____

Investments _____

Savings _____

Child Care _____

Med & Dent _____

Other _____

Other _____

Other _____

Other _____

Total _____

% of net Monthly Income

_____

Active cashflow

Groceries_____

Clothing _____

Eat Out _____

Ent. _____

Sports _____

Reno. _____

Vacations _____

Rec. Vehicle_____

Toys etc. _____

Kid's Stuff_____

Day Trips _____

Cell Phones _____

Electronics _____

Other _____

Other _____

Other _____

Other _____

Total _____

% of net Monthly Income

_____

Do you see any surprises as you examine what you wrote down? Any expenses you didn't expect to be so high or so low? What you should get from this is a clear picture of what you can control. If you don't have savings, or you aren't making room for savings in your cashflow, whatever the reason, this is a potential problem waiting to happen. Besides having more cash to work with, what would you change on the active cashflow side of things?

Your Mindset Affects How You Use cashflow

When it comes to spending, each Money Mindset has a unique behaviour. Be you Dreamer or Bunker, rest assured your spending habits can be directly attributed to your Mindset.

The Dreamer: You tend to be keen to live for today, spending very unconsciously, convinced that tomorrow will work out. Meanwhile, when you spend too loosely and without a plan, the truth is you've shrunk your access to more choices. You could have funded a trip to a great conference where you may have made amazing, life-altering connections, but you don't have the money. You've spent it, but you don't know what you spent it on. A whole lot of tomorrow slips from your grasp when you spend those hard-earned dollars on something insignificant today.

The Justifier: You would say, "I don't really spend that much. Taxes are too high. Something happened to upset my life", or any other number of reasons to not apply the control you could today. You, too, can allow unconscious, although well-explained spending, to keep you from opportunity and leave you exposed to consequences you can't control. As a Justifier, you may be inclined to section off certain expenses as sacred. For example, kids' sports, you may classify them as a need and you may even have a very good argument for doing so, but nothing is sacred; NOTHING!

The Polly Anna: You would say, "I really don't pay too much attention to the spending anyway." You'd say you were responsible and involved in certain types of household expenses but that you weren't really aware of them. It's not that you have a spending problem, but if the person who's pulling your financial strings is a spender, you could end up paying for it. This is really for your own good. It's not as scary as you think. If you can accept whatever you discover, you can do something about it.

The Brick Wall: You would say that your spending is no one's damned business. You might even feel that the thought of you making an effort to control your spending is ridiculous. So my dear Brick Wall, if you indeed meet the seven criteria from Chapter 4, then you are correct, you don't have to control your spending, which means, while you can keep reading if you wish, you are right, you know best and you don't need my help. However, if you didn't check all seven, indulge me and keep reading. Don't worry, I'm not going to tell you specifically how to spend. Rather, I'll give you a frame to work within. All decisions will remain your own.

The Undercover Agent: This makes you so uncomfortable, I know. Don't panic. Looking at, or controlling your spending doesn't mean you must announce it publicly in billboard format on your front lawn. My spending recommendation will allow you to keep that private feeling you value so much.

The Masquerader: I know you would make the argument that you do not overspend, but what you're actually doing is trying to protect yourself from judgment. Controlling your spending is going to have a lot less to do with your reputation than you think. In fact, you may be pleasantly surprised just how many people will look up to you as you morph into the financial diva you so long to be.

The Bunker: I know this whole controlling spending thing might be music to your ears. You are a total gold star when it comes to being conscious of just how much money goes out of your household. That doesn't always mean you are in the financial situation you wish to be in. So my spending guidance for you might actually highlight areas where you can indeed loosen up and spend just a little bit more, without being panic stricken by the results. For you, managing active cashflow is done for entirely alternate reasons, but the benefits are just as wonderful.

CHAPTER 6

Debt: It's All In Your Head

"When you know better, you do better."

~ Mia Angelou

Spending and debt are about as interconnected as it gets. Yet when we borrow money, only certain types of expenses get considered. Does your lender ask how much your grocery bill is each week? Do they ask what you spend on vacations most years? No. They don't take these factors into consideration, they only look at costs such as debt service (how much your monthly debt payments are), utility bills and property taxes. Debt is one of the single biggest issues of the more developed nations in our world. Both personal debt and national debt have been making headlines day-after-day. In Canada, the finance minister even launched a "Financial Literacy Task Force". Those considered the Who's Who of finance were assembled to go across Canada and bring back their findings so we could solve our problem. In the US, UK, Australia and many other parts of the world, a similar pain has been felt and financial literacy resources and initiatives have sprung up all over the place, especially online. If there is one thing I think most of us can agree upon, it is that, yes, there is indeed a debt issue!

I think it is also safe to say, and even to accept, that debt is a part of our society. What I take issue with is the fact that too many of us don't know how to take our power back and use debt as a tool. Often, when I'm speaking to a client about the drastic changes they need to make, which can involve changing banks, the conversation often goes like this:

Client: "But my bank has been good to me!"

Me: "Really? They've given you loans without putting you through a pesky application process?"

Client: "Well, no, of course not. I have to qualify to borrow money just like everyone else."

Me: "Oh, then perhaps they've extended you an interest free loan?"

Client: "Oh no, they charge me interest on my loans and credit cards like everyone else."

Me: "Then they offered to provide you with a plan to help you pay down your debt more efficiently, saving you thousands in interest and becoming debt-free years sooner?"

Client: "Well no, that's why I'm here."

Me: "Okay, to stop me from my incessant guessing, can you tell me just how they've been so good to you, so I can understand?"

Client: "Well, whenever we needed to borrow money, they gave it to us and their branch staff is always very friendly."

Me: "Okay, first of all, they didn't give you a thing; loans come with strings attached, that's why they are called loans, not 'gifts'. Just so I've got it straight, what I understand is, you qualified for a loan, they loaned you the money at the going rate, which is incidentally how they make their money, and their staff is nice. Is that right? Is there an alternative way that you would expect to be treated that makes this good in comparison?"

Client: "Umm . . . no. I never really thought about it that way. I was a qualifying and paying customer and was treated as such."

For some reason, asking someone, anyone, for money, including a formal application to lending institutions, finds us reverting back to three-year-olds, pleading for an extra cookie after dinner. I have no problem with the banks, frankly, we need them; they are good for the economy and they do have their place. However, I do have a problem with this seemingly prevalent perception that providing good customer service and lending money to qualifying individuals, who pay it back with interest, is worth feelings of loyalty that stop you in your tracks if serving your own best interests doesn't involve that particular bank. If you are best served by managing your debt in a certain way that your bank simply can't or won't provide you at this time, it is absolutely asinine and totally financially counterproductive to pay significantly more money back for the sake of feeling loyal.

No company of any kind will lend you money for the fun of it, or because they like you. You weren't so charming that the banker couldn't help but give you a break on the interest rate. Your heavenly scent didn't cause the lender to push your income up by $20,000 or ignore your credit score. You may be a good negotiator, but none of the lending institutions that any one of us deals with will lend money or base interest rates on the "likability" factor. It's math. If you get a loan, it's because you qualified for it; if you got a lower rate, it's likely because you asked for it, or that is their policy and your interest payments are the profit of that business relationship. I can't discount the value of good customer service, it is important, but it should not be solely what you base major financial decisions upon. Chances are, the same great customer service you got at one institution, you can receive at another just because you are who you are; a paying customer.

We have to stop devaluing ourselves as part of the borrowing equation. If you weren't borrowing and paying back funds plus interest, the banks wouldn't make those gargantuan profits they post—that indecently, so many of us complain about. So stand up for yourself. Stop cowering in the corner of the lender's office, as if you've just said, "Please sir, can I have some more?" Hold your head up high! Take charge of your debt. Start using it as a tool, not as something bad that happened to you, and you'll see a whole new world of possibilities unveil themselves to you.

Debt Diversification

Diversification is an accepted practice in the investment world. The idea that one should not have one's eggs all in a single basket is fairly universal—well, at least until 2008-2009, but that is a whole other book. The post-market meltdown world looks at risk far differently than it used to. People spread their risk around by having an investment portfolio of different types of investments, which in theory, shouldn't be exposed to identical risks at the same time. In essence:

Proper Asset Allocation should = growth over time

So what happens when we apply a theory adapted to ensure investments have a reasonable chance to grow and use it on our debt?

Unfortunately, often more predictably than the market, that debt grows. Debt diversification happens when we keep multiple accounts of debt; a couple credit cards with balances here, a mortgage there and a line credit over there. It all adds up, but because our debt is all over the place, for many of us, it's harder to focus on paying it down. Also, since the lowest interest rate charged on debt is on that of our homes, diversification of debts almost always means we are putting more pennies out in interest than we need to. Debt is surely one place where diversification should be avoided when at all possible.

Diversification of debt has another rather unpleasant side affect—and here is where our Money Mindset can put so many of us in harm's way. We end up paying back a lot more than we have to on borrowed funds. The status of having numerous debts, regardless of efficiency, can have what we perceive to be a psychological benefit. What I mean by this is that when you have all of your debt all over the place, you can avoid looking at or thinking about the real total. You can compartmentalize some debts as bad, some as good and rationalize others, but mostly, you can avoid the whole truth when you don't see it all at once. This is not only expensive, but far more likely to result in the odd missed or late payment to a creditor, which can damage your credit score. Your credit score is your power, folks, and if you want your life, spending and borrowing habits should be set up to protect it, not hurt it.

Debt Diversification = Debt grows, too!

Debt Doesn't Age Well

I've even worked with a handful of clients in their 80's carrying five-figure credit card debt because they felt they'd be a failure if they put a mortgage on their homes again—homes which had often been paid off for several decades. The accomplishment of being mortgage-free was so important to them for so many years that they were willing to pay 19-21 percent interest on rather sizable debt for the privilege. They were under the mistaken impression that somehow not having that exact debt attached to their home served to benefit them. Now, I'm not a lawyer, but as I understand it, in all of those cases, if they were single or widowed and their assets were all left to be split amongst the kids, the debt would be left to the estate, too, and it would be first in line before the heirs. That credit card debt would take home equity or other equity left to the estate upon their death anyway. The only thing they were accomplishing by keeping it on the plastic was maxing out negative impact of their debt in life and death.

Debt Unification

Now having said that, I do not mean to imply that you can be in a place tomorrow where you only have a mortgage and have to find the cash to pay everything down, nor do I think that if you are in your first home you magically have the ability to avoid a car loan. No, total debt unification can't always be accomplished overnight, but heading in a direction that will ultimately lead to your debt being managed all in one account, is key to maximizing efficient repayment while maintaining financial agility.

Our world is set up to keep us opening different debt accounts, to distract our focus from the total owing. Think about it; our traditional closed and fixed mortgage products, by their very construction, pretty much force us to carry at least one or two other debts or pay cash for everything—which is about as likely as a green polar bear. Our conventional and typical household use of debt practically guarantees we'll have at least three or four debts on the go at any one time. The problem with this practice is that it makes us the groveling intern to our debt products CEO when it comes to controlling our financial destiny.

When you can't get a good look at your debt any time you want, the additional effort required to tally everything up on any given day is enough for most of us to use our hectic lives as an excuse to keep us from even looking. What you don't see, you can't change; what you can't change, you can't control. That leaves you keeping on like you've been keeping on and, if you are like so many others, that means you are paying out more than you have to because your debt is not unified.

When you unify debt, not only can you focus all your repayment efforts on a single target but you can also keep your reality in check. The total liabilities facing you each month on one statement might seem scary, but the reality is that looking at the whole truth is the only way to see real progress. The first statements can be a little stomach churning, but it will just be an accurate reflection of what it was before, when you had every egg in every basket you could find; you just didn't know it.

As you go along making progress on that singular debt account, you can see every penny of your efforts come to life. You can make real plans and see real progress when you are able to see your total financial reality each month. The reality is you owe what you owe. You can decide to play your hand in your favour or you can choose to delude yourself into feeling better in the moment over getting better in reality; the choice is yours.

All of the Mindsets have different reasons to diversify their debt or even different ways of looking at a common form of debt management. It is a common occurrence to see most people diversify their debt and all Mindsets are susceptible to managing their debt this way.

The Justifier: You have a good reason to section your debt all over the place. While the truth may be that you really just don't want to look at it all together, you have a better explanation. I once had a Justifier explain to me that they needed separate debt accounts because they felt like they could keep better track of their debt that way. They felt they knew what each debt was from. A quick exploration of one of their credit cards proved otherwise, but they really believed that keeping separate accounts was helping them keep track of their debt.

The Dreamer: You just don't think it matters that much. Most of your debt you see as an investment. You may even be able to write off a fair amount of it, so what does it matter if it's not quite efficient? Well, when you spend $100 to save $50, you are still out $50. When it comes to writing off interest, it is still better the interest be less rather than more. While you can save some money in taxes, you can only save taxes, not get 100 percent reimbursement back for your expense. So keep that in mind when you are spending $100 to save $50. You are still spending $50 and every $50 that doesn't have to leave your bottom line in the first place can go toward building your dreams.

The Brick Wall: You have a million reasons not to unify debt. One: it requires trusting that one account is the best account and there could be a better one. Two: There are fees that come with a debt unification solution. You forget to take into account what fees you won't be paying if you get rid of multiple inefficient debt accounts. So make sure your research is comparing apples to apples and you'll obtain a more accurate result.

The Polly Anna: Your main reason for practicing debt diversification is to avoid having to look at your debt in the first place. It won't be as scary as you think to look at all of your debt in one place. In fact, when it's in one place, you can get some positive reinforcement from seeing results much faster. Remember, just because you don't look at your debt all together, doesn't mean the amount is reduced. So put it all in one place and take a look. Don't be a turkey!

The Masquerader: You may have trouble technically qualifying for a large enough limit when trying to unify your debt. Not that your income won't support a unified account, but because that very income often allows you to qualify to borrow far more than your primary residence is worth, you may have difficulty qualifying. The most effective tools to unify debt often involve the home, so even though you have a very high income and likely valuable home, you may still have to use some alternate strategies. (I'll tell you more about alternatives in the next chapter.)

The Undercover Agent: You like to diversify your debt because in your household, even if you have a spouse, you may still have separate finances. The separation for you may be less about mind games with yourself and more about trust. You need to ask yourself how much you are willing to pay to avoid trusting others, especially those closest to you. It is worth learning to trust enough to manage your debt more efficiently.

The Bunker: You are the most likely to have only one debt to begin with, perhaps two, if you have a car loan. The issue for you is that should you have a fluctuation of any kind, you'd be forced to borrow outside that one debt. You would rather keep your debt to a minimum than be prepared for the unexpected by using more flexible lending products.

It's not your fault

It isn't your fault that you make expensive financial choices when it comes to debt. In fact, you are pretty much pre-programmed to do so and most lending products on the shelf lead you in a direction that requires little thought or action. Actually, it's been proven that it's not your fault. But as I say to fellow financial advisors about helping clients with debt, "It's not your fault, it's not even your responsibility, but it is your problem. It's everyone's problem." Indeed, much of the way we behave with money—which, of course, influences just how much debt we end up carrying—is not our fault, but it is our problem.

We are well programmed to behave the way we do with money and I can't even blame the banks or marketers—for the programming, anyway, their knowledge and manipulation of those tendencies are their fault. No, our decision making processes are far more ingrained than that.

Professor Laurie Santos from Yale University was actually able to prove many of the financial decision making tendencies we humans show, we come by quite honestly. She and her team created a monkey economy in their lab for a group of capuchin monkeys. They wanted to see if the monkeys would make some of the mistakes humans make if they could be taught to use a monkey currency. Her experiment worked and she and her team were able to determine that our primate friends, like us, showed no natural interest in saving and were likely to take increased risks with their monkey money in an attempt to avoid loss. Rather counter-intuitive if you think about it, but it explains everything. Yes, indeed, our issues with money have had over 35-million years to set in. The good news, according to Dr. Santos, is that you and I are not monkeys and we can learn to change a behaviour if we can understand it.

So, I'll say it again, your current financial situation might not be entirely a result of you knowingly making poor or costly financial decisions. However, it is your problem and even if you are not someone who is in financial distress, you can likely make vast improvement in the efficiency of your debts. So, before you tell your-self you are stuck, or that you are just fine because you're not having trouble paying your debt, or even feel that you don't carry too much debt for your age or stage of life, decide to pay attention and man-age it better anyway.

We Borrow Like Magpies

Do you see a theme here? I'm either comparing humans to birds or monkeys (at least both are proven to be incredibly intel-ligent). I told you my educational background in Animal Sciences had been unexpectedly helpful!

> *Magpie (disambiguation): the common name originat-ing in Europe. Once called "pies", later "mag" was added to feminize the name. Magpies are so smart they are one of the few species who can recognize themselves in a mir-ror. They are members of the crow family but they are eas-ily distinguished by their white breast and wing feathers. These birds are famous for their tendency to steal shiny things.*

Yes, magpies like shiny things and they are easily distracted by them; and when it comes to borrowing, so are we. When it comes to loans, mortgages in particular, rate is our "shiny thing". We are easily distracted by focusing only on the rate of interest charged by a certain debt. Doing so leaves us susceptible to the risks that come along with ignoring the true cost of the debt. We all know that three is less than four and the banks know that we all know this. Why do you think so many advertisements are based on rate? About three hours ago, when I drove to my local café to sink my teeth into this chapter, I counted the number of bank billboards, posters or signs I saw along my way. Every sin-gle one of them had some reference to that institution's great low rates; not one of them said, "Take a $250,000 mortgage with us and if you are lucky, and rates stay similar over the next 25 years, you'll only pay us $186,000 in interest!" No, the marketing department would never approve that ad! I'm guessing in my lifetime no one who lends money is going to spend time or capital attracting attention to the total cost of conventional borrowing; not in billboard form anyway.

So many of us borrow like magpies and those who market most lending products—mortgages in particular—know that all too well. It is only fair that we pay interest on the funds we borrow. Banks and lenders are not charities, but it might do us some serious financial good to start looking at the cost over the life of a debt, or the remaining principle at our next renewal, rather than focusing strictly on that proverbial shiny thing! I'm not suggesting that rates we pay—especially on larger debts like mortgages—aren't fair; I think in many cases they are. However, the way these debts, especially fixed loans, are set up does not necessarily encourage us to repay that debt any faster unless we insist. The flow of that cashflow of yours may have a lot more impact than the rate in some instances. I'll explain more on this in the next chapter.

Metal to Manor Ratio

When it comes to buying a car, the rate is rarely the shiny thing. No, in the case of vehicle financing, the monthly payment is the shiny thing. Again, most people pay little attention to the total and true cost of the vehicle, distracted and focused only on how much it will cost them each month. The theory is still viable, we are still distracted from the total reality by another variable. This is why leasing was so popular, or as I like to call it (in far too many cases), renting a car you couldn't afford in the first place. At least that's what most people do with cars. There are always exceptions to the rule, but many people lease to keep the payment low on a car they couldn't have managed an actual loan payment on.

While I have you thinking about car debt, test yourself on

your current vehicular liability position. I do this with most of my clients by checking what I call their metal to manor ratio. I do this in one of two ways:

For younger couples, newly single or anyone who's still early in their mortgage repayment days, I check this ratio to see if their car debt costs are in line with their overall financial picture.

- In ratio-form, I show how your total car payments stack up against your mortgage payment.

  Example: Two car payments totaling $1200 per month and a mortgage payment of $1800 per month, which would give you a ratio of 2:3. When you think of the fact that you pay equal to two thirds of your mortgage payment on vehicles, it might help you be ready to make different decisions in the future. This ratio is more and more dangerous the longer the car repayment term is stretched. So, if those $1200 car payments are coming from two car loans, which are over 60 months, that can be really concerning. Just when the loans are finally paid off, the car may be entering a more maintenance-heavy stage of its life cycle. For many, any degree of unexpected maintenance cost is scary and can often lead to a rash trade-in decision.

  For those who are older, or have been in the same home a long time or who are further along on their mortgage repayment journey (or even have it paid off), I use this ratio instead:

- In ratio-form, I show you how your total vehicle purchase price compares to the value of your home.

  Example: Car one, SUV purchased for $42,000 and car two, Sedan purchased for $52,000, and a home, which is nearly paid off (only $25,000 remaining on the mortgage) valued at $376,000; you'd have a ratio of 1:4.

There isn't necessarily an ideal ratio I'm looking for, although I don't like anything over 1:2. This is just a fairly simple way to help people see their vehicle purchases in perspective. It can help one make better decisions in the future. Vehicles are a factor in many of our lives and they may be for some time. Making smarter decisions can save us thousands of dollars we can put toward other facets of our lives; if we don't live for cars, that is.

So what is your metal to manour ratio?

Ratio 1:

Car payment 1 _____ + Car payment 2 _____: Mortgage payment _____

Total car cost / total mortgage cost

Ratio 2:

Car 1 total cost_____+ Car 2 total cost _____: Home value

_____

Original vehicle purchase price/ Home value

In Chapter 7, I'll be covering my rules to managing vehicle costs as part of your overall financial picture; and don't worry, I won't be recommending you can only afford a 1980's Ford Pinto that requires you to drive it Fred Flintstone style. No, my methodology to car purchases still sees most people in a vehicle they can count on and one that will fit their needs, just at an overall cost less likely to hold you hostage later on.

Each of the Mindsets is distracted for a different reason, but make no mistake, when it comes to borrowing, most of us are paying attention to only a few variables. We forget about the big picture and it can end up costing us.

The Justifier: You are a real magpie borrower. In fact, before you know it, you'll adopt the sales pitch and use it as your explanation for that borrowing decision. It's easier to justify smaller purchases over larger ones, and you see a vehicle as a smaller purchase than your home. As such, you may be more distracted when negotiating the details of a car purchase. Really watch that. Go into negotiations knowing what you want the bottom line (total cost) to be and keep asking the salesperson to match it.

The Dreamer: You are too busy to bother to look past that shiny thing and see the reality of the situation. Until now, you may not have even realized just how much your dreams could end up paying for that level of distraction. There is no greater risk for you with homes vs. cars, although car purchases do come up more often. Make sure your major purchases support your dreams rather than take from them. You want to focus on what you can afford today so you can take all those "extra" dollars you make and put them toward keeping your success on track.

The Brick Wall: You are the least likely to be swayed by the shiny things. If fact, you sometimes go the other way and don't make a purchase because you want to be sure you are not distracted. This is really procrastination. I hope you can use your new knowledge of these "shiny things" that so many of us are distracted by, to help you make decisions you can live with. Neither type of purchase is more or less risky for you. Make sure you are listening, not trying to control the situation when you make a major purchase. You can easily miss something if you think you already know what someone is going to say.

The Polly Anna: Sometimes you just pretend to be interested in the "shiny things". Most times, you don't really care. You act like rate is important because the mortgage person inferred that it was. You say your priority is the monthly payment on your new car because the sales guy started there. You have a high risk of being distracted on either purchase. However, since vehicle purchases require less action (you don't usually have to provide a lot of paperwork or information), you are more likely to make mistakes there. You should really try taking notes during meetings about your finances. Use this book as a guide to write down questions to bring with you to every meeting about borrowing. You have to start coming to the table! When you start to ask smart questions, you will become more confident in your ability and want to be part of your financial decisions every time.

The Masquerader: I might argue that for you there are always two "shiny things": the item you are purchasing or financing itself, and then the rate or monthly payment of that item. Cars and homes are equally important to you. You believe they are a status symbol and that makes you really easy to distract. Try looking at your overall big picture. Always ask yourself why you are doing something before you do it. You don't like to think you aren't making your own decision, so make sure you aren't just succumbing to peer pressure.

The Undercover Agent: Your comfort level with things being so separated when it comes to your money, makes it easier to distract you. The "shiny thing" has greater power over you because of your need to keep things private. That can sometimes lead you to rush the borrowing process. You are at a greater risk when making car purchases because they are quicker and require less information. Be careful that you always focus on your bottom line. Write it down and bring it with you if you have to.

The Bunker: The "shiny thing" makes you feel safe. You feel comfortable when you can effectively compare offers based on facts, but that keeps you from asking for enough information to really find the true and total cost of borrowing. In your attempt to protect yourself, you are most likely to make a mistake related to guarantees, like buying warranties that may be more costly than they are worth or taking a fixed rate without doing the math first. When looking for a mortgage, ask for a print out showing the total interest and repayment costs of the proposed option. Look at the first renewal date and ask the lender to increase the rate by 2 percent. What happens? Are you ok with it? With warranties, ask to read the details before you add it on, and if you know anyone in the car business (besides the person selling the warranty), ask if they think it's worth it.

Mortgage Myopia

Humans instinctually seek pleasure and avoid pain; who wouldn't, right? Uncertainty for most of us might as well equal pain. Case in point: Fear that a variable rate could go up on a home equity line of credit could be totally counter-balanced if you structure your cashflow in a way that sees you carrying a much lower balance because you've paid it down so much faster. In other words, it's not just rate you have to keep an eye on, it's how much principle is exposed when renewal comes. Fixed products are only as safe as they seem when you are in them. If you take out a very long mortgage amortization, like 30 years, but you renew on average every five years, then every five years you are re-exposed to the rate of the day. This is what I mean by Mortgage Myopia.

> **Myopia:** *A disorder of the vision where distant objects appear blurred because the eye focuses their images in front of the retina instead of on it; A lack of imagination, discernment or long-range perspective in thinking or planning.*
>
> **Mortgage Myopia:** *Financial nearsightedness characterized by an inability to see clearly or envision the level of exposure debts amortized over long periods of time can create. Long-term financial consequences appear blurry and irrelevant when compared to the near-term situation. This common condition often manifests when one perceives the original rate and payments a long-term debt are calculated upon, will continue into the future.*

There is a danger avoidance mechanism in the fantasy land within our heads and it keeps us safe a lot of the time; it guides us to keep our hands off a hot burner and once kept us from being eaten by large carnivorous animals. Here's the thing; our brains and bodies don't know there are no more dinosaurs, no sabertooth tigers or lions waiting to pounce and eat us as we walk between shops at the local strip mall. That's why someone can have a strong and negative physiological response to public speaking even though it is unlikely they are in physical danger. Their brain doesn't know that real danger isn't present and as such, produces a strong physical reaction in the body, as if a dinosaur were about to chomp down. The very part of us that kept us alert and aware when we were a potential snack for a larger creature is the same part of us that seems to kick in when we are making decisions. It can be a good thing when we need to bring our car to a sudden stop and a bad thing when we decide what mortgage is best for us.

Making long-term borrowing and even investment decisions seems to be rather driven by that prehistoric fight or flight mechanism. We zig when we should zag because of mostly imagined consequences. Some would call it fear. I often say, "When you make fear-based financial decisions, you are sure to get scary results". But then I read a great book called *Linchpin* by one of my favourite authors, Seth Godin. I realized that I had been misusing the word fear. What I should have been using is anxiety. In *Linchpin*, Seth really opened my eyes to this fact when he reminded me of the difference between Fear and Anxiety. Fear is real. It's fair. We should and need to react to it. Fear is reasonable, like avoiding a poisonous snake or jumping out of the way of a flying horse hoof. Anxiety, on the other hand, is an imagined projection of what might happen. Anxiety robs us of the ability to make good decisions and paralyzes us all too often until after the window of opportunity has been slammed shut. So let's apply these two states of being to money:

Fear

Realistically, what is there to be afraid of with money? What physical or real dangers exist?

Anxiety

What about imagined projections? Do you really employ fear

when making financial decisions? Or are most of your so-called fears around finances really anxiety? Do you sign that fixed rate mortgage because you love the idea and you are making significant extra payments to reduce risk when the mortgage renews? Or are you signing these papers and making these decisions because of imagined consequences?

When it comes to money management for the most of us, I think our would-be fears are really anxieties in disguise. If I had a dollar for every person who came to me with unreasonable fears about money, I'd be further along my own financial journey than I am as I write this book. I, like you, am simply a person. I do not possess a super human expense calculating computer for a brain; I am not emotionless or totally rational either. However, what I have spent the better part of a decade consciously focused on—likely most of my life unconsciously—is how to work with myself, my flaws, my faults, to get what I really want from my life, in spite of myself; just as I am.

I can tell you one thing; getting what you want means learning to tell the anxiety to bugger-off. Sometimes, it means you sit with it. Let it wash over you, feel bad for a moment. You won't die if you feel bad for a moment. Anxiety is like the boogie man, it loses its power over you when you don't run away, when you don't flinch or turn, when you just sit—you win. Victory is when you can sit through the anxiety and keep going—finish. I've done it many a time as I've sat down to write this book. My anxiety tells me you won't like what I write. It tells me that I am wasting my time. It tells me to check my email or answer my phone. But the greatest things I've done with my life are a direct result of looking my imagined fears right in the face and saying to them, "I'm doing it anyway". It means finding new ways to think about many things—especially money. To put results above the imagined 'what-if's' our brains cook up in an attempt to protect us. If you want to make the most of your life, money is a big part of that and getting it right for you, means getting right with yourself. This is why working with your financial personality (or

Money Mindset) is so important in predicting your probability of success.

Our brains might not know the difference between fear and anxiety when it comes to money, but we can teach them to recognize the difference and to respond to the right impulse. You run that amazing organ on top of your shoulders and it will do what you tell it, if you know that you can!

Is it fear or anxiety?

The Justifier: You try to reason your anxieties away. The next time you find yourself doing this, ask yourself, "Why do I feel the need to explain this purchase?" The answer may be a real clue as to what spending habits are good for you and which are not.

The Dreamer: You don't think you really experience either, but you do. Dreamers often fear success; that is why the Dreamer can be so good at sabotaging their amazing potential. So sit with that thought for a moment and then ask yourself, "Am I afraid of success?" Be a silent observer in your head. What are you telling yourself? I believe that dealing with this particular issue is where your real success will come from.

The Brick Wall: Well, you aren't afraid of anything, so it has to be anxiety in your case, right? In my experience, the Brick Wall's anxiety kicks in when you are trying to exert control. The next time you feel that desire to be in charge creep up during a financial discussion, ask yourself, "Who is making me anxious here, them or me?"

The Polly Anna: You would call your financial concerns fears, but I'd call you a ball of anxiety when it comes to money. You will never gain the life you seek if you don't get involved in your own finances. So practice sitting through the overwhelming feeling you feel when money becomes the topic of conversation. At first, practice listening and taking notes, then when you feel comfortable, ask some thought out questions. You are forbidden from putting yourself down during money talk!

The Masquerader: I believe you actually feel a great deal of anxiety about money. Those who have more, stand to lose more. Why not think about losing something, a thing like your car or your home? Walk yourself through what that would feel like. Now, examine what wouldn't change if you lost those things, and what you could do to pick yourself up and keep going. The more attached you are to the stuff that you believe comes with success, the more at risk you are for losing it. I've found that loss is less likely to occur if you don't worry about it because you can stay focused on the purpose, the why behind your life.

The Undercover Agent: You can be a ball of nerves about money because you don't like to share. You may find this feeling stressful and being just a little more open to suggestion may sooth that need to hide your financial truth. Some of the solutions in the coming chapter will allow you to be private about the things that could actually hurt you, thus taking away your anxiety and giving you a way to control your spending and make better decisions without making you feel too vulnerable.

The Bunker: You can be scared of your own shadow when it comes to any degree of perceived financial risk. You can help yourself by gathering facts before completing your decision. For example, if you were certain a fixed-rate mortgage is best, check out the research (and there is plenty) about how fixed vs. variable have worked out in reality over the past 30, 40 or 50 years. You might be surprised with what you discover.

The next two chapters are all about the actions each Mindset can take to make that meaningful and lasting financial change you sought when you cracked the spine of this book.

CHAPTER 7

Baby Steps to Success

"Intention is the active partner of attention; it is the way we convert our automatic processes into conscious ones."
~ Deepak Chopra

Okay, in this chapter I'm going to, as Dr. Phil would say, "put some verbs in my sentences", and tell you what I think you can really do with your money. These Baby Steps are for all personality types, but I'll reframe everything for each Money Mindset separately. Ready? Go!

Baby Step 1—Reality check!

That's right, this book isn't just for reading; it's for doing! So read this chapter through and then make an appointment with yourself and other family members who have a financial say (even kids that are 12 and older can benefit from witnessing a financial overhaul), and just start!

In order to identify what you truly have control over, most people need some guidelines to work with. So separate your expenses first and then we'll look at the degree to which you can actually control them. What I mean by this is, for example, you can choose to never buy a latte again and you'll live. However, you can't choose to never eat again and survive. Both the latte and the food are controllable expenses but only one is actually dispensable.

In Baby Step 1, we'll be revisiting active and working cash-flow, but this time, we'll be adding in a sub-category of debt repayment to working cashflow. You should be able to save time on this and go back to Chapter 5 and grab those figures from your original working and active cashflow management exercise. Make sure these are real numbers based on past reality, not just on estimates off the top of your head.

Take your last few months' bank statements (or if your bank is offering a cashflow analysis tool, use that if you can easily figure it out). Identify the following:

Working cashflow:

Working cashflow, just as before, is made up of those expenses that rarely cause overspending and that actually tend to get us somewhere positive, financially. Typically, these costs are mostly a constant or are easy to average out on a monthly basis. For example, your utilities (which you can average out), your communications costs, your home and car insurance, the gasoline for your car, child care costs, property tax, etc. Basically, anything that is quite predictable as a monthly cost. These are expenses that won't necessarily be affected if you have a bad month. What I mean is, no one all of a sudden has a double mortgage payment one month. Again, as I mentioned, the sub-category of working cashflow I want you to recognize is debt repayment. Take a look at your mortgage payment, minimum payments on revolving debts like credit cards, loan payments and car loan or lease payments. I want you to separate these because if you work on Baby Step 3, you may find that you indeed have control over how much your debt is costing you.

Active cashflow:

These are items where the average monthly cost might be calculable, but the cost from one week to the next can be volatile and almost all of them can be influenced by emotion. For example, clothing costs could be variable for a very different reason. While the prices, of course, could go up, it's more that we don't always purchase the exact amount of clothing in a given month. Groceries and other food costs are variable as well.

So go ahead and record your fixed and variable expense totals below. Base these numbers on past statements. We are trying to get an accurate snapshot, not apply the controls just yet. Many of you may be able to use your working and active cashflow figures from Chapter 5 to help you, but be sure to confirm that your figures are consistent.

My working cashflow (less debt) is: $_____

My debt costs are $_____

My active cashflow is: $_____

My total expenses are: $_____

My total income is: $_____

My surplus or deficit is: $_____ x 12 =_____

The reason for those last few lines is that, fairly consistently, when I work with a family's cashflow figures, I find that even when they look at past spending reality in the form of bank statements, the numbers that come back tend to look like this:

> Working cashflow: $1200
> Debt Repayment: $2000
> Active cashflow: $3800
> Income: $9500
> Surplus: $2500/mo x 12 = $30,000

Yet, there is no $30,000 sitting in the bank account, nor is it hiding in investments. It is not at all uncommon for people—even with great incomes—to have a five-figure gap between what they show they are spending and what they are actually spending, based on what they have left over after 12 months. In fact, I've come across many cases with a large gap between expense figures and income, like the one on the previous page, where the debt has grown in the last year or two, meaning the real gap is even bigger than it looks. Often, after a few questions, we can figure out where a good deal of it has gone. My point is that it wasn't (usually) stolen, gambled away or spent by any other extremes. The fact is that a couple can lose track of $30,000 worth of spending over a 12-month period very easily.

Don't worry if you do have a big surplus or deficit, we'll be dealing with that in the coming pages. The figure that is most important here is the fixed costs, as we'll use it going forward.

Mindset Tips

The Justifier: Total and complete honesty about the facts with no explanations accepted is the only way for you. There is no reason good enough to not count the cost, so just do it!

The Dreamer: This is where you can finally get a good grasp on what it is that you actually need. That way you can keep as much of your cashflow going toward your dreams as you want, rather than spending it on expenses that don't matter to you.

The Brick Wall: You may already know these figures off the top of your head, but do it anyway to confirm that your estimates are accurate.

The Polly Anna: You broke the ice on this one when you did your working and active cashflow figures. So, now it's time to be brave again and figure out what your fixed costs are each month. It is important for you to understand that your fixed costs are just that, fixed. If you just work away at it, it won't seem nearly as daunting as it once did.

The Masquerader: You may be in for a real shocker. I often find your Mindset has some of the highest fixed costs due to the degree of items you may have financed.

The Undercover Agent: This is something you may have to do some digging to complete. I recommend that if you have a spouse, you do this together. Even if you and your spouse have separate finances, the responsibility of paying down your debt falls on both your shoulders equally and therefore you should both be equally aware of what is going on.

The Bunker: You'll love this exercise! It's right up your alley, so enjoy!

Baby Step 2 – Control What You Can Control!

This is where you'll take some of the figures you've been keeping track of in this book and put them to work. Here is where you learn to control what you can control. Too many times people feel—as we went over in Chapter 1—that they just aren't spending that much, yet a near six figure net annual income a couple may be earning is going poof'.

We don't feel like we are getting anywhere, no matter how hard we work at it. So this is where we get a handle on how much you really can spend at your current income level. If you aren't reaching the financial goals you wish you were, or you can't handle even a tiny financial crisis, you can't make excuses for every cost and wonder why you don't get ahead.

Controlling your controllable cashflow works 100 percent of the time. In fact, if you follow my advice, the only way to mess it up, is to do so intentionally. The time it takes to consciously disengage from cashflow control is often enough to keep many people on track. We are talking about setting up your world so you are guaranteed to apply as much control as you possibly can to spending in a way that you can reasonably manage the behaviour change.

Get ready for some serious rocket science. I call it living on an anti-budget. What am I really getting at? Cash baby! That's right. If you really want to control spending, cash is a guy or gal's best friend . . . now, there are some variable options going forward, but for at least the first 60 days of your financial evolution, I recommend the tactile, tangible variety. Good old fashioned "folding", as my husband calls it. Yes, real cash. Traditional budgeting would have you allot a specific amount to groceries, and a certain dollar amount to coffee each week. But we're not going to do that. Following a good 'old fashioned' budget is not going to work for most people simply because it doesn't work well with most financial personality types. The old way of writing down what you make on one side of the paper and your monthly costs on the other and trying to spend the difference has not proven successful in the past, so I suggest you let go of the idea.

Electronic spending, at least at first, and in general (there is a viable option I'll explain later), is the arch-nemesis to your intention to make change. It just won't work. Your bank card, connected to your chequing or saving accounts, leaves you no control. As I've mentioned before, you can't see what you are doing before you decide to do it. You can't accurately predict the consequences of your actions with most any form of electronic spending.

When it comes to actually controlling your finances rather than just trying to react to them, you have to slow down and be able to see the effects of spending in real time. Meanwhile, you systematically set things like bills, investments and debt repayment on auto pilot. Think about it, when is the last time you got stressed out and felt you deserved it, so you went ahead and splurged by putting an extra $1000 down on your mortgage? I know the risk of overspending really only exists in a few places and the good news is that in most of those areas, we are in the driver's seat.

Take a minute to gather some of the figures you've been accumulating through the course of reading this book. Record them below:

My Working cashflow is $_____
My Debt Repayment is $_____
My Controllable cashflow is: $_____
(avg. monthly income – working cashflow expenses)

So now you know just how much of your money you can actually control on a monthly basis. Surprising, isn't it? We don't often think we have much wiggle room, or much ability to control our money, but when we really look at it, many of us have a good deal more control than we think we do. Now, this doesn't mean this is discretionary money that you can just spend for the heck of it. It just gives you a picture of what you are really able to do something about; the size of the stick you have to create a powerful financial lever to change your life.

Whether you picked up this book because you feel trapped, stressed or held hostage by your financial situation or if you just knew there was a better way to manage your day-to-day finances; seeing your real degree of control is somehow cathartic. If we change the way we use our money, we can change the value it brings to our lives. We can find ways to pursue passions we thought we'd passed over. We can change a career, have another baby or start the business we've always wanted to start. By controlling our cashflow, we can prepare ourselves to be ready to lead the life we want.

So now let's take those dollars we know you have control over and show you how to manage them effectively, making this book worth a whole lot more than the price you paid for it. My mission is that everyone who ever pays me for my advice, time or services, finds that I am always worth more than my fee. I strive to find my clients more money than I cost them and my hope is that your experience is no different.

Your controllable dollars will go toward a few things, including wants and needs, which can be either emotional or unemotional. Also, these are dollars you can harness to pay down your debt faster and save for your future. In the next Baby Step I'll show you how to find even more money to take control over spending and efficiently manage your debt to ensure you can take care of all of these things!

You don't have to categorize these things or write them down; this is more of a concept to help you decide which controllable expenses your cash-budget is really for.

Most people understand the concept of wants vs. needs, although I'd argue many put a few wants in the needs category. I've only ever seen male college students do the reverse:

- needs: beer
- wants: laundry detergent

. . . or at least that's how it would appear if you were to examine their spending habits.

Let's clarify anyway.

Needs vs. Wants

- Wants are things you DON'T need to any degree to survive

- So clothing you don't need is a want:
  - If you don't have appropriate work clothes for an office job and you have an office job, you clearly need clothes, but you can still control how much you spend, right?
  - That great pair of jeans you just had to have because they made your butt look like you'd had a transplant of some sort; definite want!
  - Basically, if you won't be standing naked waiting for the bus or wearing the same pair of pants to work everyday until your co-workers begin to comment, you do not need more clothing.
- You need food, but you don't need to eat out.
  - I would agree that we all need to eat healthy, but don't use that logic to buy organic if you really don't have the ability to afford it.
  - Don't use poor money logic to support unhealthy habits. I agree, milk is more expensive than pop but tap water kicks both of their butts in the health and price department.
- You want to have the latest electronic toothbrush, but you only need the regular old drugstore, manual variety.
- You want to have a new car because you have three kids and Lord knows with today's child safety regulations, it's hard to fit three kids in anything but a mini-van or SUV. However, there are some car seat manufacturers who've been working on that problem. So, perhaps, you need a more expensive car seat system but do you really need a new car?

Emotional vs. Unemotional

- Groceries are emotional. I don't care who you are. From the health nut to the junk-food-etarian. Shopping in most of the stores where we buy our food is emotional. Food stores don't just sell food anymore, which increases the risk of spending more than we mean to.

- Gasoline is one example of a controllable and variable expense that is not emotional (at least in most cases). I've never seen anyone buy more gasoline than they needed for pleasure. Or rush to fill jerry-cans full of it when it's on sale. For most of the population, gas is unemotional.
- Clothing is always emotional, even when it's a need.
- Family fun, toys for our kids, eating out, coffee, sometimes even the little extras at the drugstore all add up and are all emotional expenses.

The easiest way to determine if something really is emotional is to imagine going without it. If we could all avoid paying for gasoline tomorrow, not one of us would clasp our chests in sorrow. However, if someone told me I couldn't have a latte again, I'd be brewing up an argument as to why that wasn't reasonable in a heart-beat. So, the degree to which you are attached to the expense will give you an idea of whether or not it has an emotional bend to it. Don't even try lying to yourself here. I'll tell you what I tell every client. If you want to live in denial and exclude clearly emotional expenses from your cash-budget then that's fine; just remember it's your money and it won't affect my lifestyle if you find yourself on the cat-food cardboard diet in retirement. Sometimes, when someone gives us spending advice, we tend to shoot the messenger, even acting as though they may somehow benefit from your sacrifice. For example, just because you don't buy those hot jeans because you don't have enough cash left, doesn't mean those funds you aren't going to spend are instantly wired to my account. We all know that it's not rational, but it's what we do. So we aren't rational, let's get over it and do something about our finances anyway.

Essentially, cash should be used on all expenses that are emotional; period. For example, the following regular expenses would be emotional and controllable, so I'd recommend they be paid for in cash only (using a pre-determined weekly cash limit):

- Clothing, shoes and all accessories
- Groceries
- Eating out
- Coffee and other treats
- All entertainment, like movies, books, magazines etc.
- Sports activities (yes, even for the kids)
- Toys and play equipment
- Magazines and books
- Make up and accessories

You can see this does take some degree of planning, at least at first, but mostly it takes paying attention; we are all capable of that.

The good news is that what I'll be recommending you do will allow you the room for needs as well as some discretion for wants. You'll have to learn to re-prioritize some things, but overall, you'll be redirecting cash toward the things that truly make life worth living and stopping all the leaks to the stuff that doesn't really mean much . . . at least to you.

So, just how much cash can you use? Well, there isn't a hard and fast rule but I would recommend you start with no more than 15 percent of your net income.

Example 1) monthly salary

Net income $7000 monthly pay
15 percent = $1050
Weekly cash-budget ($1050 x 12/ 52) $242

Example 2) bi-weekly salary

Net bi-weekly income $3500
15 percent = $525
Weekly cash-budget ($525 / 2) $262.50

So, in this example, if you make $7000 net a month, you'd have a starting cash-budget of $242 a week. But if you really earn $3500 bi-weekly you actually get $262. What does this mean?

In most cases, people can really afford to spend 15 percent of their income on groceries, clothing, coffee, eating out, and movies and so on. If you'd have trouble managing with this amount of cash with an income of $7000 a month, that might show you right away how your spending measures up to your income.

This is just a start; a 60 day (minimum) exercise. If you continue on, you'll see that you can increase this amount if you find it tight, but the fact that there is a limit is the most important part. If for 60 days you could use cash to buy groceries and discretionary items using 15 percent of your net take-home income, how many decisions do you think you'd start to make differently?

I dare you to try it. We'll work through some other parts of your spending and debt reduction plan, but for 60 days, right here and right now, commit to a cash only existence based on 15 percent of your take-home income for groceries, wants and other day-to-day expenses.

Example:

Net Income Monthly $7000
Controllable Cash $4000
Cash spending $1050
No Excuses. Savings Amount $700/mo!!! Period!
Leaving $2250 controllable cash to work with.

Now, most people's instinct would now be to take the $2250 and start divvying that up over their various spending categories but not so fast! Baby Steps 3 and 5 will put those dollars to work.

The Justifier: You are one of the Mindsets likely to have trouble discerning your wants from your needs, so cash spending works really well for you. It takes away the risk that you'll try and talk yourself into a different reality. You should stay on cash for all recommended active cashflow categories. Only switch to a limited amount in an account linked to your debit card with EXTREME caution.

The Dreamer: Cash spending is a gift to you. It doesn't bog down your daily thought process with a bunch of inaccurate mental math. You can go along and work away at your dreams with a clear and concise idea of what you have to work with each week. It will take some getting used to, but you are one of the most able to adapt Mindsets. You can do this! You should stay on cash for discretionary expenses indefinitely.

The Brick Wall: I know, I know, you are probably thinking, "this is stupid". Or perhaps you think you don't need to do this, but this would be a great idea for your spouse or your kids. I still think you should do it. You might learn some interesting things about yourself that will help you continue to make great decisions.

The Polly Anna: You will likely gain quite a bit of relief from the idea of cash spending. It's limited. You can go about your day focused on what you like to focus on and the amount of money you have to spend is already worked out and taken care of.

The Masquerader: You like the idea of cash, you might even have a money clip or be used to carrying cash, but the limited part you might not be so keen on. It all comes back to this. Do you want to change something about your financial reality or not? If you don't, then give this book to someone who does. If you do, trust me and do the cash thing. It's not forever. You should switch to a debit card as recommended after 60 days. You'll still have a limit to work with, but since you are likely to make a higher income, you are also likely to have a higher cash amount, making cash less practical for you. I'd still recommend you use cash for your pure discretionary money each week.

The Undercover Agent: Cash works just fine for you and the limit isn't necessarily a problem, but you are going to get a rude awakening if you don't pay attention. You'll run out of money fast and if you want meaningful financial change, you must stick to it. No "sneaking" extra funds.

The Bunker: You love this idea and are all over it like dust on Velcro. In fact, you probably do it already. If you are married to another Mindset (besides Brick Wall), then I'd suggest you keep on the cash idea permanently. You can both feel more confident going forward if you can trust what is going on with the funds and cash is the best way to monitor them.

Baby Step 3 – Unify Your Debt

Okay, now all that debt diversification and consolidation I was on about in the last chapter is coming into play. Unifying debt is the solution for real life in my opinion. Life is not linear. None of us go from the point A to the point B of life in a straight line. Our lives are filled with potholes, forks in the road and the occasional need to go financial off-roading. I believe that in our current world, the reason people have so much trouble managing debt is because they can't accept that it's fluid. It isn't reasonable for many to be debt free all of the time or even to decrease your debt each month. People often think that paying down debt every single month by exactly the same amount is the definition of financial perfection. As soon as our life does something our plan doesn't account for, however, we freak out, throw up our hands and give up! When what really matters with debt is flexibility. Yes, flexibility. You might be thinking, "Flexibility? Isn't that part of the problem? My credit card is flexible and that's the issue, isn't it?" Well, it can be if you don't know how to manage it. However, not knowing how to manage it is now the world's most pathetic excuse. Remember, you are starting to know better so now you can do better. Debt is just a tool and the products you use when you borrow are just tools, too; nothing less and nothing more.

What if I were to hand you a circular saw and you'd never used one before. Then, I showed you a sheet of plywood I wanted you to cut precisely in half, and then I blindfolded you and spun you around a couple of times. Could you cut the plywood safely and accurately? Of course not, but is the saw the problem? No, the tool isn't the issue in that case, and the debt tool is usually not the issue when it comes to repayment. It's the fact that far too many of us are walking around with figurative missing fingers—or even limbs—because someone handed us a debt tool and not only did we not learn how to use it, we've blindfolded ourselves from ever learning how. One thing we need to come to terms with is that in our haste to accept money that someone is willing to lend, we become part of the process that keeps us blindfolded.

I've lost count of the number of people who say to me, "Stephanie, I can't unify debt into only one account because if it's flexible, it could allow me to borrow more and then I'll get into even more debt." This is code for, "I'm worried I'll overspend. And rather than learning how to make a massive positive financial change and incorporate new money skills, I'll keep paying exorbitant amounts of interest over multiple inefficient accounts and wonder why I'm not getting anywhere; the risk of success it just too great!"

Does that even make sense? I don't want to learn how to act in my own best interest because I don't know how to act in my own best interest. So quit cutting off your nose to spite your face and do the right things with your debt. Focus your energy on modifying your spending behaviours. If you want to cut the wood, are you going to learn how to use the saw safely and properly, or are you going to use the safety scissors to guarantee you won't cut yourself?

All-In-One Pot!

So where is all of this talk of debt unification going? Ideally, I'm pointing you toward the use of All-in-One mortgage products. I'm a huge fan of using these things to make debt/cashflow and retirement plans work. I stress that these particular debt tools (as with all others really) should be used as part of a plan. They are, in my opinion, the most efficient, flexible and effective ways to pay down debt quickly while allowing the homeowner to fund retirement savings and manage fluctuations in expenses. Not everyone in every country has access to such products and of course, not everyone will qualify, so I'll go through other options. My main message is that the lower the number of debt accounts you have, the better. It is key to your financial agility that at least one be what is called revolving, meaning you can pay it down as much as you want in the lower expense months and re-advance on months with higher or annual expenses.

Essentially, these all-in-ones work like a huge line of credit, mortgage, chequing and savings account, all under one roof, so to speak. All of your income goes right into the account and is instantly applied to the principle of your mortgage. From the moment it is deposited, your paycheque is saving you interest. Of course, we both know that you have to spend money each month, but you only pay interest on what you owe each day. By managing your spending (what goes out of the account each month), you can make a massive dent in your debt much faster than if you were using a conventional mortgage or other debt options. You can reduce your balance more effectively by putting every dollar to work. It's like a vicious cycle, only for the first time, it's moving in the right direction. The dollars that aren't in use in your active or working cashflows are sitting there saving you interest against your total debt. Also, when lump sum expenses like vacation, snow tires (for some of us), car repairs or school fees come up, you've been paying down debt rapidly but you can access the extra when you need it. While your balance will go up and down from one day or month to the next, by managing your active cashflow, you'll see astounding results from year-to-year.

If there is anything I can promise you, it's that in a given year, something you didn't plan for will happen. Something will break; someone will break or even break-up. If you are focused on what you can control and you have your maximum debt re-payment and a good amount of savings running on auto pilot, you'll be a lot better equipped to handle what is going to happen anyway. So, set your sights to run your spending and debt management plan at 100 percent and accept that success probably looks like 80 percent, which is a heck of a lot better than most of us are headed for with no plan. A word of caution, however; if you only aim at 80 percent, you are sure to achieve less success. So work toward 100 percent financial efficiency and be very happy with achieving 80 percent of your goal.

The reason I like to use this type of account (and yes, you better believe this is what I use) is because I can focus my clients on the real issue, keeping them conscious of the active cashflow. The working cashflow can do its work unencumbered in an All-In-One account. This helps me keep my clients concentrated on the things they can control, like cashflow and slowing down spending behaviours. Simultaneously, it's keeping them out of the way—in their own best interest, since maximum debt repayment, monthly savings/investments and bill payments become automated. When used properly, the decisions that get you ahead financially are automated and the risk behaviours are managed by Baby Step 2.

Example:

    Net Monthly Income: $7000
    Controllable Cash: $4000
    Cash Spending: $1050

No Excuses Savings Amount: $700/mo!!! Period!
Leaving $2250 controllable cash to work with

Using our earlier example from Baby Step 2, the full $2250 could be left in the all-in-one account, rapidly repaying debt. However, what would be even better, is to split up that money, sending some to savings/investments and creating assets while debt is simultaneously repaid. In this situation, $1000 a month could be redirected and invested long term and there would still be significant debt repayment. This person can have a life, pay down debt quickly and effectively and save for their future all at the same time. How would you feel if you could change your financial stars by restructuring your debt, controlling your spending and using the money you already have to live the life you really want?

What I've discovered is that when the actions the client must take to follow a debt repayment plan require manual input (meaning each month the person has to identify an amount they can put against the debt and then physically pay those funds to a given debt), the likelihood that they won't stick to it is very high! So I've made most of the debt management plans I create to take that risk out of the equation. I know that in most cases you won't manage a high degree of efficiency if you have too much time to think about making extra payments toward debt. There are a few reasons for that. One, the internal dialogue we have with ourselves, which says we might need that money so we'll pay some extra, but not as much as was recommended. Or, we'll look at the overall repayment goal date and decide we'd be happy with half of that and start to pull back on debt payment. Either way, humans and extra monthly debt repayment as a monthly task, don't mix well, so when I can avoid it, I do! I want you to succeed, so I want to give you my best advice based on observations I've made over the many hundreds of cases I've worked on. When it comes to debt, automated repayments at maximum efficiency are your friend. Remember to *speed up and not interrupt good financial actions* and *slow down and interrupt high-risk financial decisions.*

I think you really need a financial plan, which includes cash-flow and debt management as well as access to regular professional guidance when using an all-in-one mortgage solution. Having said that, I think if you want this type of planning, this book is a good start to get you in the right frame of mind to do so. There isn't room in this book to fully educate you on all-in-one accounts or to give you enough information to do your own plan with your exact situation. Every person is a little different from the next as is their financial situation. What I want you to take away from this possible solution, is that you should consider it. If you can't qualify for an all-in-one at this point, it should be a goal, and you should demand the type of planning you need to manage your debt most effectively. If you and I, and everyone who reads this book, don't speak up, it will be our own fault if we don't get what we need. As it stands now, many financial advisors or other financial professionals don't provide this type of advice, and if we aren't loud about its importance, they never will. Remember, I told you this book isn't meant to be a cure, it's meant to be a catalyst.

Alternatives

Of course, as I mentioned, not everyone, everywhere in the world can even access an All-In-One or they may not qualify for one. So what else can you do? *The answer:* A lot.

If there was only one acceptable solution, there would have been a lot of people I've worked with throughout the years that I wouldn't have been able to help.

Two is Better Than Ten

The next best solution for homeowners is a combination of two debt types; a mortgage and either an unsecured (not attached to your home, but usually higher interest) or a homeowners line of credit (this would be secured to home equity and usually is the lowest rate debt you can get). Obviously, your mortgage could be fixed but what you would do is put your debt repayment dollars, which would have lived in your all-in-one on your line of credit until it's gone. Accept that you might have to re-advance every now and then, as life happens. Again, your focus on spending and working with cash will be instrumental to your success.

Still Can't Work It? Then Snowball it Baby!

If all else fails (maybe you have wounded credit, or all of your debts exceed any home equity you could access, or maybe you don't even own a home), don't worry, all is not lost! You can still snowball it, baby. You are probably thinking, "She's lost it now. What does a snowball have to do with debt?"

Snowballing is a common term used to express a process of paying off multiple debts. If you go online and search snowball calculators, you are sure to find something you can use.

Basically, the concept of snowballing is taking any number of debts and organizing them in a specific order. Some recommend paying multiple consumer debt accounts off in order of interest rate, paying the highest rate debts off first. While others suggest it is more motivating to pay off a few small accounts first, even if they aren't the highest rate. Quickly getting the number of accounts from, say, seven to four, can help you to focus. For the most part, interest rate order is the most cost-effective way to rid yourself of pesky and costly consumer debts. However, as discussed throughout this book, our behaviour and motivation are as important as the math, if not more so in many cases. Once you have the debts in order (again, there are several free online calculators that can do the math for you), your objective is to take some of that cash you've freed up for additional debt repayment and put it toward Debt #1. Then, once Debt #1 is paid off, you roll the original Debt #1 monthly payment and the additional debt repayment funds to Debt #2, on top of that debt's regular monthly payment. This is one snowball that will roll in the right direction and you'd be surprised at just how fast you begin to see results!

In general, this concept can't be as automated as an all-in-one solution, but you can and should set things up so that you don't have to add the extra debt repayment dollars each month. Rather, adjust your automated payment to reflect the old payment plus the additional debt repayment dollars on the debt you are focused on at that point in your repayment plan. Just make sure you keep an eye on when you are supposed to roll your gathering snowball of cash onto the next debt. I recommend marking it on your calendar or even setting a reminder in your smart phone or online day planner. It is certainly less than ideal to keep debts in multiple accounts like this, but when the ideal solution isn't for you just yet, don't let that hold you back; or worse, become your excuse!

Mindset Tips

The Dreamer: Those dreams of yours will be limitless now if you keep focused on Baby Step 2 and implement Baby Step 3. It doesn't bother you to see your debt anyway and anything that requires less of your time to manage it will work for you. Make the time to set up automatic payments and get your pay coming into your All-In-One account. A few extra minutes now saves you hours every week.

The Masquerader: You are the most difficult Mindset to get approved for All-In-One products because of your "debt metrics". As I've mentioned before, sometimes your income is often great and you can easily borrow because of it. Because you can easily borrow, you can end up in a situation where there isn't enough equity in your home to put all of your debts under one roof. I've seen many Masquerader Mindsets unable to qualify for All-In-One products because they have too much debt, even for their great income. No matter how much you make, there is always a limit to how much money anyone is willing to lend you.

The Justifier: Oh, this thought is just messing you right up. Telling yourself stories is much more difficult when you have to look at the reality of your debt each month. However, if you want to see real change and stop feeling like you have to come up with a reason for your money being the way it is, Baby Steps 2 and 3 will get you there. Just trust in the process. Focus your energy on Step 2. Step 3 takes some work to set up, but then it will run on auto pilot.

The Brick Wall: You don't like this idea only because you weren't the one to discover it! That really doesn't matter; you can tell everyone it was your idea if you like. Do you really want control over your money? Baby Steps 2 and 3 are the key to that. So analyze whatever you need to make you feel better but make sure you do apple-to-apple comparisons. There are online tools to help you do that, so look for them and use them well.

The Polly Anna: This thought just freaks you right out. To that, I say, "Oh well, do it anyway and take the time to make sure you understand it." You don't get to shrug off your power to make meaningful financial change on my watch. So sit with that anxiety, ask questions and make a plan to incorporate Baby Step 2 and 3 into your finances.

The Undercover Agent: You don't like this idea at all. Not only will one, perhaps two people (some all-in-one products come with an expert or consultant that deals with both the financial advisor and the client during the application process) really have to know your total financial picture to qualify you for and provide you with a plan to manage an all-in-one. This will seriously push your boundaries, but in my experience, it is worth it. You can still maintain your own money. If it is helpful to you, you can have your cash amount split and go in two separate accounts for you and your spouse. Combining the big stuff for the sake of better financial freedom and knowing you and your other half are on the same page can be a good thing and it doesn't mean you have to give up control.

The Bunker: You have no problem with the idea of having only one debt account. You don't like the idea of having access to your home equity or the fact that because these products are line of credit based, they have floating rates. If you are a bunker, you are likely to pay off these accounts even faster, saving even more in interest than anyone else. However, you should compare facts rather than feelings. If you barely have five years left to pay the whole debt off, your interest costs compared to principle are teeny-weenie anyway. However, if you are just coming off year five of a 25-year amortization, keep your balance in mind at renewal. How much will be exposed to the rate of the day then? You are often a good candidate for these types of products, but you should insist on a plan so you can feel comfortable that you are on track as you go.

Baby Step 4 – Budget for the Big Stuff

Unless you are never going to buy another car or you can somehow guarantee that you'll never have another vacation or even unexpected expense, you are likely to have to borrow again, at least until your savings are huge. What can you do about it? If you haven't caught on to the theme yet, the answer is: you have to plan ahead. So let's review a few of the more common major expenses that can come up every year, or even every 3, 5, or 10 years and go over just how you can plan ahead. Knowing what to do when faced with your next major financial decision is one great way to keep yourself on track. Of course, you shouldn't expect perfection, but you should expect to do better with each financial Baby Step.

Metal Masks

Or as we more commonly refer to them, cars. Our vehicle choices are one area where we can have some of the greatest effect on our overall debt and cashflow picture. Of all debt, I hate car debt the most. I have seen more people stuck in financial corners even I can't get them out of very fast, all because of vehicle purchase decisions. I can't stress enough how important it is that we start making major purchases, like cars, part of our overall cashflow and debt planning. If you take nothing else from this book, I hope you take the advice I'm about to give you on car purchases.

Buying

I prefer to see people buy their cars. I also firmly believe you should only purchase a car that you can afford to pay off in three years or less. This belief is based on years of working with people's cashflow and having dealt with thousands of car payments inside many a client's financial plan. Without exception, paying off cars in 36 months or less makes a huge positive impact on overall financial progress in every case I've worked on. It has been my experience that if you have to stretch it further than that magic three-year point, especially on an older car, you set yourself up to be forever with a car payment. Worse yet, when you stretch out a car payment over 4, 5, 6 or even 7 years, you are really tricking yourself into thinking you can afford just about any vehicle. Let me share some more of that rocket science of mine with you; when it comes to cars, what you get approved for and what you can afford, are two very different things.

One thing with car loans you should avoid, as if your life depends on it, is purchasing a new car before you paid off the old one and rolling the old debt into the new loan. This is a financial nightmare! I know you walk into the dealership and they "make it go away", but the problem is still the problem. Piling new car debt on old car debt only means that you owe that much more than that new vehicle is even worth, and that's before depreciation, which is lost the second you drive it off the lot. Bottom line is if you can't afford the payment over a 36-month term, then you are buying a car you can't afford!

Leasing

My best advice for leasing a vehicle is DON'T. In my opinion, it is not the best choice for most people. There is an exception to this. Anyone who can legitimately write off at least 50 percent of the entire monthly costs of the vehicle for business should lease. If you are a business owner, you should check with your accountant to confirm whether or not you can deduct the costs in your situation. Having said all that, I don't like leasing for the most part for a very specific reason; most people lease to gain use of a car they can't really afford. Someone once told me that smart people rent depreciating assets and buy appreciating assets. Okay that's fine, I just say that a really smart person would only rent something they could have afforded to buy in the first place and then they put the difference in payment to work.

I'll use myself as an example. I lease my own car and have for the last nine years. My vehicle is used almost entirely for my business, to the extent it is generally parked all weekend long (unless I book it to Starbucks on a Sunday morning to write in peace). Remember, in the introduction, I told you I've learned many of my lessons from doing the wrong things and then working to keep myself and others from making the same mistakes? Well, here is one of my mistakes.

Learn From My Errors

When I returned from Alberta, I didn't have much to my name, except my dog, the clothes on my back and my 1996 Dodge Neon. I know, I know, the makings of a good country song, right? In any case, I nearly had that car paid off, which I had purchased over four years. With a very manageable payment of only $250 a month, it wasn't too much of a strain on my budget (while I was employed anyway). However, three months before I paid it off, I was T-boned and my poor little green Neon-that-could was toast! I got a payout from my insurance company based on the value of the car and was told to go shopping. Keep in mind that at this point I've been a financial advisor for just over a year and I've discovered very little about debt and cash-flow. In a panic, I called around to a few dealerships, trying to get a handle on what I could buy. I didn't really know what I was doing and I didn't know much about cars and frankly, I didn't care that much. I drove a lot in the winter and I needed something that would stop, go and be safe in the snow. I decided on leasing a Subaru Forrester, which I loved. It was a manageable payment (note that shiny thing, the monthly payment had me in its grasp) and I was able to write off most of the cost, as my car was used almost exclusively for business. Everything ticked along.

Now, here comes the mistake part. I didn't know how to take advantage of that low monthly lease cost to create more savings or help my husband pay off his car. When that lease was up, I took over my husband's vehicle, which we had taken out a loan on over . . . wait for it . . . 60 months. It was a piece of garbage and I hated it. It was bad on gas and even though it was only a few years old, it seemed to always be falling apart. The final straw was when I was getting barely 300 km of driving out of a full 60L tank of gas. This was a little four-cylinder engine, it shouldn't have been eating gas like that. So, after a multitude of mechanical issues, I realized I needed a different work vehicle. By now, my husband had another vehicle, which we had been smart enough to save for. We owned it outright (and as of the writing of this book, still do). It was reliable, mechanically sound, good on gas and just an all around great family vehicle. We weren't going to sell or trade in Mr. Reliable and keep Mr. Ridiculous. I had to find a way to get rid of the awful vehicle I was driving.

So, I made a call to find out what we owed on the garbage car. We'd purchased the car two years prior and you could have knocked me over with a feather when I was told we owed nearly $18,000 on a $24,000 car. So, here was my lesson. We'd bought a demo and financed it through the dealers financing arm. We'd been loaned money based on the original sticker price (less our negotiated discount) but because our car was a demo, and it was last year's model, it wasn't worth what we'd been lent, even before we drove off the lot.

If we'd applied for that amount of a loan against that vehicle at a bank, they would have told us the book value (fair market value) was far lower than the price we were being charged. On top of that, our interest was paid almost 100 percent from our original payments but little was put toward the principle until they'd taken their five years of interest first. So, in reality, we'd paid $14,000 in car payments over 24 months and put only a $6,000 dent in the loan. I was gutted. I couldn't believe I hadn't understood all this. I ended up going back to Subaru and negotiating a good enough trade-in value for that sorry excuse for a car, put a good lump sum down to erase most of the leftover loan and went back to what was best for me business wise — leasing. It was an expensive lesson, but I've used it to create great value for those who I work with and I hope it will bring value to you.

I did make a different choice leasing from Subaru that time though. I leased a car I could actually have afforded to buy over 3 years. I stuffed the difference between my real lease payment and the would-be loan payment aside so that we could continue on with my family's personal financial goal, which is for me to lease a low-cost vehicle and save up for my husband's cars and buy them in cash. I've recently leased my third Subaru and with a very small lease payment, I can afford to save that difference I told you about in order to make sure we can buy our family car for cash!

Example:
- My lease payment is $329/mo over 48 months
- We would have afforded a $850 loan payment and I had $5,000 saved for a vehicle down payment.
- We tucked the $5,000 aside and we are topping it up with $521/mo over the next 24 months
- We will have nearly $18,000 ready to buy my husband's next car (or make a large down payment and take on a small payment for 12 months)
- We can keep at this pattern for the rest of our working lives if we pay attention and make a plan on how we buy cars

People sometimes tell me how hard it is to save for cars or how if they bought cars they could afford, they'd be driving a heap of scrap metal. Then I share my own situation with them, pointing out that we always lease one new and arguably good car but base model and always buy one good quality used car. While we don't have a fancy ride, we are not driving buckets of bolts either. The market will come to meet us if we show it what we want. If we all start to be smarter with our vehicle purchases, there will be more affordable vehicles to be had. If we are all leasing $40,000 SUV's, then that's what will be available.

Miscellaneous

There are a number of other things that can crop up and would qualify as major expenses, like renovations, buying a business, buying a rental property or going on the vacation of a lifetime. You can still do these things, but it doesn't have to be at the expense of your financial success. These are individual things and therefore require an individual goal. So here is my ten cents on these types of costs:
- Make a total debt repayment goal:
  - Make a plan to get your debt on track and when planning for a major expense, work on getting your debt down below a certain amount then you'll know when

you reach that number you can go ahead and do that renovation or book that trip (on a pre-determined budget, of course).

- This is one place were a budget will really work:
  - Sit down and figure out how much you are willing to put toward that major expense.
  - Write out where you think the funds will go on different areas of the expense.
- Record quotes as you get them against your budget, as well as costs as you spend funds, this will keep you from going over budget.
- Decide what debt repayment goal you must achieve before moving on to the next goal on your list.
- Repeat, repeat, repeat!

Mindset Tips

The Justifier: You are at high risk for overspending on major purchases. Pay close attention to the tips in this chapter to avoid falling victim to traps you may indeed unintentionally set for yourself. Pay special attention to details when you are making purchases and bounce your choices off others before committing. If you hear yourself justifying something, you may want to reconsider that choice.

The Undercover Agent: You are a lower risk Mindset to overspend on the more obvious major purchases. Still, stay alert and don't be distracted by the shiny things.

The Dreamer: You are a very high-risk person when making major purchases. You have to keep focused on the present when considering what you can afford. Take a look at the guidelines provided to you in this book and use them to make sure your financial decisions are consistent with your dreams.

The Brick Wall: You are at a much lower risk of overspending when it comes to major purchases. You'd be almost embarrassed to pay full price for just about anything. However, add the tips you've learned here to your research tool kit and keep on track with your active financial management, being careful not to expect the impossible, of course.

The Polly Anna: Your Mindset is high risk for major purchase errors. Take this book with you if you have to the next time you visit a car lot or appliance store. Don't give in without considering your options first. Keep learning and getting more comfortable with financial decisions and they will get easier and more natural to make on your own.

The Masquerader: You are definitely one to blow your budget when it comes to major purchases. You don't have to drive a heap of metal or live in a shack, but I would suggest agreeing to limits with a spouse (or other significant person in your life if you are single) for such things as how much you'll spend in a year on vacations, or your next vehicle for example. Trust me, people have way too much to do to really get wrapped up in the fact you are keeping your beemer for a few more years than you did last time. Thanks to the economy, it is far more socially acceptable, almost chic, to be a little more practical with big stuff these days.

The Bunker: You almost don't need anything here, except that you can use some of these ideas to get your non-Bunker spouse on board with some of your ways of doing things, and that is sure to make you feel more comfortable.

Baby Step 5 – Make Investing/Saving a Bill

If you're going to take my advice, I recommend you take it all. From the very beginning of this book I introduced you to the idea that savings isn't just about safety and being ready for an emergency, it's also about being ready for opportunity. After I present a plan, people often ask me how long they have to do the "saving part" for. My answer is always the same. "Until you are dead or independently wealthy, whichever comes first." I truly believe that we should always be saving. That is not to say we can't spend any of our savings; that is not my point. But if we are always saving and we commit to never dipping down below eight months of living expenses as our balance, there isn't much that we won't be able to handle. Savings won't make us infallible, but it gives us space and time. The space to sit back and make the best decision when we lose our job and we have to find another. Time to deal with a life event we could deal better with if our finances don't make us rush to decide.

My rule when it comes to savings or investments is that they should be treated like a bill. It never ceases to surprise me that so many of us value our utility provider more than we value ourselves or our family. Now, of course I don't think we actually feel that way, but if you looked at the evidence, it tells a different story. So many of us will pay a lot of other people before we'll pay ourselves in the form of savings. Does that even make sense? If you treat savings and investment as if it were as non-negotiable as your monthly bills, you can really get somewhere.

From a behavioural standpoint, it is important that you change the way you look at putting money toward investments or savings differently than you may now. You must let go of the thought that saving money is about "not getting to spend it". When tasked with saving money our inner teenager really seems to come out. As I mentioned a few pages ago, we sometimes act as if money we save for ourselves is somehow providing funds for someone else. The fact of the matter is that even the financial professionals in your lives, who likely make a commission from your investment purchases or savings deposits, aren't going to get the value from those dollars that you will. Savings is about you! Investing is about you! And if you are ever going to develop into the financially independent person you and I both know you can be, you are going to have to commit to putting money away every month. Until what?

"Until you are dead or independently wealthy, whichever comes first."

So when it comes to putting money away, and to work, I like to see at least 10 percent of your take-home income—read carefully—10 percent of your take-home income, not 10 percent of your controllable cash, MUST go into savings. Ideally, 10 percent to long-term investments and 10 percent to short-term savings. Have a look below at how that would affect our earlier example:

Example:

> Net Income Monthly: $7000
> Controllable Cash: $4000
> Cash Spending: $1050
> No Excuses Savings Amount: $700/mo!!! Period!
> Leaving $2250 controllable cash to work with

When we look at our previous example, they could take my rule of thumb below and still result in very significant debt repayment while saving for the future.

> 10 percent net take-home = $700 50/50 investment and savings
> Total Money For the Future = $700
> *Leaving*
> $1550 for additional debt repayment
> OR

10 percent of net take home = $700 savings
10 percent of net take-home = $700 investments
Total Money For the Future = $1400
Leaving
$850 for additional debt repayment

What opportunities could you have had if you'd been saving like this for the last ten years? Better yet, what opportunities will you be able to take advantage of if you save like this for the next ten years? My advice is never about what you can't have or what you can't do with your life; it is just the opposite. Most people aren't managing the money they have in the most effective way and for the most part, it's because of the way we've been trained to use money. But you don't have to do it that way anymore. Now that you know better, you'll be able to do better with your money.

This book is not about investments or how much risk you should or shouldn't take. It's about working with your personality traits and helping you make better decisions so you can find the money to do things like make investing a bill. You pay your phone bill, right? You consider it to be important enough to prioritize and pay right away. So treat your own investments, as if they were that important and make them like a bill. It's so easy to talk yourself out of investing or saving. Sometimes you're able to get started and then something happens and you feel you should cash out. Managing your debt, spending and cash flow so that you can commit to long-term and patient investing can make a huge difference in just how financially independent you become. Most people only really invest to create future cash flow. Every time you feel the urge to pull the plug on putting money away, think about how you'd feel with even less money because that is what you'll be setting yourself up for.

The Justifier: You have a million reasons why you don't invest, or why you used to have investments but had to cash them out. Don't even go there. What's done is done and you can do things differently now. Automating investments is key for your Mindset. The less action you need to take to put your investment dollars to work each month, the better. The all-in-one idea I told you about earlier in the chapter will smooth out your cashflow over the year, allowing you to be more committed to investing long term.

The Dreamer: Just think of investing as if it were a company you were building on the side to sell "someday". Don't look at it like it's a "piggy bank". You may want to divert some funds from those brick and mortar type investments you like so much. Unless you are positive that you can sell a property at any time (ever tried to do that? It doesn't always work out), you should consider the kind of investments you can liquidate with a phone call.

The Brick Wall: You are the most likely not to need any encouragement to invest. However, if your assets leave anything to be desired, you might want to use what you've learned here to free up more cashflow to build them up. It makes you feel safe to be in control, but being a little gentler with those who work with your assets on your behalf might have them bringing more initiative to the table.

The Polly Anna: I know this stuff freaks you out. So start out easy. Freeing up the cashflow to invest is the first step. You need to find a professional who is as much a teacher as they are an advisor or planner. You have to tell them you want to learn and start out slow. If you ask for what you need, most of the time, you will get much closer to it.

The Masquerader: For you, freeing up the cashflow isn't necessarily that difficult, but resisting the temptation to just pull money back out is where you will have to fight with yourself. If I were you, I'd discuss with your advisor/banker/planner that you'd prefer to stick to the plan and ask them to more seriously question a withdrawal, just to slow you down long enough to think. In the end, the choice is still yours and so is the result.

The Undercover Agent: It's really hard to give you advice on your investments because you tend to be all over the place. This could inadvertently result in you getting unsuitable investment advice because your professional is missing some key facts. So, you either need to be far more involved in your investment choices, so much so that all you need is an order taker, or you need to start finding people you trust more. Either way, keeping monthly investing and saving systematic and separate is ideal for you.

The Bunker: You don't need to be told that saving or investing is important, but you should likely learn more about investing and base your decisions on fact rather than feelings. Having said that, avoiding any risk can still result in enough assets, as long as you save more than someone who is willing to take a risk. It is important that you have a plan and that it includes your debts, assets and spending.

What life dreams could you accomplish if you could harness the money you are wasting on inefficient interest, unplanned major purchases, and buying things you don't truly value? I'm about to put it altogether for you so keep going, there is only one more chapter left!

CHAPTER 8

It's All You!

"Be the change you wish
to see in the world."

~ Mahatma Gandhi

I would paraphrase the above quote as, "Be the change you wish to see in YOUR world". If you want more from the money you earn, and the work you put into this world, then you need to act, not wish for change to happen to you! Change will happen to you if you choose not to act, but it may not be in the direction you want or even anticipated.

One of the most common questions I am asked by my finance professional peers is, "Stephanie, does your advice work?" My answer is, "Unequivocally, yes, 100 percent of the time it works!" Now, that answer always gets me a teenage-style eye roll and exaggerated sigh. I know what they are thinking . . . I bet I know what you are thinking. No one can say they have 100 percent success. But I didn't say that people listen to me 100 percent of the time. It does work 100 percent of the time if people follow it. Actually, a lot of advice works like that. If 100 percent of *Weight Watchers* members did exactly what the program told them to do, they'd have darn close to 100 percent success. If 100 percent of recovering addicts . . . well, you know where I'm going with this.

What I've come to accept is that there is a very volatile variable (say that three times fast) to financial math, food math, exercise math . . . really, the math of life. It's us; we the humans, who mess everything up. We'd be living in an utopian *Star Trek* world by now if it weren't for us. Think about it, the greater good is not served by poverty, war, obesity, out-of-control debt, unkindness, drug addiction or any other imperfection that seems to come hand-in-hand with humanity. We are all capable of excellent productivity, fit finances, a healthy body and absolute and unconditional kindness. We all realize that expecting to live in a world that is always running at 100 percent of what it could be is ridiculous. I accept that, too. We are all a work in progress and maybe we always will be—I know I will. What I don't accept is that this general population really has anything to do with what I can create in my own world. Many people struggle with debt, but does that mean that I can't change my life so I can do a better job? People are starving in the world, does that mean I have to eat when I'm not hungry? There is war, poverty and general unfairness all around this, but does that mean I get a pass for being unkind to anyone? Comparing ourselves to the population at large in order to relieve ourselves of our responsibility to live up to our own greatness—that is what is really ridiculous.

Watching a financial show where the couple featured has $50,000 in credit card debt isn't a reason not to make a plan to get rid of your $5000 credit card balance. We are not better or worse, we just are. If we started trying to be the most financially balanced versions of ourselves, we'd really be getting somewhere.

Someone actually said to me recently, "Stephanie, if everyone follows your advice and stops overspending that could have major repercussions on the economy." My response? "Yes, that's it. Me and my little book, or even my regular rantings, are going to single-handedly collapse the economies of the free world. After all, what could stop a robust economy from being held together by people's credit cards?"

Classic Brick Wall question ,though. Look, I know as well as you do that every single person who reads this book, or sees me (or any other personal finance expert) speak, or watches TV money shows like *Till Debt Do We Part*, isn't going to run out and become a financial superstar. That's okay; frankly, if that were even possible, there would have been one personal finance book written decades ago and a simple annual update to keep us all on track. The reality is that not everyone will do something with even great advice when they hear it. My question to you is: *"What does that have to do with you?"* If everyone threw their money off a bridge . . . well, you know how that sentence ends.

This is your choice, your life, your money and using a perceived economic fallout resulting from a change in your spending behaviour is just an attempt to avoid dealing with it; so stop right now! Consider this instead: *What value can you put on saving yourself from the personal economic, emotional and/or a relationship fallout that comes with spending money you don't really have.* How can you continue to buy goods and services and support the economy if you run out of money and eventually, out of credit? Is the economy really less vulnerable if it doesn't ride on the backs of our debt?

Don't worry. You and I, and anyone else choosing to learn how to change the way they spend—and stop wasting money on things they don't value—will not bring about economic disaster. We might just prevent it to some degree, though. Without a doubt, if I could get everyone to follow this philosophy by simply wiggling my nose, then yes, there would be an economic effect. Even so, it wouldn't be quite as Armageddon-like as a financial collapse. Rather, I think what you would see is that businesses that people didn't truly value, or products that weren't worthy of our hard-earned cash, would suffer. But in my opinion, that's great news. It's better for business on the whole and outstanding for consumers. There would still be competition for your dollars and deals to be had, but people and companies might just have to work a little harder to earn your dough. I just don't think that is a bad thing.

So, to that nagging voice in your head, or tugging feeling in your gut that is making you second guess if you are really capable of change, I say "Mess off!" You might think you are hesitant, anxious or even afraid to make changes because you believe you might fail. But here's what you really are; afraid you'll succeed! What? Afraid of success? Who's afraid of success, right? I think most of us are. We might tell ourselves we don't do great things or make great change because we are afraid we will fail. But if you don't try, then you've already failed, so you can't possibly claim that fear stops you from doing what you are already doing? No, I think if you really think about it, you'll discover what is truly holding you back are questions like: "What if I can do this?" "What if I've wasted years of my time and thousands of my dollars by borrowing and spending the way I do now?" "What if it works but I don't keep going?" "What if I make enough change to know this will work and then bail because I don't feel like working at my money?" "What if I can't blame the government or the bank or . . . well, anyone but me for my financial circumstances?" "What will I do then?"

Ladies and gentleman, if these thoughts are running through your head even on a subconscious level, you are not alone. Here come those dinosaurs again. Your brains, and even your emotions, are playing with you. There are no dinosaurs and no man-eating predators around the corner, but reacting to fear stimulus is part of our makeup. Instead of dinosaurs, we have debt and we are reacting the same way to that debt as we would to a T-Rex.

It's Just Like Riding a Bicycle

Making sweeping financial change is just like driving a car. Remember when you first learned how to drive? Do you remember how many steps you had to consciously run through; sometimes, you may have even said them out loud.

My experience went something like this:
My first driving lesson was that afternoon. I'd spent all of the

previous night thinking about it and most of my school day day-dreaming about what it would be like. My driving instructor pulled into my driveway. Before I even got out the door, I grabbed my wallet and double-checked that my beginner's license was in it. Then, I ran through the rest of my mental check list. Sunglasses? Check. Purse? Check. Coat? Check. Hair tied back? Check, and so on. Then, with butterflies fluttering in my tummy, I stepped out the door. The instructor began to explain what we'd be doing during the lesson and showed me his passenger side brake pedal. Finally, it was my turn to take the wheel. Here is what went through my mind:

- Walk around the car then get in the driver's seat
- Adjust the seat so I can properly depress the brake pedal (I'm really short, this is always a step for me)
- Do up my seat belt
- Adjust my side mirrors
- Adjust my rearview mirror
- Hands at 10 and 2
- Depress the brake pedal
- Turn the key
- Slide the gear stick into drive
- Take a few deep breaths
- Look around, checking all directions and blind spots
- Slowly release the brake pedal
- Slowly depress the gas pedal, feeling for when the engine engages
- Keep the lines on the road at the centre of the hood and corner of the passenger side of the window
- Signal at least five telephone poles before I need to make a turn. Etc . . .

Can you imagine how painful driving would be if you were still slowly and meticulously reviewing these steps in your head each time you jumped in the car? Can you imagine the danger you'd be on the road if none of these steps had become smoother in transition, more natural? You'd be that person slamming on their brakes four blocks before they actually had to turn. Or, what if you stressed yourself out for hours before your first drive, running through all the things that could go wrong? How well would the drive go then? What if you still did that every time you drove now? Hint: if you do, you probably shouldn't drive.

Learning any new skill or taking on any new task can seem overwhelming and full of cumbersome steps. But trust me, it just seems that way. We are adaptable creatures and once we get the hang of something, it becomes part of our natural behaviour. Learning to drive can be a huge task to wrap your mind around at first, but the payoff is great enough that most of us will do it anyway. At one point, learning to tie your shoes was overwhelming, too, but we mastered it anyway. So, too, will this change seem overwhelming at first. Do yourself a favour; turn down the volume on your internal dialogue. Stop yourself when your mind starts rattling on about what you can't have, or how hard you work or what you deserve. Shut your thought process down when you find yourself dwelling on what purchases might not be easy with cash or how your changed spending habits could collapse the economy. You are welcome to be anxious if you like, but do yourself a favour and sit with that anxiety for a bit, then make the change anyway. The less you give in to that scaredy-cat part of you, the less power it has. Once you look behind that curtain and discover the powerful wizard is just a scared version of yourself, there isn't much to be afraid of anymore.

Just like driving a car, which most of us can master and become competent at—at least on some level—you can turn new financial behaviours (especially spending), into a very natural feeling routine.

Tips to Keep Financial Behaviour Changes in Check

1. **Anchor it!:** Remember the 'why' behind your commitment to making financial change. If you are making this change to follow a dream or to get your life back on track or even just to

feel in control, keep that in mind every day. I often keep a playing card (or something else out of place and eye catching) in my wallet where my debit and credit cards live. There are expenses that I still use those methods of payment for, albeit they are few and far between. But I keep the playing card in my wallet because it is out of place. Every now and then, I even change it up. Because the playing card is out of place, I notice it. When I notice it, I remember why I put it there, which gets me thinking of the purpose behind my own financial change. I am instantly reminded of my why and therefore, completely and totally conscious before I make a purchase with those higher-spending risk methods of payment.

2. **Break it Down!:** Don't let your mind run away with the scope and size of the change this books suggests you make. Break it down to the real meat of the change, the part you manage everyday. The spending part. When it all seems too overwhelming, focus on the cash spending money and nothing else. Remember everything else should be on autopilot, or worst case scenario, there will be a few days a month you have to actively bank or pay bills, but most weeks, your job is to take out cash and stop spending when you run out.

3. **Shine the Light on Your Pre-Existing Valuables:** When this is all seeming too hard and life starts to get hectic, take just a moment to appreciate your life and all your current positives. Writing down what you are grateful for in a journal, or even on a sticky note, can help keep you from concentrating on what you didn't buy that week. Taking time to read an extra bedtime story to your little one or turning off the TV and actually talking to your spouse, costs nothing extra and can keep you on track.

4. **Monthly Money Meeting:** If you take my advice, you will see progress in your debt repayment, but if you don't pay at-

tention to it, you might not appreciate just how far you've come. Once a month, set an appointment with yourself (and anyone else with financial say in the household) and review your progress. You can get a notebook at any dollar store with some of your weekly cash and keep track of your monthly progress in that if you like. Whatever you do, schedule it. Even months where there have been lump-sum expenses and you see the debt go up or not reduce as much as it has been, your notebook will help you see that you've still made progress since you started. This is a great time to review some major purchase goals, too. If you only have $5000 more to pay down before you can renovate the bathroom, then reviewing the fact that you paid down $4000 in three months can really encourage you to keep going and show you just how close you are. You can't manage what you can't measure, so go on and measure it regularly.

5. **Make Fun A Requirement:** If you start to feel deprived of a life on your cash budget, take a minute to carve out some fun money each week. Get the kids to help you research some finance-friendly activities. Have a picnic lunch in the middle of the living room or in the backyard, or even a family camp out on your lawn. Often, annual family museum passes are an inexpensive way to have a day of family fun every few months. Exchange movies with friends regularly. There are a million things we can all do that are fun and won't have you living in overdraft.

6. **If you've got it, use it!:** If you already have a boat, a cottage or recreational vehicles, then be sure you haven't wasted your money by taking the time to make use of them. Often when I meet with people who want to buy such items, I send them away to look at their daily life schedule and figure out how much use they'd realistically get out of said item. I do find that many people are better off renting these types of items if they aren't likely going to make extreme use of them. Yes,

owning something means it could go up in value, which is probably more likely in the case of a cottage than a boat. However, if you can only make time to use a cottage a few weeks a year, you'd probably be better off renting one. That way you have to make sure you have the money before you do it each year. Years that come with too many unexpected expenses, you can choose not to rent, whereas you can't choose not to pay a mortgage or property taxes on a cottage you own. Many people will come to me with this thought: a mortgage on this cottage would be only $800/mo but renting it for a month is $2500, so clearly buying makes the most sense. But hold it right there. If you only have a month to enjoy the cottage anyway, that's $2500/yr. The mortgage option would be $9600 a year plus property taxes, upkeep etc., etc., etc. And yes, that $800 mortgage payment may eventually yield a profit when you go to sell, but for many, that profit still wouldn't be equal to the value of never having spent the $9600/yr + + +. While, at least emotionally, most people would feel owning the cottage is better, this is one of the places where you have to override emotion to see if it makes financial and family sense.

7. **Review it:** Your debt progress and cashflow accomplishments should absolutely be part of any review process you go through with your financial advisor, banker or anyone who manages assets or debt of any kind for you. If they aren't willing to include these goals in your financial plan, or even provide you a plan in the first place, then my best advice is find someone who is. If you start to lose track of where your debt fits into your financial picture as a whole, you could get discouraged more easily. For example, during the market turmoil of 2008-2009, if you'd been working on a debt-repayment plan, you might have been down in the market but you could still have had a positive effect on your net worth. When you look at your finances as a whole, debt and cashflow become just as important as assets, because essen-

tially, that's what they are. When you make them a priority, you can do a much better job of weathering the market, both financially and emotionally.

8. **Plan Those Major Purchases:** Before the first one sneaks up on you, you should draw out what kind of major purchases you are either going to want or need to make in the next 5-10 years. Do this right from the get go, don't go along following a debt and cashflow management plan and figure you'll get to these things when they start to happen to you. Look firstly at when you'll need to replace vehicles and then any major repairs, possible education costs, etc. The stuff that you will likely have to take care of first and the stuff you want second. Again, these things are a work-in-progress, but if you didn't know what you were going to do in the first place, you can't make adjustments as your circumstances change. If you go back to just guessing, you'll have difficulty making the best financial decisions.

9. **Share it:** Please don't try to keep the amazing financial changes you've made or are making a secret. You'll serve no one but your own ego. Tell your friends and family all about what you have chosen to do with your money. I can't stress how important this is. As long as shame and money hang out together there will always be far more financial struggle than there has to be in this world. By keeping your problem, or room for improvement, and subsequently your progress to yourself, you rob others of the chance to learn from your experience. Can you imagine how much less effective my advice would be if I tried to pretend I'd never made a mistake? You learn a lot less from doing something perfect the first time. You learn even more when you share your experiences. Do you have to wander around with your total debt painted down the side of your car? Of course not. However, keeping your own discoveries on the down-low will not help you in any way. If you don't talk to those closest to you about what you are doing and at-

tempt to cover up your changes in their presence, it will likely lead to overspending again. If you don't want to face additional pressure to go right back to what you were doing, you have to talk about it. I think you'll be pleasantly surprised how other people follow your lead and look up to you when you don't keep these changes to yourself. *Remember, you aren't living on less, you are living for more.* As humans, I really think we all want to live better, and you and your change can be a positive influence on the rest of us. So, go on and share your story of financial change, and progress of course!

Your Money Mindset is the key to your financial freedom; it also poses the greatest risks to it. Remember all those scores you tallied in the second chapter? We are going to re-visit them again.

The Justifier: You have all the tools you need if you just look around you and stop making excuses. Your Mindset is just one part of the puzzle.

Money Management: Active money management is not required for all categories. For you, it's mainly about your active cashflow and major purchases. You should review your monthly bank statement, but you should also have savings deposited, investments made and bills paid automatically. Be very active by using cash for things you can control and you'll be well on your way.

Financial Agility: Remember, if you have low agility, your ability to deal with change or opportunity of any kind is low, so working on savings and finding access to empty credit is important. If you focus your spending and line up your debts in an efficient manner, you'll increase your agility quickly.

Mental Math: Anything above 4 is great; don't worry too much about that score. Since most people's mental math is flawed, I give you cash instead so you don't have to rely on it.

The Dreamer: You just need a tweak in the way you spend day-to-day and make financial decisions to reach your true potential. You'll be ready to take on the right opportunities when you are in your best financial shape.

Money Management: Remember, it's most important that you become more of an active money manager when it comes to day-to-day spending. Using limited amounts of cash for spending is a key step for you to take. You can also apply that step to business expenses like lunches, coffee and the like.

Financial Agility: Being a Dreamer doesn't mean your finances are in jeopardy. In fact, all of the Mindsets can be in great financial shape. Your Mindset only shows some tendencies you may have. If your financial agility score was under 20, you want to really work at cleaning up your spending, paying down your debts (unified hopefully) and putting savings away to increase your agility.

Mental Math: Don't worry about your mental math, I don't want you to use it anyway. Focus on the cash. Set up everything else automatically and slow down your major purchase decisions.

The Brick Wall: If you are not content with your finances, you are more than capable of doing something about it. Working from cash may require you swallow your pride a little, but you can handle it.

Money Management: Working with the ideas in this book, you can encourage your family to be more active with their money management. This will help you learn to trust their judgment and make money a happier topic in your home.

Financial Agility: A Brick Wall can swing either way when it comes to agility. If you are honest with yourself, you know you should make increasing your financial agility a top priority. Make sure you have access to inexpensive credit and build your savings so you can be ready for both opportunity and crisis. Saving takes time and waiting until you need to borrow money doesn't usually go so well, so start now.

Mental Math: You were most likely to have a good mental math score. While I'd still suggest you take my cash spending recommendation for the first 60 days, you can switch to your debit card by transferring (from your All-In-One or regular account) a specific amount to a "spending" account, but I would recommend you keep on top of your mental math.

The Polly Anna: You can do this. But, if you only kind of take your power back it will only kind of work. If you are brave enough to really take your financial power back, it will really work! Even if you are afraid, start taking Baby Steps. One by one, you'll get to a point where money is not scary for you anymore.

Money Management: You have to work to become a more active money manager. If your score there was lower than 20, you could be in real danger of finding out about any financial issues by surprise.

Financial Agility: You want an agility score of more than 20, so you need to look at your current access to inexpensive credit and start to build those savings. Agility gives you time to think, time to think keeps your financial power where it belongs—with you.

Mental Math: Don't get too wound up about your mental math score. I'd like you to really focus on the cash spending. Remember, you can only control certain expenses, so focus your energy on them.

The Masquerader: A lot of what I've told you to do in this book may be hard on your ego. You need to decide if your financial independence trumps the perception of reality you've created. Change is completely up to you.

Money Management: You should aim to improve a

low score here. Look at some of the items that were classed as active money management behaviours and add at least a few of them to your repertoire. Start with cash, but you can switch to debit as long as you are separating your active cashflow.

Financial Agility: This is an important one for you. If your finances are at all delicate, you could be in a world of hurt if one variable changes. Start working toward unifying your debt and managing spending to create a two-sided cushion of savings and credit. You need a plan that includes your debt and cashflow, so start asking for one.

Mental Math: This isn't a worry as long as you stay on cash, but if you switch to a debit card, you'll want to keep an eye on the balance to avoid any embarrassing episodes.

The Undercover Agent: Like all the Mindsets, you need to decide if something is important enough to do it. You must have picked up this book for a reason and somewhere through these pages, you've decided making the most of your money is either worth it, or it isn't.

Money Management: You are more likely to be leaking cash in the form of frequent but small purchases. Focus your energy on being most active in your management of the day-to-day spending.

Financial Agility: If your score was lower than 20, you really want to find a way to unify your debt without feeling like it is too much change at once. Having separate spending money for yourself and your spouse, either in the form of cash or two separate spending accounts, may be beneficial. Do what you need to do in order to manage your feelings, but make sure you unify your debt.

Mental Math: I'll bet your mental math score was really low. If it was, that is even more reason to focus on spending cash. Your brain can't change the amount of cash left over.

The Bunker: I really hope this book can help make you feel two things: one, proud of the fact you already know how to control your spending and two, confident enough to make better decisions even when your fear wants to win.

Money Management: Your score was most likely very high here. You might be the only Mindset to whom I might suggest you tone it down just a notch. Or, at least try not to let your goal to become financially healthy make you a stress case.

Financial Agility: If your agility score was under 25, I would be concerned about your access to credit. You are good at saving, but you are often afraid of having access to credit. Even if you feel safe, you never want to put yourself in the position where you need credit and then have to apply for it after the fact

Mental Math: If anyone had a good score here, it was likely you. No need to improve your mental math. If you like the cash idea, I say stick with it. If you'd prefer the separate spending account idea then by all means, go with that option.

Ready Set Go!

So now it's all you! It's up to you to make the changes. You have the tools now. You can choose to ignore them and continue to cut off your proverbial financial fingers to spite yourself or you can choose to be better, do better and have more. With my own clients, I help set up a structured plan and provide them specific advice appropriate for their situation, but I can't really make change for them either. It's up to you what you do with what you've learned here, but I hope that you will take it one Baby Step at a time and take your financial power into your own hands.

Let go of what you have done in the past. Any mistakes

you've made should only serve as great lessons and nothing more. Guilt, regret and worry will only stop you in your tracks. So, don't even go there. Decide that you know better now and you'll do better now and accept the past for what it is; behind you!

Money is something that touches many moments of our lives, but it doesn't have to run our lives. When it comes to money, you can control it or let it control you. The choice is yours.

So what's it going to be?

GLOSSARY

Active cashflow:
The monthly funds that go toward expenses. Money you can apply some degree of control over. *Example:* Food

Active Financial Behaviour:
Financial transactions or actions, which are done with much care and focused attention; example: reviewing your bank statement monthly, looking for out-of-place items.

All-In-One Account:
A lending product available in some countries. It combines a line of credit (secured to your home), a chequing as well as savings account, and a mortgage into one account. All-In-One accounts allow the borrower to deposit their income directly onto the balance of their mortgage, paying interest only on the exact amount of money owed on a given day. The borrower can also set up regular bill payments to come out of these accounts, just like a regular bank account.

Debt Diversification:
The spreading of household debt over multiple accounts.

Debt Unification:
The reduction of debt diversification with a goal of getting all household debts into one account.

Financial Agility:
The ability to adjust to life events and changes from a financial perspective.

Investment:
Money deposited in a financial product or the purchase of a hard

asset with the goal of making a profit is considered an investment.

Mortgage, Fixed Rate:
A mortgage contract generally with a fixed interest rate and a fixed term. Such mortgages often have penalties if you try to pay them off early (however, some contracts do allow a borrower to leave without selling their home). They often allow pre-payment over and above the payment structure and it is expressed as a percent of the borrowed amount.

Example:
$170,000 mortgage, 10 percent pre-payment per year privilege. Meaning, the borrower could pay an extra $17,000 per year without incurring a penalty.

Mortgage, Variable:
A mortgage contract with a floating interest rate usually related to prime.

Example:
Prime + 1 percent

These contracts generally allow the borrower to lock in the rate (usually with specific rules). Variable rate mortgages can be for a fixed term, like 3 or 5 years, but they could also be open. This means there would be no penalty to change products. Often, changing lenders will charge an administration fee to release even an open mortgage.

Passive Financial Behaviour:
Financial transactions or actions, which are done without much care or focused attention; example: using a debit card day-in and day-out without keeping a running total.

Retirement Savings Account:
An account that may or may not be registered (or qualify for spe-

cial tax benefits), in which a person saves or invests funds for retirement.

Snowballing:
The ordering of multiple debts in order of interest rate or balance for the purposes of repayment in an efficient manner, as the first debt gets paid off, that debt's original payment is applied to the next and so on and so forth, until all debts are paid off.

Unsecured Line of Credit:
A line of credit, which is not secured by the borrower with any property, cash or investments (there is no collateral).

Working cashflow:
The monthly funds that go toward expenses. You have little control over these monies. *Example*: Utility costs

A Coming of ROSES

Patricia Hingle

Home Plates of Ascension, Inc.

FIRST EDITION

Printed by
Printing Incorporated
3019 Plank Road, Baton Rouge, Louisiana 70805

Library of Congress Catalog Card Number
88-81870

ISBN 0-9620595-1-X

Hingle, Patricia Landry
A Coming of Roses

Permissions

Dedication

A Coming of Roses is dedicated
to my immediate family —
Walter, Chipper, Allyson, and Alexis;

to my original family —
my late Dad, Mom, Joe and Paul;

and to my newfound family —
those who have been touched by cancer.

Introduction

At first, Pat Hingle fit into our "Make Today Count" cancer group like most others on their first visit. Not only was it natural and obvious that she had those tragic feelings and questions of what was to take place within herself physically, but also thoughts of her future.

As a cancerous parent of young children, the sorrow was even heavier within because of the thoughts of the children, husband, and other loved ones.

"Make Today Count" is a session of cancer patients and/or families and friends of cancer patients. The group meets twice monthly at the Perkins Cancer Center and is part of the Cancer Society of Greater Baton Rouge. For many, the first visit can be most difficult. Prior to entering the room, there is that reality that you are truly a "cancer patient," and secondly there's the thought, "I've got my own problems being a cancer patient. Why waste time with other people's problems?"

As a brain cancer patient, those were my first thoughts, and I'm sure Pat felt the same. But to almost everyone on his first visit, entering the room makes you feel like you are visiting someone at the hospital, so enter "quietly." To your surprise, what's truly taking place has the sound of a party!

Yes, it's a gathering of people who have become friends because of some cancerous similarities. Everyone wants to hear from the other how things are going both physically and personally. Also, there are moments of tears and sadness, but for the most part, then comes courage and positive direction.

Pat and I have many differences in our types of cancer, surgery, and treatment. But like so many others, we have a great deal of similarities in coping with reality. Cancer was the most disastrous experience in our lives, yet by facing reality, and making extremely positive changes in our lives, we were able to create wonders for ourselves.

For Pat, this book has put a big smile on her face, and it has already brought courage to many. Read it and remember: there are many negatives in our lives, but if we add them together, they can create new positives.

Gary Hendry
President, Make Today Count
Board Member, American Cancer Society

Foreword

I wrote this book to fulfill, initially, a selfish purpose. For when I was diagnosed with cancer, far from home, far from friends, far from hope, I wanted to grab everything I could get my hands on to read in order to give myself a quick-fix education in what was turning my life inside out. I scoured the shelves of the library at M.D. Anderson Hospital and Tumor Institute in Houston, Texas, where I hoped to find something specific about what I had, what I would encounter, what I would experience, but what I wanted was not there. I found writing which was clinical, technical, and medical, and it was grounded in doubt, tempered with caution, and mired in devastation.

Contrary to what I was reading, what I was feeling was a different thing. I knew there was hope. I wanted to read somewhere, to see in black and white, that others had been where I was now, and that they had survived. I knew that they were out there, for God never leaves us alone in the universe with a unique problem.

Now, two years from my diagnosis of cancer, I am reaching out to tell my story not so much as a diversion for myself nor as a catharsis, but to sow the seeds of hope, to give those who will be diagnosed with cancer (next week, next month, next year) the courage to prevail through it and to re-find and refine their lives because of it as I have done. The journey has not been easy.

I wrote this book during the darkest hours of my life, sometimes in a neighborhood skating rink watching my children strive to attain balance, sometimes in a karate dojo watching my son struggle to gain his higher levels of self-discipline, sometimes in a health club by the indoor pool with one eye on my children and the other on my manuscript. I wrote this book alone but never lonely because I was always surrounded by love, though I was often unaware of its presence.

I wrote this book because God was guiding my hand, allowing me through His grace to support, encourage, and love cancer patients, their families, and myself. The writing has been the greatest learning experience of my life. My encounter with cancer has changed my life for the best. I hope it will do the same for you in your time of need.

Patricia Landry Hingle

Acknowledgements

For me, saying "thank you" used to be perfunctory. Not so anymore. For now, after my cancer experience, I have gained a humility in the capacity to give thanks for all the wonders of living, in the understanding that "thanks" is a joy because it signifies a mutual sharing, an established reciprocation, based on heartfelt satisfaction not so much because of one's own accomplishments but because of the enhancement of one's life resulting from the sincere contributions of others which effect the "thanks." There can be no "thank you" without another person, and the elemental sharing which results from being touched by another often gives greater rewards, accept-ances, gifts, and trusts than we can ever initially anticipate.

I am thankful and grateful to the following acquaintances, friends, and loved ones who contributed significantly to the reality of *A Coming of Roses*; I did not and could not have done it alone.

Thank you to those who read my manuscript, to those who helped me to fine-tune it, to those who laughed and cried with me during the telling of the story, but more importantly, through the living of it. Comments are imprinted in my soul. They are my treasures. One friend said after reading the manu-script, "I just wish you had taught my children English!" Another exclaimed, "My God! This is so powerful! And you are still teaching." A doctor of mine called to say, "It brought tears to my eyes." My friend, a cancer patient, said, "This is how it really feels."

Special thanks to my editor, Diana S. Welch, who listened and suggested; to my artist, Judi Betts, who shared and guided; and to my printer, Bob Gullic, who anticipated my needs and who added a special polish to the production of the book.

To all of my support systems (colleagues, students, doctors, friends, and family), I say "thank you" for being there for me. I cherish you.

Pat

Table Of Contents

Chapter 1

Contemplation

"Eternally, woman spills herself away in driblets to the thirsty, seldom being allowed the time, the quiet, the peace, to let the pitcher fill up to the brim."

Anne Morrow Lindbergh, *Gift from the Sea*

Cancer saved my life. I never wanted to die an early death. Even before I had ever heard of Percy Shelley and his wise words so freely given, "I fall upon the thorns of life! I bleed!" spoken with the exuberance of knowing the necessity of suffering in order to be able to embrace fully the joys of life, I knew as a child that I would set my goals, strive for whatever it was that I wanted, eventually accomplish the task, yet maintain my balance during the process of living, a process which I believed would be long and fruitful. The maintaining of the balance, though, would be the hard part, the part that required the greatest sacrifice, yet I forged ahead.

First thorns materialized in the form of nettle grass hiding in my grandmother's back yard, separating me from the chicken coop, alive with music of the birds and feathers flying, from the picking of brown chicken eggs, an act which I loved. The nettles in the grass were as mines in a minefield; as my eagerness to attain my goal overpowered my common sense in planning my route and in carefully checking it, I found I was in the middle of enemy territory with no contingency plan. My feet began to smart from the sting of the plants as soon as I realized what my impetuous behavior had cost me—fruition.

Backing down was no fun—I would not turn back. However, I could not stay there forever, and the thought of causing a commotion in the henhouse as I dethroned the mistresses of the mansion to steal their treasures was too delicious to abandon, so I carefully inched across the rest of the yard. The eggs would be mine. The victory would be mine. The next time, though, I'd take a hoe.

And I did. And the nettles did not kill me. And I began to learn the importance of balance. And I thanked God for my first encounters with those nettles with their prickling, awakening stings as I faced the greater foe, cancer.

Other encounters with thorns settled in and left blood, sweat, and tears. As a child, my reveries of independent thinking allowed, though infrequently yet involuntarily, the wrongful entry of the symbolic thorns which transmogrified, like some terrifically quick, bizarre cartoon sequence, into a wall too high to climb. Sometimes, as I rode to school, the image would enter my brain out of nowhere and occupy my thoughts until the bus squeaked to its final stop.

At first, the mystery and remoteness of the wall promised temporary escape; it became my buffer zone, a force outside myself intruding harmlessly in the beginning, and then annoyingly as time passed. However, I rejected the wall which seemed to loom higher and wider. For a while, though, it became an entity that moved and changed its size, always oblivious to everything else around it so that it was imminently obstructive. It was a fascination which began to border on obsession, and I began to fear its power over me. In my life's odyssey, it came to symbolize something terrible; it blocked out things and people I loved, threatening to separate me from life itself. I cried. I knew then the meaning of Frost's "Something there is that doesn't love a wall. . ."

I would not allow the wall to overcome me, I did not need it, and so with my childlike power, I replaced it for what I though would be forever with a positive force, that of learning. Learning became the focus of my life. Somewhere down the line, I

announced to my mother that I would abandon dancing \
must have been about six) in order to study and to learn. "I
want to learn everything," I stated.

Awed by my comment, she understood. I know now that she
devoted herself to my goal by not putting demands on me like
helping her to clean the house or wash the dishes. My work was
more important to her, and because of her attitude toward my
decision, I realized at an early age that the quality of selflessness was never so intrinsic in any other human being as it was
in my mother.

Eventually, though, the selflessness gave way to an arche-
typal self-effacement, and in the transformation, her own walls
would be silently established. My daddy would grumble sometimes about my not helping around the house, and she would
quiet him in her own way by assuring him that I was working all
the same and that I was not to be disturbed.

As I lived, I learned how to cook and clean and plan and
nurse my children and care for my husband, knowing that my
mother always felt that as long as I was pursuing work that I
loved, I could always do whatever else needed to be done. It
was the love of work that was beginning to take form at an early
age for which I thank my mother. She allowed me freedom to
understand myself so that I could realize the importance of
love of work, even if at first the work was in the form of study for
me. But the walls would reappear and take on different mean-
ings later.

A nail, one singular rusty thorn in a board turned temporary
baseball bat, almost claimed my brother's eye. We were outside playing, having abandoned the usual bicycles for awk-
ward though irresistible self-made "toys." As the neighbor boy
swung the hand-fashioned bat, my brother's scream pierced
my soul. Blood spurted out of his eye. That was the first time I
remember seeing someone I loved being physically injured,
and I knew that it might be serious and permanent. He was
about seven and I was about nine.

"He needs his eyes to play baseball!" I cried to God whom I
believed could not hear.

I ran with him, screaming, to the house. I remember arguing
with my mother about the dress she hurriedly put on me as we
dashed out. How pre-occupied we are with appearance even in

nes. I can still see the patient doctor
my brother's eye, asking him what he
brilliance, and said so. The whole time, I
im, and with Daddy. My mother was in the waiting
ne knew he could see when we came out. His sight had
en spared within a hair's breadth. Such a tiny distance would
also spare me later on in my life.

And the thorns surfaced many times in the next years. My
mother suffered from an illness which caused her to retreat
from the world, to shut herself away, to allow depression to
rule her. It was not so much agoraphobia as it was a dis-
quietude, a despondency, and I vowed that I would always be
strong for my children if ever I had any, that I would embrace
the world and its events together with my family as we lived. I
also vowed that my mother would come to my high school
graduation. I would get her out of the house, and I did. She was
with me when I delivered my valedictory speech. She began to
go out again into the world of church and of stores and of
people. I never wanted anyone else I loved to feel that sort of
anguish again.

Yet, sometimes the thorns seemed unrelenting. They were
in the forms of the intrusion of the Vietnam war which gouged
out the eyes of my generation, and not just those of the men
but of the women who loved the men; of the loss of my first
child through miscarriage; of the loss of my first husband,
physically, in an automobile accident; of the loss of several of
my husband's jobs in my second marriage. The sustaining
force in the losses, though, was the fact that disasters brought
change and change brought hope.

Shelley's words held a literal meaning for me every day when
I began to grow roses in 1981, one of my hobbies which has
given me great pleasure. I did not awaken one morning pro-
claiming that I would grow roses; indeed, the decision was
based on a tragedy, the death of my father-in-law, on New
Year's Day. My mother-in-law decided to sell the family home in
Baton Rouge, a home surrounded by rose bushes. She offered
us whatever we wanted. It was with mixed emotions that my
husband and I uprooted the plants, many of which had been
his grandmother's, to bring them to our home in the country.

January was a good time for transplanting rose bushes.

However, knowing that fact regarding roses was about the extent of my knowledge, and I learned that life in Louisiana was not necessarily most conducive to producing extraordinary blossoms, particularly because of the plant being prone to black spot, a devastating fungus, which was difficult to control because of such a high-humidity climate. I struggled to foster their beauty. First blossoms were always a miracle; I noticed, however, that almost always the outermost petal was ugly, malformed like some growth gone awry because nature could not be ever watchful. That outer petal was the rose's salvation, though, I learned—it protected the bud and allowed it to reach its fullest beauty; the outer rim of the petal, the crescent, was most worn but ever vital in the life of the whole bud.

At first I couldn't get Wordsworth's ". . . little we see in nature that is ours" out of my head. His phrase bothered me. However, my ambivalence toward that first color, that fragile skin, always gave way to acceptance and admiration, for without its presence, the bud had a limited chance to flourish. Humanity, as I later analogized, was much the same way. It was not until cancer crossed the borders of my protective outer layer that I appreciated the full meaning of the Lake poet's nature reference.

As I enjoyed seeing the roses in their fruition, so I reveled in my teaching career. Grandeur of satisfaction was so often found in my job, in the joy of teaching, especially in my senior honors English classes, at East Ascension High School in Gonzales, Louisiana, where I taught for fourteen years. I loved my work, and I loved my students. Whether it was explaining a concept in grammar, or relating a particular nuance of a sonnet, or exploring a writing technique, I was "into" English. E. M. Forster's "Only connect . . . " on his title page to *Howards End* became my basic teaching philosophy.

I believe that English is one of man's basic connections with his fellow man—it is that part of the element of humanity identified by language, feeling, and expression. It is the story of man's account of living on the planet, of experiencing and of loving life through all of its possibilities. I naturally connected in the classroom with my students; most often we were attuned to one another and to the subject at hand. No force could stop us when we wanted to experience the learning process together. The classroom was my "mini" world which brought all of the individual talents of humanity center stage. The experience of working with my students will be a time in my life which I will always cherish.

Again, there was an intruder who was beginning to infringe on my territory in the classroom as well as in my private life. It began so innocuously that I was hardly aware of it, yet innocuous would turn insidious, and its diversionary power would grow so that it would almost engulf me. 1985 was the year I took on too many activities, wore myself down, stressed myself out, and left myself open to cancer. One of the major reasons was that I was not a person who could say "no." Whenever anyone wanted me to serve in some capacity, whether it was as a member of a school committee, as a church paper editor, as a writer of an article for a publication, as a grader of a few extra English papers, as a wife who ironed one more shirt, or as a mother who allowed her children one more treat, I did it. In fact, I expected people to call on me, and in my expectations, I became my own worst enemy. In my doing for others, I had no time for myself. My head was a constant checklist of "must do's"; the checklist prevented fun or escape.

I began to wear thin. Super Mom/Teacher/Wife/Woman was not super at relaxing. In the classroom, I began to notice that as I read aloud a particular literary work or passage (Truman Capote's "A Christmas Memory" stands out most in my mind), I would begin to lose my voice. At first, the students would be minimally annoyed because they would be engrossed in the lesson; later, though, they hated it when I threw their trains off the tracks by stopping at a critical point for no apparent reason. I stubbornly plodded on, incessantly clearing my voice, as I distracted them from the greatest works known to man, because of my hardheadedness.

'What's wrong, Mrs. Hingle?" they would ask. "Could I get you water?" each seemed to ask with concern.

I fought an inner fury which would almost surface as I realized that getting through a masterpiece like *The Eve of St. Agnes* would be the hardest thing I would ever do on a given day.

Other signs of the impending illness, the wall, were an exquisite tiredness when I could not even begin to think about grading several sets of papers a night, a slight sore throat when I would leave the house at night, and headaches which I attributed to sinus complications that would stop me head-on during a lecture. I ignored them all.

It is human nature to attempt to measure life's desires in future time blocks. For instance, we all say, "In 5 (10, 15, 20) years, I will have a home, money in the bank, a Mercedes, a master's degree, four children . . .," or whatever it is that we believe we need to fulfill our own particular definition of happiness. What we plan, though, may never come to pass. One lesson that I learned from cancer was that one cannot systematically plan his life, for there are too many factors which enter the scene which we can never anticipate. Unplanned forces in the forms of accidents, natural disasters, other people, and just the turning of the globe dictate, to a large degree, directions. We do have a choice either to "divorce," "untie," or "break" those bonds which hinder us from realizing our dreams or to "whisper" to our "souls" of desired objects "to go" as John Donne offered in order to effect our own changes. Who we have become and how we have become ourselves influence our choices. As I focused on earlier years to glean the reasons why I had become a person who could not say "no," I realized that certain things for which I had never striven or never expected also entered the picture.

1982 started as a marvelous year for my husband and me as we delightedly awaited the birth of our third child, but we realized early in the pregnancy that we would have to enlarge our home to accommodate a growing family. In the midst of doubling the size of our home at the beginning of that year, I'd come home exhausted from the school work, wanting sleep, but facing workers from four to eight every evening. I was without my kitchen sink for about ten weeks. Washing dishes in the bathroom was no fun.

I remember once when our son, who was almost five at the time, told me, "You're lazy," when I did not get up immediately upon his demanding a drink of water. Devoted to my family, I was broken by his comment. "Lazy" was something I was not. "Lazy" was Garfield the cat, dogs idly lounging and scratching, flowers swaying in the field on a hot summer's day, and men dozing on park benches. No, Momma was not lazy. Quickly slapping him for his innocently-chosen word, I realized that he could never understand why I was so harsh with him. I immediately burst into tears.

I knew then that I needed a rest, and I needed it soon. I decided that I would take a sabbatical leave for the next school year, because I had never taken off any time, including summers, from the rigors of my work, and that would give me the time for the needed rest. The idea began to appeal to me more and more as I constantly faced the growning stacks of senior essays that spring semester. Some days the papers seemed almost to reach the ceiling, but I was secure in the knowledge that my students would be able to handle any kind of writing assignments encountered in college.

When I approached my assistant principal with my decision to stay out a year and enjoy my child, she reacted negatively, telling me that if I left, there was no guarantee that I would get my same classes, including Advanced Placement English, when I returned. I didn't care. I had been the departmental chairperson since 1976, and it was time for a rest; furthermore, I was eligible for it. My mind was made up. Although I had earned my master of arts degree in English in 1976, I decided to continue my education during the sabbatical because I had committed to a professional improvement plan offered by the state guaranteeing teachers a higher salary upon completion of the program, and also because of "extra's" for the household addition. The decision meant that I would have to take at least two graduate or post-graduate courses in the fall semester and three in the spring of 1983 in order to fulfill the requirements for my professional improvement and my sabbatical. I realized too late that I had overdone it again. Those 15 hours were wrenching, especially as I trekked across the Louisiana State University-Baton Rouge campus while still committed to nursing my baby at home. I was almost too tired to return to school in the fall of 1983.

The baby, Alexis, was a beauty. It was one of the joys of my husband's life to see her born. He had been cheated, he felt, out of the experience of the births of the two older children, both born by cesarean section, and it was only because of some serious talks with my obstetrician that I convinced him that my husband, a former United States Marine, would not faint at the sight of my blood. I still remember the operation. Lexi had blue eyes, and she was also so strong that the nurse in the operating room commented about it as she lifted her up by her fingers moments after birth. The baby clung on. My husband kept exclaiming about my various body organs after the baby was delivered. He described my appendix to me, and I barked at him. We broke up the operating room. I remember quickly consenting to the removal of the appendix before surgery, a routine procedure often accompanying cesarean sections.

Indeed, there was a history of appendix-related problems in my family. My grandmother had died in her early forties from a ruptured appendix, leaving behind three young children for my grandfather to raise. He died a few years later and my dad and his two sisters were on their own. I wanted to be around for my three children for a long time.

The ride from the hospital was too short. We came home to a house with furniture so rearranged because of new flooring that it seemed a hurricane had passed through. I believe my dining room set was stacked in the middle of the old bathroom. I settled into the only room with old carpet and began to nurse the baby. I wanted to go back to the hospital.

When I returned to school in the fall of 1983, I had my same classes with the exception of a ninth-grade remedial class, and all of us in the department had committed to teach at least one remedial class a year. I was happy and even happier when my principal called me in to tell me that he had chosen me as the school's nominee for the 1984 Louisiana State Teacher of the Year. I thanked him. We went through the preliminary steps which I looked upon as extra work which I really didn't need as I returned with a new baby and a new course to teach.

It was during a test on Shakespeare that I was called out of my classroom in order for my director of secondary education to tell me, "You are one of twelve state finalists in the teacher-of-the-year contest!" He was almost crying over the telephone (he had been my senior English teacher), and I believe he was more excited than I.

The award, though, took me away from my students too much. There were so many meetings and interviews that I began to regret it all. The students were annoyed. I almost wore out my smile trying to placate them when they said, "We don't want a substitute. We want you."

In addition, the recognition made me feel I had to be as accommodating as I could to everyone involved because now the "reputation" was established. Teachers hardly get any positive recognition, and they deserve it more than any other professional group. I was merely a representative, yet I wanted more than ever to be back in the classroom with my kids. The summer of 1984, though, saw me finish my "thirty plus" requirements while helping to write a syllabus for a ninth-grade pilot program in writing. That year I would have six lessons which included honors twelfth-grade English, two senior academic English classes, Advanced Placement English, ninth-grade remedial English, and ninth-grade writing. They would do me in. More than anthing else, I wanted to step back, to relax.

I decided to take the summer of 1985 off, and I looked forward to it so much that my supervisor must have been sick of hearing me exclaim over the possibility of doing nothing; other summers since my graduation from high school had included working, completing my requirements for an additional English degree, having babies, teaching summer school, and writing.

Doing nothing during the summer of 1985 was short-lived. It was about that time that I started waking up in the middle of the night, every night, in cold sweats. The wall was back, only this time it was in the form of a barrier that separated me from my children. My husband awakened me many nights when I cried out in my dreams for my children. At first, I thought that the sweats were a result of wearing certain kinds of sleepwear to bed. I must have tried six or eight different kinds of garments and materials, and then nothing, before I realized that the sweating was caused by something physiological, still nothing seemed to be wrong. Somehow, though, teaching and living were losing their quality of joy.

In contemplating where the joy had gone, I looked back on much earlier summer school teaching assignments. I even had fun teaching summer school with inordinate class loads and students who only wanted to be there because they needed grades in order to move on. It was during the teaching of summer school that I gained a heightened realization of the importance of giving individual attention to every student who came my way. There was a young man who was 6' 7" and had a criminal record, but he knew not to disturb my class of 60 students ranging from ninth to twelfth graders. Once, during the course of the summer, he sent his friend to tell me he was in jail because of a shooting but to send his work because he wanted the credit to graduate. I sent the work with a note, "Do it." He did. He graduated.

Then there was another, one so pregnant that I knew that I would have to deliver her baby while explaining the dynamics of subject-verb agreement. She would come into the classroom with fluffy pink slippers because of toxemia, and I even let her bring an oversized glass of water one day. That was a mistake, for the other students heard her drink it quickly, and one exclaimed, "If I had known you would have been so thirsty, I would have brought a hose pipe!" The kids were having fun, at least, and so was I. The time would come in my life, though, when not even a drink from a hose would cool my throat so sore from radiation. My student was lucky.

The "fun" nature of the job began to wane when I began to force myself through the motions because I was so tired. I really began to worry in January of 1986 when I was scheduled to cover a school board meeting for a local publication and to write an article about the nature of the public school system in my parish. I had to take off school that day in order to feel energetic enough to make the night meeting. That was definitely not me. I was even beginning to feel ambivalent about my roses.

Though I had symptoms of the flu, it was the lump in my neck that finally pulled in the reins on me. My first thought was of cancer. I feared cancer, but not too much not to do something about it. I went to the doctor the day I found the lump. As I was examined on January 23, 1986, by otolaryngologist Dr. David G. Fourrier, answering all of his questions, I still felt uneasy. Dr. Fourrier, a careful, knowledgeable man, checked me thoroughly, asking me pointed questions about the lump on the right side of my neck. From his preliminary exam, I could tell that he was concerned, but he found nothing unusual in the ear, nose, and throat area, nothing which obviously startled him. I asked him what he thought it was, and he stated that in all probability it was an infection or inflammed lymph node. Under no circumstances, though, was I to get upset. He gave me erythromycin to reduce it.

I asked him what the chances of its being cancerous were, and he said less than ten per cent. When I returned home and told my husband, he calmed me, suggesting that I take the medicine and wait for positive results.

I was at home recovering from the bout with the flu and worring about the lump when the Space Shuttle fell from the sky. I could not help but question why Christa McAuliffe was taken so suddenly, when I was lying there watching the shuttle plummet to earth, contemplating the implications of death by cancer. My birthday was February 1 and I was 36. I was too weak to cut back my roses. My husband did it for me as I watched him from the window in the den. I wouldn't be strong enough to touch the rose bed for another year.

Soon, it was St. Valentine's Day, and the medicine had done no good. When I went back to Dr. Fourrier's office, he had to give me a Valium to calm me down, worrying that I would wreck my car before I got home. That morning I threw plates, knowing that I had cancer. No diagnostic tool had to confirm it. I just knew. Again, my husband calmed me and our three children who had been scared to death by my actions. They had never seen me so out of control before. The balance was gone. My husband had enough presence of mind to joke that he was glad I hadn't been close enough to the china cabinet to let the crystal and china fly. But he was worried.

In order to appease me, Dr. Fourrier gave me more medicine, then arranged for tests at Our Lady of the Lake Hospital in Baton Rouge. They consisted of an esophagram, thyroid scan, full body scan, and bloodwork. The sneaky thing about my cancer was that there was no obvious primary site. Dr. Fourrier was working according to what he could see, and there was nothing there. The first test was one of the worst that I have ever undergone. Anyone who experiences an esophagram for the first time never forgets the cups of barium which must be swallowed while the body is angled back and forth and up and down to check the progress of the liquid. I never could take milk of magnesia. I changed my tune, fast, though. Lights flashed, machines whizzed and whirred, my body was poked and prodded. Other tests were not so unpleasant, and yet the only thing revealed was a lump on the right side of my neck which could not be definitely analyzed without more sophisticated tests or surgery.

When I went back to the classroom, I forced myself to teach, something which I had never done in my life. The students definitely knew something was up when I was out three days in one week for tests. I began to tell them that I was undergoing routine tests at the hospital in order to prepare them for the possibility of my not being there for their graduation. They wanted to know why. I pointed to the lump. They hadn't even seen it.

A while later, however, one student commented to the class, "Mrs. Hingle is not the same since she had the flu." Very astute. Very mature. "If you only knew," I thought.

March found me panic-stricken, but I was a good actress, and the students were still under control, but the maintaining of the balance was the most difficult juggling act ever. Tuned in to my distress, my husband went to see Dr. Fourrier. They talked. Dr. Fourrier had set the operation for mid-March, but my husband asked him where the best cancer hospital in the country was, just in case there was a possibility of my having it. Fourrier, a skilled surgeon, suggested M.D. Anderson in Houston where he had recently visited his colleague Dr. Oscar Guillamondegui in the Head and Neck Clinic, Station 52.

I was still in the classroom, lecturing, when my husband came to school and called me into the hall. It was fourth-hour senior academic English. I gave them a break. They knew that something was amiss, because nobody stopped one of my lectures without a good reason.

My husband and I paced the hall down to the water fountain. I kept thinking as we walked, "Here's Pam and Mary and Sylvia on the right and Kris and Audreye and Birda on the left, friends and members of my department." I didn't want to hear what he had to say, but I had to listen. As we reached the water fountain, I just kept my hand on the button until the water almost ran over the sides. I was playing a little game with it like the kids did in order to avoid his eyes, his words. He told me, "We are going to Houston."

I could not go to a hospital distant and remote to me, and I told him he was crazy. In that instant, I could see how much he loved me, how much he wanted me not to fight him, how much he knew that I would, though, for he knew me. I fought back the tears, and I asked him to wait until I got the kids out of the classroom. When I returned, they thought *I* was crazy because I let them go to lunch ten minutes early, something for which they always begged, but hardly ever received. I can still hear them now, "But we're seniors (emphasis on first syllable). Aren't we special?" It seemed I struck them dumb, and I received so many looks of incredulity as they left the room that I was beginning to wonder if I had come back without my clothes.

Somehow, though, the balance had to be maintained. I finished grading term papers the weekend of March 15-16 and asked my friend who also taught senior English to take over my presentation of the American College Testing English workshop April 1 if I didn't come back from Easter break. She asked, "What's wrong?" admitting that she could never see me out of the classroom. I could see a look of terror, of panic (the god Pan was having a field day with us), in her eyes when I began to talk. I was very controlled when I told her I might have cancer. She was not.

My last day to teach school was March 21, 1986. As I completed the report cards for the third nine-weeks period, I kept thinking that I might be leaving my room for the last time. I gave the old bulletin board a pat. I closed the door to Room 77. No one with whom I taught wanted to believe that I had anything wrong with me, especially cancer. My dear friend and colleague Linwood Holdridge, the only realist in the group at that time, did say to me that if by an unbelievable stretch of the imagination I had cancer, I was going to the right place. He told me that they had kept his dad alive for 30 years after they diagnosed his cancer. Linwood did not know what an incredible comfort his words were to me at that moment.

As I walked out of the school, I kept thinking of Anne Morrow Lindbergh's inspirational *Gift from the Sea* where she defined the concept of womanhood, especially where she states the following:

And then home, drenched, drugged, reeling, full to the

brim with my day alone; full like the moon before the night has taken a single nibble of it; full as a cup poured up to the lip. There is a quality to fullness that the Psalmist express- ed: "My cup runneth over." Let no one come—I pray in sudden panic—I might spill myself away!

Is this then what happens to woman? She wants perpe- tually to spill herself away. All her instinct as a woman— the eternal nourisher of children, of men, of society— demands that she give. Her time, her energy, her creative- ness drain out into these channels if there is any chance, any leak. Traditionally we are taught, and instinctively we long, to give where it is needed—and immediately. Eter- nally, woman spills herself away in driblets to the thirsty, seldom being allowed the time, the quiet, the peace, to let the pitcher fill up to the brim.

I wanted my moon to stay full. I did not know how I could keep this particular cup from running over, from spilling, from destroying the lovely balance of my life. All I knew was that a part of me was beginning to die. I was beginning to die an early death. Where was fruition for which I had so striven, the fruition which makes our life's work worthwhile as we are engaged in our individual journeys, as we long to flourish along the way? All I could see was a wall of cancer. My full moon was waning, the wall was converging on it, and all I could hope for, out of the blackness, was a crescent.

Chapter 2

Realization

"Alien they seemed to be:
No mortal eye could see
The intimate welding of their later history, . . .
Till the Spinner of the Years
Said "Now!" and each one hears,
And consummation comes, and jars two hemispheres."

Thomas Hardy, *"The Convergence of the Twain"*

Initially, I was never told by a doctor that I had cancer. I confirmed what I had suspected by reading my own medical charts in the hall of M.D. Anderson Hospital and Tumor Institute, and then I calmly told my husband.

"It's cancer," I said, just as if I were looking out a window, reporting that it was raining. "I guess I'm in the right place after all." He gave me one of those looks which intimated that I couldn't read, that I couldn't be right, that I couldn't comprehend results of reports, that I was not really standing there, reviewing the situation. My detachment soon gave way to a fear so fierce that I thought the growth in my neck would become a hand and strangle me. I fought the floor moving out from under me.

The roses were in bloom at M.D. Anderson March 25, 1986, the day of my diagnosis. At home, they usually didn't open until mid-April, barely in time for my mother's April 17th birthday. Upon entering the building, I kept thinking how ironic it was that there was so much beauty and life outside when there was so much ugliness and death inside. I was wrong. "Anderson," as it is called by those who are closely associated with it, is a rose-pink marble structure dwarfing most of the surrounding medical institutes in the area, but more importantly, it is one of the finest facilities in the country for treating cancer. The surrounding rose gardens were carefully tended by a woman whose salvation is in nurturing them, in having something positive to do.

The diagnostic procedure was preceded by completing what seemed to be reams of paper filled with all sorts of questions pertaining to cancer, especially those relating to environment, diet, and job experience. I can remember trying to decide how many times a week I had eaten barbecue, had lain in the sun for any particular length of time, or had been exposed to smoking or had smoked at any time in my life.

The process of diagnosis was quick and accurate, considering my symptoms. Since Anderson is a teaching hospital, I was surrounded by several doctors, including the one who was to be my chief surgeon, throughout the preliminary examination of the head and neck area. Since I was a teacher, I was not bothered by the presence of people in the process of learning; in fact, I welcomed the idea of some other patient perhaps profiting from an experience similar to mine because a doctor had been observing me and had remembered some pertinent bit of information gathered.

Everyone was quiet in the room during the examination of the lump on my neck which was high and to the right, and about the size of an olive. I answered the doctors' questions as a person undergoing an eye exam for glasses answers the optometrist. It didn't seem to matter what the degree of the condition was to me or what had caused it; it simply was there and that was enough.

After several polite but uncommitted comments from Dr. Guillamondegui, who explained the next procedures carefully and calmly, I found myself undergoing the first of many sophisticated tests—fine needle aspiration. The aspiration is a form of biopsy whereby a needle is inserted into the suspected area, fluid is removed and examined, and then a preliminary diagnosis is made by staff members and recorded while the patient is still in the room.

When I entered the room for fine needle aspiration, the doctors directed, "Take your blouse off." I was shaken since my problem was in my neck. I suddenly realized that the doctors in the examination room, all women, had assumed that my lump was in my breast. I pointed to my neck. They profusely apologized and set to work. It was no small wonder that they had assumed breast, since my doctor at Anderson told me later that the type of cancer I had, squamous cell carcinoma, was generally found in men in their 50's and 60's who smoked and/or drank heavily. I didn't fit the pattern. Three times a needle with a syringe the size of what seemed to me a small bicycle pump was inserted into my neck. I found it hard to believe that so much lymphatic fluid could be drawn from such a small area.

In addition, the size of the needle not only facilitated an accurate diagnosis but also limited the spread of the suspected tumor in the process of aspiration. I could hear the word "feathery" in the doctors' hushed conversation. Their faces said it all. They wished me "Good luck," and as soon as I was able to read the chart, I knew. I also underwent various scans, X-rays, and bloodwork. But they all seemed superfluous in terms of aiding in the diagnosis.

My head and neck area had been a virtual palimpsest of problems from the start. It began when I was in the womb.

My mother had once told me, "When you were born, you were the ugliest baby I ever saw." It seemed that when I breathed, upon exhaling, I looked like a little frog. The doctors had never seen anything like it before. Deciding simply to prick the area in order to see what it contained, they released, in the process, water. I suddenly began to attain beauty, according to my mother. Other medical problems with the head and neck area included two tonsillectomies, one when I was 5 and the other when I was a college freshman. Also, during my routine physical for college, my general practitioner noticed a lump on my thyroid gland which he ordered removed immediately. His wife was dying of cancer at the time, and he was taking no chances with me. Fortunately, it was a benign cyst. The scar disappeared quickly. However, until the time I became an adult, the only surgical operations in my life had been confined to the head and neck area. So would be the most serious one of my life.

From the day my cancer was officially diagnosed, I began to live in a world where the ubiquitous presence of cancer became such a powerful force that I really began a struggle to fight the feeling, hopelessness, moreso than I began one to fight the disease, cancer—at least at first. Emotion overrode reason. One lesson I learned is that I could not allow cancer to play "mind control" with my psyche. I learned very quickly that I had to be the most stubborn woman on the planet as far as the self nurturing of a positive attitude was concerned. I would not die from cancer, I told myself, as I remembered the words of one of my doctors at Anderson who quickly intervened when he saw me starting to spiral out.

"What you have is fairly common," he said. "I can't tell you if you'll live three months or 30 years, but you'll probably die from something else besides cancer." Thank God for caring doctors who know what to say at the right time.

Daily scenarios, though, were always played out to their fullest in my head. One day, for instance, I was deliberately sharp with my healthy, loving, bright, beautiful children who had nothing but unconditional love for me, because I felt that if I died it might be easier for them to accept my death and to move on more quickly since I had been so hateful.

"Maybe they won't love me so much," I told my husband when he came home, listening to my confession of unwarranted anger directed against the children.

"Nothing, especially cancer, could ever change their love for you," he countered.

Love is more powerful than any of the negative possibilites that cancer can evoke. I would never again deny the children the spilling away of myself, no matter how much suffering might be entailed. It would be better for them to experience all facets of living honestly than to be exposed to a world where cancer or some other unacceptable force controlled my actions or their actions. They would get clear signals from me rather than confusing ones, no matter what the cost. It was the only kind of truth that they could ever trust, the only behavior from me upon which they could build their lives as they became less dependent on their mother. They simply had to learn about the thorns at early ages, too. It was the only way.

When cancer crashed into my life, there was no contingency plan. The man in the moon was laughing at me, telling me that my moon would not stay full. Perhaps there was a grand design in God's plan for me, something providential, perhaps His guiding me down a path to allow me later to embrace a more enriched life in the form of career or other person or self or all.

But now I felt as Macbeth did when he confronted Banquo's ghost at the dinner table. I had taught the passage for many years, never really being able to relate to it, at the point where Macbeth screams to the ghost to take any form (bear, rhinoceros, tiger), but to become tangible so that he can strike out at it. Cancer was my ghost. I couldn't pierce with sword or sue in court or spurn with emotion this "alien" which I could not see as it welded itself to me, beginning its evil consummation. All I could do was to try to understand it. I had one more barrier to overcome, one more wall to cross. I put myself in God's hands.

It is one thing to express how one who has been diagnosed as having cancer feels and another to try to define cancer. The feeling and the definition often have little to do with one another, and each is exclusively powerful in its own way. Initially, I felt that my collision with cancer was imminent, if not immediate, death. Death had been personified so many times in great literary works which I had taught, and one of my favorite expressions of the personification was in John Donne's "Death Be Not Proud" wherein death would be destroyed, paradoxically, by everlasting life. However, that was not nearly so consoling a thought to this cancer patient as it had been to that classroom teacher who had never been close to death.

I didn't want to die in order to live. I was in my mid-30's, married with three children, and involved in a career which I enjoyed. Life was good. Death was not a viable alternative. I wanted to sit across a table and bargain with God. There was so much unfinished business, so many things left undone. I felt that an invisible hand had stopped me right in my tracks. I was in a long, dark, room, continually walking, as on a treadmill, which got me nowhere. I was Sisyphus pushing his rock up the hill, not gaining any ground. I had always flown through life, embracing it. Now I was in the twilight zone, in T.S. Eliot's dead land, on some strange planet out of a Star Trek episode, floundering.

Something that had perplexed my doctors and which would always trouble me was that my type of cancer had begun elsewhere in the mouth area before migrating or metastasizing to the neck. If only the primary site could be found! I underwent an examination with a fiber-optic instrument called a Machidascope which explored the nose, mouth, and throat areas for tumors. Nothing was there except for a webbed area in the nasopharynx region which yielded nothing in biopsy. Surgery would evidence nothing as various sections would be routinely biopsied.

Thankfully, what was known was that the tumor was in one lymph node in the neck, localized. At no time did the conversation ever turn to death or even prolonged, agonizing hospitalization. Yet I still feared death for the first time in my life.

I feel that until people can become better educated about cancer, about its limitations rather than about its devastations, then the race is doomed to an inordinate fear of cancer which may be unrealistic, naive, and more deadly than the disease itself. It is true that more people die from cancer than are saved from it, but greater strides in technology are accomplishing an almost 50% survival rate. Even odds are much more promising that absolute equation with death.

People panic when they hear the word "cancer." So many people who fear that they may have the disease put off going to the doctor until it is too late. For instance, I taught with a woman who doomed herself to the ravages of breast cancer because she was single and did not want her doctors to think that a man had ever touched her breasts. Until our generation can throw off the Victorian attitudes surrounding cancer, we are indeed lost. Others act in time. Another former colleague, a breast cancer patient, acted and is alive today because of her actions. No one must ever be afraid to effect whatever may be lifesaving for him.

People, including most doctors, dance around the word "cancer." There were those who used as many euphemisms when referring to my having cancer as they use substitute words for sexual intercourse. I was always astonished when someone would refer to my "illness" or "setback" or "disease." It was as though their tongues would catch on fire if they said "cancer."

Thankfully, I have been a woman who has tried to communicate effectively my thoughts and feelings on every issue, and cancer wasn't different from anything else. For example, I spoke at a Women's Health Foundation meeting about my cancer experience. One lady who was there told me that if I ran for governor, she'd vote for me! "Maybe our high Louisiana cancer rate would go down then," she said.

Looking back, I figured that if I could explain the concepts of human sexuality to my 8- and 10-year-old children as they asked pointed questions, then I could surely address the pertinent issues surrounding cancer. The problem, however, was that people do not want to hear about cancer, especially if they don't have it. If they do have it, they don't want to be reminded of it. It has been my experience that the head-in-the-sand attitude of dealing with life's problems only gets one a mouthful of grit.

I have prayed "The Lord's Prayer" countless times, always pausing at the phrase "Thy will be done on earth." I have, after many hours of soul searching and pondering, come to believe that the will of the Father may be what we unconsciously will for ourselves as long as it is good in His eyes. In other words, I feel that He will act through us as long as we honestly feel that what we effect for ourselves is the right and just thing to do in order to enlarge our spiritual lives as we attempt to grow closer to Him in our earthly journeys.

For all cancer patients, that means continually striving to live as we act on the choices available to us to prolong our lives in order to live full lives. In our illness we must gain strength for healing, and then, ultimately, for growth, the key to living. Anything else may be defined as "death," a word that we should not allow in our vocabularies. Most often, it is the power of mind over matter. We may all possess regions in our brains which are as yet "undiscovered" by scientists but which nevertheless exist solely for the purpose of healing our bodies from the most serious illnesses known to man. It is our duty to attempt to discover and activate these regions for our total health.

I never thought that I would trace the etymology of the word "cancer." In all of my graduate and post-graduate courses in English when I dealt with semantics or rhetoric or the growth of the English language, I never thought I was preparing myself to make the major inquiry of the *Oxford English Dictionary,* that of going to the "cancer" source. From the more obvious "tumor, according to Galen, . . . so called from the swollen veins surrounding the parts affected bearing a resemblance to a crab's limbs" to the figurative (an evil figured as an eating sore), exemplified by "Sloth is a Cancer eating up that Time Princes should cultivate for things Sublime," the word connoted a sense of thievery, destruction, and dread. Wouldn't it be something, though, if once we figured out cancer's operational abilities, we could harness them for the good of mankind? For instance, from some of the deadliest diseases came some of the saving antibodies for mankind. Perhaps our technology will unlock the mystery of the cancer cell in our century.

But unlocking the mystery will not be the answer to the world's cancer problems. People will continue to get cancer even when we know how it is caused and how it may be cured because they will continue to drink and smoke and pollute as long as there is humanity.

I remember dear friends, who when smoking and blowing their smoke in my face after my surgery and radiation therapy, lamented how sorry they were for my having had to live through the ordeal. People will not stop smoking even when they are confronted with cancer on a constant basis. For example, my friend's mother, dying in the hospital from lung cancer, continued to smoke a pack a day until she died. We all have stories to equal this. I feel that it should simply be a matter of human will to effect the best health for ourselves through ourselves while maintaining a positive attitude.

And even that will not be enough. My doctors speculated that I could have gotten cancer from inhaling someone else's cigarette smoke. Exposed to cigarette smoke on a daily basis in the teachers' lounge at my school, I was in an environment of no ventilation because the windows were hardly ever opened to let in fresh air. We were inhaling the same stale air every day. Today, the lounge is worse because the windows have become walls to accommodate the growing school facility.

In addition, until we compensate for our polluting the planet, the world for our children will be gloomy. Though cancer strikes on the average of one member out of every family, the chances of that figure rising are great, since we do almost nothing to stop hazardous waste dumps, unlawful carcinogenic emissions from industry, and spills of undetermined pollutants into our waters. The choice is ours.

In addition, stress, though an unproven factor in the causation of cancer, surely should be addressed. All of us who are in stressful occupations should provide ourselves with effective mechanisms for managing the daily stresses of our lives. Employers should be aware of job situations which alleviate stress of employees to some degree. These mechanisms can begin to exist only if we demand them as an interested and vital work force. Again, the choice is ours.

When I arrived in Houston, I immediately called my dear friends from college, Patty and Ken English, whom I had not seen in a while, to let them know why we were there. Immediately, Patty began to ask a lot of questions. Her dad had just recently been diagnosed with lymphocytic leukemia, and the doctors had given him about a year to live, yet he was undaunted. She urged me to call her back as soon as I knew something definite. That night, she received my call. She knew, too, without having to be told.

"Come right over," they said. We did. It was good to be among people who loved me. They and their three children who were the same ages as ours provided a surrogate family which I desperately needed at that moment. She had cooked a great meal, but I couldn't get through it without crying.

I kept repeating, "What will happen to my children?"

"You will not die," she kept saying. "My daddy will not die and neither will you." Calming words, they worked for a while.

Yet it was the going home that was difficult, the having to tell family face to face that I had cancer. Friday we decided to drive home for Easter weekend and to have as normal a day as possible before driving back Sunday evening to prepare for Monday surgery.

Family reacted much more calmly that I expected, probably because of the initial shock. (Over a year later, though, my sister-in-law finally confided to me that my brother, a singer, could hardly contain his frantic feelings. He was a wonderful actor for me, though.) We didn't have time to worry with pity. I immediately called my principal and supervisor to let them know what to expect as far as my job performance was concerned, and that was uncertainty. Initially, I thought that I would be out until the end of the school year, and then return in the fall. Radiation therapy changed those plans.

Friends and relatives started coming over and calling all weekend until we left, bringing great support and encouragement. No one cried.

The worst thing that happened was that my children opened the armoire in our bedroom and discovered all of the Easter candy which I had not yet arranged into the baskets. I hurriedly told them that the Easter bunny was in a rush and had planned to come back to finish their baskets. Things just really weren't working out as I had planned. I kept thinking of Robert Burns' poem about the best-laid plans of mice and men going awry.

Saturday night we watched Chevy Chase in "Vacation," which was a welcome relief from the rigors of the weekend. (When we got back to the hospital, I had some really good laughs with one of my doctors about the movie.) That Sunday we went to early mass, feasted on turkey, and drove back to Houston.

Settled in my room, I was prepared for my surgery. One of my doctors and I got into a lengthy discussion about roses. He was ready to spend some money investing in a rose garden, but didn't know which varieties to choose, so he asked me to make him a list. At least I could gain some vicarious pleasure from a "rose" conversation. The next morning, however, as I looked up into my doctor's pentrating eyes, all turned to blackness.

Chapter 3

Salvation

"Wert thou my enemy, O thou my friend,
How would thou worse, I wonder, than thou dost
Defeat, thwart me? O, the sots and thralls of lust
Do in spare hours more thrive than I that spend,
Sir, life upon thy cause. . . .
Mine, O thou lord of life, send my roots rain."

Gerard Manley Hopkins, *"Thou Art Indeed Just, Lord"*

Robert Frost had stated that the greatest salvation was in surrender, and so I surrendered myself to the capable hands of my doctors and my God.

I awakened from surgery euphoric. I was experiencing one of the greatest states of well-being that I had ever known, and ironically, it was because of cancer surgery. I knew, though, that it wouldn't last forever, but whatever the doctors had talked about during the operation or whatever they had said about my chances of recovery must have been wonderful, because I was ready to click my heels in the air. I stopped short when I saw the bandage in the mirror.

I started tugging at it right away, knowing that it would be covering a modified radical neck dissection, an incision starting under the center of my chin, coming straight down to my windpipe, and curving slowly upward to the right where it would end at my hairline about an inch from my ear. In my mind, it was already a capital "C" for "cancer." I would never model necklaces, I thought, and I hadn't even seen the cut yet.

As I continued to look at it, the bandage began to remind me of one of those Oriental collars which I thought quite fashionable. "At least it's not an 'X' across my face," I thought, and said aloud, causing my husband to come to my side quickly. Nothing that he could say could make me smile. Suddenly, the depression began to set in.

As I looked around the room, I saw flowers surrounding me. I started to cry. The phone began to ring. From that moment, I have always associated the ringing of the phone with depression, bad news, and lousy days in general. I generally avoid the ringing of the phone. If there is anyone else in the house, even my five-year-old daughter, I let her answer it. It's like hiring a maid to clean your house when you cannot bring yourself to do it for whatever reason. Someone has to do the dirty work, though, at a price.

I realized that I had lost about a day because of the surgery. It seemed as though I had stepped out the door, and when I returned after a brief moment, someone had changed the calendar all too soon. The first day of true awakening was April 1. My first phone call was from my friends at East Ascension. They were delighted that my voice was so strong after surgery, thinking that I would be too weak to talk. We exchanged several "April Fool's" jokes, and we were amazed that we could laugh after cancer. Yes, there is life after cancer, I realized.

I remember saying, "I hope y'all didn't think that cancer could ever shut me up!" Later, though, during radiation therapy, I would have to eat my words as I completely lost my voice for several weeks.

The week before the surgery as we sat in our hotel room in Houston during the truly intense worrying over the cancer, through the tear-stained pillows and late-night caresses, my husband and I retreated to laughter to break the tension. It was the only device to maintain sanity. Humor in dealing with cancer, especially on a daily basis, is crucial to the patient, family, and doctor involved. It is great medicine. For instance, at one point, my husband told me that the only alternative he could have offered would have been to take me to a neighboring parish to a voodoo doctor who might have been able to "spirit away" the lump. When we laughed, he didn't know then how I was almost ready to believe that it might have worked.

I hated how I looked when the bandage was removed. I hate it when people act as if it is no big deal when any unveiling misses the mark or absolutely backfires, and everybody in the room was hitting me with that pretentious air of "well-it's-not-so-bad-after-all" when they were really thinking "it looks like hell, but we're trying not to let you think it does." Often, when displayed, the sculpture is really hideous; when performed, the allegro fizzles; and when consummated, the longed-for sexual encounter disappoints; yet everybody tries to cover up. The only person in the room who was ready to be Oliver North in the confrontation was me. The neck was not pretty.

I had been told what to expect, but the reality was almost too much to bear. I know that I must have cursed so much to myself that God was covering his ears. He probably couldn't believe that any woman could ever think the words I was thinking, and especially with such vehemence. I thought aloud, "I am the bride of Frankenstein. No make-up artist could ever do such a fine job as this. Maybe I could be in a horror movie."

I had never been beautiful, nor had I ever wanted to be. But I didn't want to go through life with such an ugly neck. I thought of the play *The Elephant Man* and cried. Somewhere, though, a tiny voice intruded on my thoughts and said, "You had cancer in the best place for a cure. So what about the scar? Count your blessings." Still, acceptance would be long in coming.

The staples and stitches looked like tiny little thorns, about 50 or 60 of them, slashing across the neck area. I quickly learned how to take care of the dressing myself, and when I went to the area on the 5th floor set aside for the cleansing of the incision, I began to meet wonderful people who were much worse off than I.

When I saw the anguish with which others had to contend, suddenly my curses turned to prayers of thanks for life, and I begged God to forgive me for my self-pity and to heal those around me, for we all wanted life, and that is when my healing truly began. I stopped thinking of myself and began thinking of others in the room, and on other floors, and in the other areas of the hospital where cancer was master. I remembered Sister Alice, a great comforter at Anderson, telling me that she had been several days before with a husband who had had to decide about his wife's quality of life. She had been kept alive for over 200 days by machines.

I then realized what God was trying to tell me through Sister Alice. The message was that my cancer was as a mosquito bite compared to what others in the hospital were facing, and with greater courage than my own. I saw that courage in the face of a man with a reconstructed nose, in the faces of three children accompanying their father who was pushing their mother in a wheelchair, in the face of a man whose body seemd tied up by countless bottles dangling from the ends of tiny tubes. Throughout my ordeal, people would tell me how much courage I had. I would say, "No, I'm just doing what I have to do. It's those patients still in the hospital beds at Anderson who have the real courage."

That's when the humility began to have a settling effect on me. I realized the "oneness" of all of us who had undergone the cancer experience, and I saw that we were brothers and sisters. The poet in me spontaneously surfaced as I thought of Walt Whitman's *Leaves of Grass* where he states, "Of all mankind, the great poet is the equable man . . . He sees eternity in men and women . . . he does not see men and women as dreams or dots. Men and women and the earth and all upon it are simply to be taken as they are. . ." I embraced them and their cancer. We embraced one another, and I was uplifted.

Even though I had had a wisdom tooth extracted during surgery and was suffering a sore throat from the operation, I was still hungry all the time afterward. My husband seemed to be constantly sneaking food into my room, including pizza and ice cream. I was ravenous as I would eat three meals for supper. My doctor was stunned at the appetite of a 5'4½", 124-pound woman who liked hospital food. But my days of living to eat were idling downward.

Dr. Guillamondegui, my chief surgeon, always did and always will have a calming effect on me even by the very nature of his presence. His visits would encourage me and buoy me up, especially the one when he told me that, luckily, the tumor had not penetrated my jugular vein. At least the circulatory system was unimpaired.

He also stated, however, that I would seriously have to consider radiation therapy as a follow-up deterrent to my cancer, especially since the point of origin was unknown. It was better to take no chances in the recurrence of the disease, though, ultimately, I would have to make the choice. After weighing the risks and alternative consequences, I opted for the radiation therapy.

Immediately, the discussion turned to where I would undergo treatment. The doctors were reluctant to allow me to leave Anderson where they could keep a close watch on my progress. Because of the nature of the disease, my treatment would be intensive and exhaustive, directed at times from areas under my eyes to the lobes of my ears to my clavicle. It was essential that a radiation oncologist know what he was doing when it came to my treatment. I explained that I really wanted to be home to have the support and comfort of my family during the 7-week ordeal. Dr. Guillamondegui finally asked where I lived and when I told him 20 minutes from Baton Rouge, he smiled. An Anderson radiation oncologist who specialized in treatment of the head and neck area had just made the move to Mary Bird Perkins Cancer Center in Baton Rouge where I would undergo what was to be one of the most grueling experiences of my life. God's hand was guiding all things.

Immediately, I took comfort in Shelley's "Ode to the West Wind" which reminded me of the "destroyer and preserver" quality of the radiation therapy which would destroy and yet preserve a part of me much like the power of Shelley's wind as a force which would motivate and uplift his life. Sometimes, the paradoxes of life are the most rewarding, though we don't realize it at the time they are happening. The choice was made.

I went home five days after the operation, and I visited my school three weeks later. My students couldn't believe I was back with them after a bout with cancer surgery. I wore a blouse with a high collar and spent the day with them in a laid-back atmosphere. They were so concerned and loving, and I was still concerned and anxious about their completing their writing assignments before graduation. We hugged and kissed and laughed and cried. One of the high points of my days throughout the radiation therapy was when the kids sent me a 20-foot banner upon which they had drawn and/or written all kinds of wonderful messages to me. The love would always be there.

My colleagues were wonderful, also. The day the teachers returned to school after Easter break was a sobering one. They all knew that I had cancer, and we were all powerless. Immediately, those who could, especially those friends of mine who were English teachers, counselors, and librarians, devised a program of action to take over the teaching of my classes on an emergency basis, taking on an extra class as they gave up their free time in order to give of themselves for me and for the students. They did it cheerfully and unselfishly and lovingly, and their acts will never go unappreciated in my salute to them.

The school was in its 20th year and cancer was devastating one of its own. That was all they knew and all they dwelled on. My fellow teachers (we were about 80 on staff) did something so selfless that I am still in awe when I think of it. They set up a network of delivering food, completely cooked meals (my students and their parents were also involved), every day from the time I began radiation therapy at the end of April until the end of the school year in June, until about a week before my treatment ended.

Every day, several of my friends would come by with the food and we'd visit. They were undaunted by the seemingly thousands of red, green, blue, and black markings all over my face and neck marking the field of radiation as we joked and laughed. (I remember how shocked I was the first time I saw markings denoting radiation therapy on patients at Anderson, and I remember the reactions of my children the first time they saw me marked up. No matter how prepared one is, one is unprepared).

Everyone, young and old, man and woman, black and white, teachers with whom I had taught all my life and those whom I hardly knew, came by the house to lift me up. They shared their lives and similar cancer stories of parents and spouses and relatives, saying, "You are not alone."

I remember the last time I salivated over food which they brought. It was for a pizza with everything on it, a thing of beauty, which I encountered during the end of the second week of radiation therapy (a period to which my doctor referred as my "grace" period because the going really got tough the third week of treatment). Unfortunately, the radiation therapy would take its toll on my salivary glands and after it was all over, I would have very little saliva again. The glands would be literally burned out, but it would be a small price to pay to destroy any remaining cancer cells.

When I met Dr. Robert Fields at our initial consultation governing the treatment involved in radiation therapy, I remember his saying, "I can cure what you have, but it won't be easy on you." It all went back to that unknown primary. A few days before the treatment began, I noticed a small lump on the right side of my tongue, and I told Dr. Fields about it. He postponed the treatment, and he sent me to Dr. Fourrier for a biopsy, hoping, as I was, that it would actually be the source of the problem. The excision of the growth was no fun, for I felt as if my tongue would fall out as Dr. Fourrier grasped the suspicious area and pulled. Unfortunately, the biopsy results revealed nothing unusual. I would have to undergo the rigors of the full radiation treatment after all. We had tried.

One of the most exhausting phases of radiation therapy was the initial one, the simulation exercise, with its positioning and balancing, in order to prepare me for the actual treatments. It would be crucial in my treatment because the right spots had to be exposed to the radiation at the right times, and the marker lines had to be applied by an artist.

By the time we were through, my face looked as if I had run into a barbed wire fence, as if a drunken clown had applied my make-up, as if a map had been used as a face cloth and it had run all over me. I had even talked with one of my priests about attending mass because I was sure that the congregation would be aghast, and he agreed that it would be more calming for all if I received communion at home. So for several weeks, he visited me at home. I felt that my face was really horrifying to look at, yet I knew that I was still loved.

Radiation therapy was my personal trial by fire as it initiated me into the scope of my human suffering, but it was also a very powerful catalyst, an unplanned force, in helping me to come to terms with many difficult decisions following the running of its course, with decisions not related to cancer, for it strengthened me.

I am an absolute believer in the curative powers of it in overcoming cancer, yet many cancer patients who require additional treatment after surgery or treatment in lieu of surgery do not agree to it because they fear it is too debilitating. One of my friends, a cancer patient, had three similar operations on her neck because of recurring cancer until she finally agreed to radiation therapy. She has been five years cancer-free because of her decision. It is a formidable power.

The area around the excised lymph node required the heaviest dosages of radiation in order to ensure containment of any closely-associated cancer cells which may have remained after the surgery. The shape of the incision, the crescent, always brought to mind a word my chemistry and physics teacher had given me in high school, a word which stayed with me, haunting me, until the cancer was discovered. It was "meniscus," a word generally dealing with the concept of capillarity of a liquid, especially water, as it rises to the rim of the container and actually crosses over the boundary of the rim of the tubular shape yet still remains absolutely contained because of the bonding of the molecules of the liquid to the rim of the container.

Though the fluid has obviously made its way out of the container, has become a crescent and can be easily viewed above the rim, it is poised and intact. It seemingly breaks the laws of physics as cancer breaks the laws of cellular division, with the basic difference being that the liquid remains controlled in its ascent out of the cup of the vessel, looking much like a scoop of ice cream sticking out of a cylindrical cone, while the cancer breaks the bond of the cellular wall and runs amok.

I kept thinking that perhaps the secret to cancer containment was in the cellular wall rather than in the cellular division, and that perhaps a very simplistically early intervention, perhaps a chemically-induced fine-tuning of the structural make-up of the wall (maybe even moments after birth), could result in some as yet undiscovered phenomenon, one which would govern the ability of the cancerous cell wall to turn upon itself early in its manifestation and make its own adjustment or even effect its own destruction owing to an anomaly only recognizable to the particular cellular entity predominant in the lining of the wall. Somehow, for some reason, it was that "something there is that doesn't love a wall" again, yet I was no scientist or researcher; however, the premise would be a forever-nagging one. It would elicit my further attention.

I prayed for the wall of the incision to act as a containment for the cancer so that it would not metastasize to other parts of my body. However, the job of irradiating the proper field would be in the hands of Dr. Fields, that young, excellent doctor who would combine his talents of persistence and knowledge with my determination to eradicate the disease which had entered my life. We were both committed to doing whatever was necessary to obtain our jointly-desired goal of restoring my health.

There were problems which were encountered along the way in the course of the treatment, as we anticipated. For example, the sore throat hit me the third week of treatment and did not leave me for three months, and even though I had been forewarned, I was not fully prepared for what seemed like all of the rose bushes in my garden shoved down my throat at the same time. I took about an hour to eat each meal because of the anticipation of the pain.

Dr. Fields told me, "Don't be a martyr" when I was reluctant to take my medication for fear of addiction after having taken it over an extended period of time. I did what he said, and the pain in the throat would be alleviated at least to a degree where I could swallow without crying too much. I vowed never to eat mashed potatoes and soup (any kind) after the treatment. My weight dropped about 13 pounds before Dr. Fields promised to stabilize it via a feeding tube if I didn't stop losing it. I was down to 111. I told him he would have to catch me first, and I was fast. My own children could attest to that fact as I would outrun them in races in our yard.

In addition to the seemingly endless sore throat and lack of saliva and hoarseness which would eventually cause me to retire from my teaching, I also had to contend with swelling and soreness around the teeth and jaw areas which also had to be treated. I blessed my parents whose attention to my dental care as a child kept me from suffering the loss of any teeth immediately before the radiation therapy. I could not lose a tooth after it was all over, either, and I would have to have fluoride treatments daily for the rest of my life.

About the time the treatments were ending, I had a small piece of lead accidentally dropped on my neck by one of the technicians as I underwent a more superficial skin treatment on the second machine (I underwent treatment with two different machines almost daily for the duration) for the incision encircling the back of the neck. It was very upsetting though it happened only twice, yet Dr. Fields would calm me, soothing my anxieties, reassuring me that the end of my treatment was near. And finally, on Alexis's 4th birthday, I underwent my last treatment. The marks on the parched neck came off, and I began to feel human again. A week or two later, though, I noticed strange electrical impulses or sensations down my spinal column which seemed to result from the bending of my neck. I did not associate it with the treatment; indeed, I sought out Dr. Ed Vinci, an internal medicine specialist, whose determination led us back to the cancer center to find out that I was manifesting what was known as Lhermitte's syndrome, a temporary condition infrequently caused by radiation therapy. It would gradually diminish as time went by.

The scariest result of it all was the closing up of my throat, especially the choking when I swallowed food. The edema, caused by the radiation therapy, was severe enough at one point that Dr. Fourrier and Dr. Fields cautioned me to go to the hospital if I felt faint or unable to breathe. However, in time, the throat began to open again. I still had to, and would continue to have to, take a drink of water in order to swallow anything again. My taste buds, too, had been altered somewhat as a result of it all. So eating became an activity that I pursued in order to live rather than the other way around, and in South Louisiana with the greatest cuisine around, that was almost a penance.

One of my friends, another English teacher, brought me a framed copy of Hopkin's "Thou Art Indeed Just, Lord" during my radiation therapy. She knew me well, as we had gone through school and college together, and we were on the same "wavelength" as English teachers. The poem, an admonition to God wherein the speaker, a good man, asks why sinners' ways seem to prosper while the ways of the "friends" of God seem to be thwarted, is an exercise in patience and in humility.

The universal plea calling for an end to disappointment in the life of one who follows the rules and yet is unable to attain his desired object (for example, the conscientious student, a perfect paper; the dedicated architect, a memorable design; the loving man or woman, a partner worthy of being called "beloved"; the cancer patient, life) points out to God that all who seem ambivalent or even arrogant about His plan thrive while those who earnestly seek fruition flounder and are frustrated.

The speaker, confused though persistent, asks for one thing from God in order to effect his worth, his growth, and that is "rain," or the nurturing power of God which touches us, revives us, and grants us that object for which we strive. The poem helped me to realize that wonderful things would occur after the cancer experience as long as I had my faith, a faith which someone pointed out to me in Hebrews 11:1 which was defined "Now faith is the substance of things hoped for, the evidence of things not seen."

In accepting the limitations that radiation therapy had imposed on me, I also accepted the wonders of the healing process and what was involved. I desired a full, loving life, and cancer, hopefully, would not stop me from having it. Indeed, cancer would always be a great teacher of mine which I would cease to fear and learn to respect.

As I visited the cancer center for one of my check-ups, I was able to bring roses from my garden to cheer the other patients who were again undergoing far worse than I was. Recovery was imminent for me now, and my cup was beginning to fill itself again, yet the healing process would involve other situations with which I would have to grapple, involving people close to me.

Yet I was willing to risk mistakes and hurt because I knew that all relationships leave us open to pain as well as pleasure. I also knew that life was about other people and loving, and I wanted that. I would risk all to have all. My moon was changing from crescent to quarter to half, and I was becoming keenly aware of it.

Chapter 4

Procreation

> ". . . He learned all there was
> To learn about not launching out too soon
> And so not carrying the tree away
> Clear to the ground. He always kept his poise
> To the top branches, climbing carefully
> With the same pains you use to fill a cup
> Up to the brim, and even above the brim."
>
> Robert Frost, "Birches"

It was because of radiation therapy that I awoke looking Kermit the Frog in the eye. As a result of the radiation therapy, mucus would build up in my throat which would choke me out of a sound sleep if I were lying down, so often I would grab any exra available pillow to prop myself up for the duration. I dreaded nights. I averaged two hours of sleep a night for several weeks until exhaustion would finally overwhelm me. It was on one of those nights that Kermit imprinted on the pillow case became by bedfellow (bedfrog?).

On that particular occasion when I was startled out of a sound sleep because of my inability to swallow, my eyes slowly focused and settled on the quintessential amphibian entertainer playing his banjo with his most winsome look. During that moment between sleeping and waking, I expected him to jump right off the pillow case and to start singing. When I was finally absolutely awake, I wondered how my Diane von Furstenberg linens had been transformed into Kermit print.

I shouldn't have wondered, though, for so many nights the children and their treasures (Monkey Shine or Kanga Roo or the Yellow Blanket) wound up in bed between my husband and me, and I would sometimes silently slip away when I was awake enough, for fear of smothering someone so tiny and beautiful because of an unconscious movement. The nights I stayed, though, were better, because the children wanted the security of the family bed and always slept better for it.

The most memorable nights were those chilling ones, the ones with the frost on the window panes, spent under the mounds of warm blankets with one of the children nursing at the breast. The child and I would both drift off breathing in unison, and sometimes disturbance would be too much for me to bear as I tried to switch the baby to the other breast, knowing that I would be slightly uncomfortable at sunrise if the baby slept rather that completed nursing. But it would be worth it because of the blessed serenity which ensued.

I believe that nothing smells so much like life itself as a baby freshly bathed and just nursed. It is a sweetness that transcends all of nature's and man's most wondrous perfumes, an irresistible force that melts even the most macho man who longs in his masculinity to touch and to love a child. A baby is God's grandest gift, woman's affirmation of womanhood, but man's legacy to the world, for the child is proof of the individual man's existence, of his essence. "Have a child," he is taught. Woman is the conduit, but man is the fountainhead of creation.

I felt wonderful during my pregnancies. I did not have any major problems. One of my minor problems, however, was that I never seemed to be able to get enough sleep when carrying my children. Every easy chair, couch, and bed would beckon to me for a stolen nap. Another problem was that I could never forgo that plate of ice cream every night during pregnancy. My obstetrician told me he was going to make a pesonalized sign for my freezer stating "Keep Out!" During it all, I never ceased contemplating the wonder of what had happened to my body and what was going on inside myself,

especially when the babies stirred. Comprehending the building process of impregnation, pregnancy, and birth was as
awesome as comprehending the tearing process of cancer.
Both were cellular in origin, and both controlled to some degree, though at different times, my physical being.

We know that the child is the result of the action of the sperm
hitting the wall of the ovum, a cellular penetration as intense as
a singular lightning bolt plunging downward to stun the entire
earth in a motion. What happens when the cell membrane is
actually touched by the sperm is uncertain, but something in
the cell wall is activated, weakened, strengthened, stimulated,
or changed to allow the process of procreation to occur. As the
cell wall changes to admit the sperm cell, so does the earth
tremble when it is struck by the lightning bolt, an awesome,
brilliant force which, when harnessed, lights up the periphery
rather than darkening it.

As the ovum embraces the sperm and begins the eternal
dance of life with child finally emerging from woman at full
crescendo, so the crust of the earth absorbs the energy which
converges upon it and flashes outward, even though there may
be an initial burn at first. It is the disturbances in the fields of
these walls of human cell and mother earth that effect the
processes of life. Disturbances in the fields of cancer cells also
occur. In cancer formation, is there an initial burn of the cell
wall before it changes from normal to abnormal? If so, what
force sets it off? For every action, we have been taught that
there is an equal and opposite reaction, but what force brings
on the initial action? The wall wants to be studied.

I remember the first flutter of each child's life inside my
womb. Each time it was like a feather drifting through air
landing to touch my face, yet the reality was happening deep
down inside my protective envelope safeguarding life. It bog-
gled my mind. I know that the womb is man's, as well as child's,
refreshment. I believe that men are attracted to water because
it is life giving and mysterious. Poets have been best at captur-
ing man's attraction to and the universal significance of the
life-giving power of water.

For instance, in Percy Shelly's "The Cloud," his cloud speaks
as a force able to regenerate water to and for humanity. Indeed, the cloud describes itself "like the child from the womb"

which will ''arise and upbuild.'' Water and man are the end results of the processes of regeneration, for while the cloud's force builds during constant change to effect life-giving rain, so the process of building continually occurs in the womb where the actual child is encased and nurtured in the water surrounding it.

The poem obviously reveals that water is the end result of the creative processes of the cloud, but there is also an implicit statement that man is the end result of the more critical creative powers of the universe—he is holy and whole because of all else that contributes to his formation, especially water. Indeed, all other processes merge for the good of the formation of the greatest force of all—man. The differences in the significances of the two creative situations can be likened to the differences between the situations of falling in love and actually being in love. The falling in love, though grand and universal, is a prelude, simply a step, which may or may not result in the formation of real love—it is temporary. If real love does occur, it is rare and elusive. Once found, however, it is precious and permanent, a model for mankind. So the presence of mankind's watery creation and nourishment is a step in complementing his being; the presence of the truly beloved, however, illuminates eternally the essence of the worthy partner. A rare merging must occur for the complementary forces truly to become one.

So as Shelley's cloud speaks of passing ''through the pores of the oceans and shores,'' emphasizing ''I change, but I cannot die,'' the power of the cloud's force is naturally capable of enhancing the power of mankind's force as his being sweeps across the beaches of the world, constantly existing in a state of self-perpetuation.

Women feel that there is something profoundly serene in the man who loves the beach and who longs to return to it for his solitude. Wordsworth captured the moment when the man sees himself in the child, when he can briefly relive those blissful moments of childhood spent at the shore, when in his ''Ode: Intimations of Immortality from Recollections of Early Childhood,'' he offers the following:

> Hence in a season of calm weather
> Though inland far we be,

Our souls have sight of that immortal sea
  Which brought us hither,
Can in a moment travel thither,
  And see the children sport upon the shore,
And hear the mighty water rolling evermore.

The transport to the shore in his mind's eye is one of man's most wonderfully vicarious experiences as he lives it through children. Though long out of the womb and grown, the man who loves the water walks to an unmistakable cadence all his own marked by waves lapping shore, matched by contentment. His action is understandable as he is refreshed by the womb of the earth.

Babies move from the womb and grow up. Marks on the bedroom wall are proof irrefutable. I do not want to wallpaper the nursery walls where all the children spent their first years, though the room in an incongruity surrounded by other rooms with wallpaper abounding. I still measure and record each child's growth on the wall—shoes off, back to the wall, no standing on toes. We are delighted to see the progress made, and each child compares his growth with the others for the same age span. Before I have the heart to re-do the walls, I want to remove the imprints of the markings from the walls and save them in some old attic box as a child is inclined to save a butterfly's cocoon as he detaches it from a tree. It usually breaks, though. It can only be perfectly salvaged in the mind. And so I save the children's formative record in my memory.

The room has heard countless lullabies sung at midnight while the nursing child nestled peacefully in my arms. When my son was small, I especially remembered Dante Rossetti's "... the curled moon/Was like a little feather/Fluttering far down the gulf" as I would create a little melody all for him. As he grew older, he would run to the window to search for the moon, but to his dismay, it was always on the other side of the house when he looked for it. And as the moon rose, the marks climbed up the wall as the children grew, yet their greatest growth was in facing and in handling my cancer experience.

My three children reacted to my cancer in their individual ways.

When my son found out, he could not eat. He became physically as well as emotionally affected, and my instinct told me that I had to have a heart-to-heart talk with him before he was overcome by depression.

He was sitting at the dinner table, alone, arranging his crawfish stew (something which he loved) into various shapes. I touched his shoulder, and he buried his face in my breast. "I don't want you to die," he repeated over and over. For the first time in my life, I saw terror in the face of one of my children. At that moment, I silently praised God for that "teacher" aspect of my nature which helped me to detach momentarily from a crisis in order for me to think during that precious second so that I could aid any child. This time, though, it was my child asking for help, asking for an acceptable solution. I brought him into the bedroom, away from the younger children, and I began to talk calmly and carefully. God was in the room with us at that time, because what I said (I do not remember the words, just the feeling) erased his fears. He was like a crippled child who had miraculously regained his balance. He left the room serene.

My middle child was outwardly courageous. Throughout the cancer ordeal, she maintained her straight "A's" in school, and her suffering was not nearly so evident as my son's, but it was omnipresent for her. She didn't say anything to me about it, so I didn't say anything either, not because I was avoiding the issue but because I didn't believe that she was affected.

I was wrong. One night when we were watching a movie together, she burst into tears when the scene turned to a parent dying and leaving a child behind. She said, "I see us like that in my dreams every night." It was her first looming wall. I encouraged her to continue talking, and by the time she was finished, she was much better. Every night we have said "Sweet dreams" since then.

My baby, a trouper, took it all in stride. Once when she and my son were helping me load the dishwasher, he hurriedly closed the door as I was trying to squeeze in the last glass. She told him, "God! Don't break Momma's arm in the door. She's already had cancer!" For her, as long as I was there in any shape, everything was all right.

My children began to learn the fine art of balancing because of my cancer.

My son, especially, became masterful at balancing during the middle of my radiation therapy. His balancing became clear to me on a Saturday, on a baseball Saturday, one when I was vomiting uncontrollably because of radiation therapy. The rest of the family had already left for the ball park with a promise from me stating that I would make it if I could.

I would not allow cancer and radiation therapy to ruin that day, even though every time after surgery when I touched a baseball, I was reminded of my neck surgery because of the stitched curves on the ball. I shook it off. I put on my straw hat, sunglasses, sunscreen, and high-collared blouse to avoid exposure to the sun's rays at that critical time of my treatment, and I watched my son attain balance. Though I had been cautioned by my doctors to stay in the sun no longer than fifteen minutes per day for two years following the radiation therapy, I cheated. The rest of the ball game would be mine that day. Cancer was not going to claim any more victories over me.

Our pitchers were off the mark. For some inexplicable reason, we couldn't get the ball over the plate. My husband, who was coaching, tried a couple of players who had never before pitched, but they weren't able to effect a miracle. Then I saw my son walk from his position at second base to the pitcher's mound. I wanted to stand up and object, but I knew that I had to stay controlled and to allow him the opportunity to do his best. It's that feeling that every parent gets when it's time to let go. I asked myself what was the worst that could happen. His trying would be better than his never being allowed to know his full potential as a ball player, though he had never before pitched. He saw me and smiled as he reached the mound.

I knew his heart was pounding, but he was attaining the poise in his life which I had prayed for all my children to gain. He looked so confident. Had I been a batter, I think I would have been better able to face a major leaguer than to face my son as a pitcher at that moment. He struck out the first batter who faced him, walked the next, and struck out the next two. The game was over; we had won. But he had gained a greater victory for himself that day. He knew what he was capable of in the face of adversity, and I felt that in some way my presence had given him courage. At that moment, I knew that cancer would never control me again. I had also regained my balance. The feeling was affirmed when my son ran to me after the game and hugged me (red marks and all), not speaking any words, not caring who saw, including his teammates. I will carry that smile of his in my heart forever.

My son was Frost's swinger of birches. He was the eternal risk taker, the boy growing to manhood (something many men never attain, yet he was nine in his initiation) who was learning about bending trees rather than not even attempting to climb them or not knowing when to let go to keep from breaking them. He had kept his poise to the top branches, and I was delighted to know that he had "climbed carefully," utilizing "the same pains" one uses "to fill a cup to the brim, and even above the brim." He was beginning to suffer legitimately, but he would grow as a result. He understood about containment. I felt that down the line, he would choose to cast off the shallowness of hedonism as he lived in order to understand the joy of delayed gratification. He was in the process of learning the only respectable way to live. He was becoming Meister Eckhart's definition of an "active, alive man" who is "like a vessel that grows as it is filled and will never be full." He said to me that he figured if I could handle cancer, then he could handle a few batters. Again, I thanked God for all of the thorns that had given me balance in order for me to look cancer in the eye and not turn away. We had both learned that launching out when the time was right was not always easy, but it was the only way to grow, the only way to gain our objects of desire.

All of my children were conceived in the early fall of the years. It seemed that when the leaves began to fall, they were signalling me that my yearning for a child would be answered. As God drew the trees' sap back into the earth for a specified time, so He allowed life to enter me in all its grandeur. I would always know from the moment of conception that I was pregnant. It was similar to the feeling I had when I knew I had cancer, an intuitive reality. No test had to confirm it. I just knew. My husband would always be thrilled, for he loved his children deeply, for he loved his part that he played in the process of the effecting of life, but it was all happening inside of me. My ultimate prayer was for healthy children, and it was always answered.

Each season brings the joy of shared experiences with the children. In the fall, we love to ride bicycles down country roads which are lined with thick muscadine vines and honeysuckle bushes. One of my fondest joys with my children is when we light a fire in the fireplace in the early winter, and we gather around to read a story, or better yet, to tell one. The wind and rain and cold outside cannot invade our world of familial love— our bond. The spring finds us together in the rose bed, weeding, fertilizing, and spraying. There is an animated conversation about which teacher gets first roses and why. Summer is relaxed, sleeping late, baseball, water sports, movies, and friends.

The seasons come and go so swiftly, and the country home is the center of time passing, of trees changing hues, of children growing and learning. Our home is a wonderful place for raising children. It is set on two acres of trees, an old/new structure, and sprawling. I can never get it all clean at once, partly because of the thirteen rooms, partly because I cannot and do not live in a perfect world. Kids track mud, spill dog food, leave hand prints on walls, drop clothes, and forget toys on stairs. I stopped struggling long ago to be the perfect housecleaner because it is impossible.

Too many other things are more important—helping with homework, drying tears, reassuring doubts, giving lots of hugs and kisses, listening, loving, teaching discipline (what works best is not shouting or spanking, but humility—" I can't believe you did that. You know that you have been raised better and your behavior has disappointed me.") There is a reduction to tears, a realization, a tension, but later a smile.

Children grow up fast, and I know that I will have to let them go their own ways. I pray for their self reliance and independence and closeness to God. Those are the greatest gifts.

My children have given me great gifts. I remember helping my son learn to ride his two-wheel bicycle. I helped him get his balance from off the front porch. I gave him a push and commanded, "Peddle and ride!" until he got it. I can still see him heading down the driveway on his own. It was great to be alive to see those spokes shining in the sun with him in command.

On the other hand, my middle child is my thinker. I remember the two of us sneaking outside to the porch, away from the madding crowd, to talk. She loved to be with me on the porch swing, talking about babies, the sun, the moon, the solar system, creation, life, school—there was nothing we didn't talk about. She is awed by the world and everything in it—I remember that feeling as a child and I hope to regain it as an adult.

My baby has alway been curious about life's tangibles. She has always been my third arm when I cook, for example. A gleeful child, she loves to drop a raw egg and listen to it "splat." She has my laugh, one which starts from deep inside the solar plexus and emerges hardly knowing when to stop in its throatiness. She is five, yet capable of doing or saying anything. She has shocked my sensibilities so many times that I would be bored to have her any other way. Once she ate a raw chicken heart before I could stop her. She laughed about it with an abandonment so clear that all I could do was admit that I would always have a free spirit, untamed, on my hands. I knew I would have to let her go early.

As a result of my radiation therapy, I could not read aloud to my children for prolonged amounts of time, for I would lose my voice. We began to work around that, though, as the older ones would take turns reading with me. Our favorites are *Charlotte's Web* and *Rikki-tikki-tavi*. Spider/pig/rat/mongoose/snake have captivated us for days. My children learned early the significance of Alexander Pope's "a little learning is a dangerous thing." They are constantly probing, asking questions not only about what books contain but also about what life contains. I pray that I have some acceptable answers for them through the years.

As long as my children have their childhood's faith, then they will have it all. They cannot be overprotected from life's problems, and then be expected to enter a real world where decisions have to be made constantly, where rationality must prevail. They cannot be overindulged, ignored, shunned, or put down. They will be recognized, treated fairly, guided, encouraged, and loved. And then they will be let go to fly. That is the only way they will ever voluntarily return to me.

As Wordsworth closes his "Intimations," he laments the loss

of those "fugitive," fleeting moments of childhood, "Delight and liberty, the simple creed/Of Childhood, whether busy or at rest,/With new-fledged hope still fluttering in his [Childhood's] breast," and, more importantly, of the loss of the child's innate ability to question "sense and outward things" as the world encroaches upon him, enclosing him. I want the world to remain open for my children so that delight and liberty can prevail in their lives, so that they will eternally question its ways. Despite whatever traumas come their way including our bout with cancer, I know that they can be happy and full, that their cups can rise over the brim because of my love for them. God is allowing me the time of my life.

Chapter 5

Occupation

"For there is a perennial nobleness, and even sacredness, in Work."

Thomas Carlyle, *Past and Present*

The *Playboy* centerfolds wallpapered the photography dark-room at school. As I looked from wall to wall in disbelief, I finally understood why my yearbook photographers had been so accommodating, so eager to anticipate and grant my every request as they seemed almost to overindulge me when dead-lines loomed ahead, when stacks of yearbook pages had to be proofed and shipped on time. It was a highly unusual occur-rence when photographers did not have to be threatened, cajoled, bribed, pampered, and stroked in order to get me the necessary photos to send to the publishing company for the yearbook; indeed, the securing of the photographs was usually worse than trying to get a man to straighten up a room, to pick us his clothes after himself, as the anxiety caused by the red-circled date made my wits go out the window.

Since I had been a high school yearbook adviser for nine years, I had almost begun to believe that my prayers for effi-cient photographers had finally been answered as I noticed how smoothly the deadlines were met, how the other staff members were easily placated, and how this adviser kept a smile until the pages were in the mail. I don't believe that I even had to resort to Valium one time that last year as adviser as I coaxed a roomful of high school seniors through the un-forgettable phases of "yearbooking."

But the centerfolds were a problem with which I had to deal immediately. What caused me to check the darkroom was the fact that a professor from Louisiana State University was com-ing to teach a night course at East Ascension in audio-visual aids, and he would probably need access to the room, so I wanted to be sure that he had everything he needed. It was a good thing that I scanned the room when I did. I hurriedly gathered the pictures together (it was during a duty shift before school) and presented them to my principal. If he wasn't com-pletely awake when I walked in and nonchalantly tossed the photos on his desk, then he was when he opened them up. "Who?" he asked, as he scrutinized the content, keeping the evidence for future inspection, along with God-knows-what else in his infamous file cabinet. When I told him (the "culprit" was one of the most brilliant, darling young men who had ever gone through the public school system), he roared with laugh-ter. We left it alone, but I decided to confront the student at sixth hour, hoping that he and the others would not use the darkroom that day, at least not until I got my hands on them. It was too delicious a delight to abandon.

When I cavalierly mentioned to my student that his principal had viewed the wallpaper in the darkroom, he said, "But Mrs. Hingle, they were really my Dad's." "Right," I thought, "and I can fly to the moon without an airplane." Oh, the joys of teaching!

I had risked quite a bit as I allowed those students the virtual unlimited use of the darkroom, but I had also risked quite a bit by leaving the kids in the mall unsupervised as I checked the room itself. The students had to be constantly spot checked for any sexual activity, covert smoking (kids can smoke in front of, talk with, and charm an inexperienced teacher all at the same time without allowing even a wisp of smoke to exit their bodies), or plot against the administration. And all of those activities generally occurred without the students ever having hall passes.

Hall passes give students more power than anything else in the realm of public education—they are promises of adventure, freedom, and of absolute mischief. Trusting students with hall passes is like trying to pinpoint the exact landings of the projectiles from a shotgun blast without the benefits of physics formulas. The meekest, most reliable student becomes a piece of buckshot capable, at least, of ricocheting, of disrupting the calm, the peace, of the halls of the school. Others go on rampages. The pass is the key to Pandora's box, to the "cure for what ails you," to the secret of life itself. Getting caught without the hall pass is tantamount to what a criminal experiences as he is mercilessly grilled for hours on end with a spotlight glaring in his face. It is a grave situation. But giving my photographers the key to the darkroom in addition to the hall pass was like giving an arsonist a match when he already had the gasoline. It was a heyday for them. Seriously, though, they would all come through for me whenever I needed them. And that was one of the great joys of teaching which I will always cherish.

Each teacher has her own set of RULES and REGULATIONS. We would be sorrowful examples of the teaching profession if we didn't, for teachers are expected to keep kids in line, no matter what, and the rules always seem to be written in blood. The problem, though, is that they always vary from teacher to teacher to such a degree that the student is placed in the impossible predicament of remembering who wants what and how much of it when. Several of my classroom rules, however, were sacred and inviolable, ranging from the ridiculous to the sublime. For instance, the first was "Nobody messes with Hingle's thermostat." I had taped a sign onto it and I dared anyone to touch it. Nothing could rattle my cage more than a student adjusting the thermostat without my permission, an action which I likened to unwanted hands touching my body. The message was, "I am in control here, this is my domain, I am ringmaster. Touch the thermostat and I will be on you quicker than a samurai warrior chopping up a foe." It was a wonderful attention-getter, one which demanded respect and distance.

Another of my rules of which I was very fond was "Do not talk when I am conveying information to the class." I was wonderfully sarcastic as I effectively trained the students to listen, especially when I had to resort to that ever popular "Do my ears deceive me, or is someone attempting to speak as I make this elucidating presentation?" It worked. They listened. They wanted to get to the bottom of "elucidate," at least. Perhaps it sounded provocative, slightly sexual, eliciting visions of nymphs clothed in transparent garments being pursued by young robust shepherds running through fields of green grass. Who knows?

Another rule, a more serious one, dealt with the students' feedback. The rule was "Ask me questions if you don't understand the material. I am here to help you understand." We always had lively discussions, questions, comments, and just plain fun, a lot of laughter.

Laughing was a great deal of what learning was all about. My own definition of education, that of bringing out the potential in the human being, often led me to potentials in students which were delightful, unexpected, and unpredictable. Some students tried so hard to please me and often wound up in predicaments because of their pleasing natures. I remember when a pressing (weren't they all?) yearbook deadline was on us (1976), and I had only one typewriter (second-hand, manual, the days before Apple IIe computers abounded in the public school system) in the room which worked. A dear student volunteered to move it for me to a more convenient place, and just after I said "All right," he dropped it on the floor, resulting in tiny pieces of steel, all shapes and sizes (springs, sprockets, keys), flying at me, threatening my eyes, my body. He was so apologetic that I could hardly be angry; instead, I told him we needed a new one anyway, and we did; my principal came through for me again that day.

Another incident about which I laughed after all was said and done was the occasion when one of my ninth graders, an expert in the art of legitimately securing a hall pass from me (I was not the world's most liberal teacher in handing out passes after the darkroom incident), had finally pushed me to my limits in his endless requests to leave for the bathroom, locker, water fountain, forgotten P.E. clothes, . . . I told him "No! You cannot leave unless you have a serious medical problem." The next day, he asked me for the tantalizing pass again, and I glared at him. He assured me that he had forgotten his "medicine" and he needed to call his mother so she could bring it. It was striking me that the crises of his life always seemed to occur when he entered the threshhold of my room, yet I gave in one more time, saying "No more after this." When I went to the office after lunch for supplies, I noticed the secretary waving her hands, exclaiming incoherently about the same student to whom I had been so accommodating. As I got closer, she kept repeating his name over and over, as if he had committed some heinous crime. When she saw me, she called me over, telling me what he had been doing as he left my room on those seemingly innocent but endless occasions. It turned out that he had been calling his mother who owned one of the best restaurants in the area to let her know what to bring him to school for lunch every day! On this particular occasion, though, the principal had been passing in front of the school and had caught him in the act of bringing in the food from the outside. The student never bothered me again after my principal was finished with him.

Another incident, humorous though serious, forced me to confront a student who had acted inappropriately and indecently toward me, the only time a student did anything downright disrespectful while knowing what he was doing. It related to an original writing assignment, a ballad, which was required of all senior English students. I explained the criteria, emphasizing that it would be graded, finally, not so much on form as on originality, but I did explain that though the topics could be varied, they had to be acceptable, a request which had never resulted in any problems during my years of teaching the medieval ballad. The papers were handed in, and a few of the seniors began to smirk as I arranged the stack. I looked at them and waited for an explanation. One said to read a particular student's paper.

As I began to read, the hairs began to stand out on my neck as I realized that the topic was masturbation, that the foolish senior boy had tried to set the teacher up with his little prank. The bell rang as I kept my cool and continued to read the paper to the end, remaining unruffled. It was surely original, all right. I had to give him that. As he sauntered out of the room with a grin on his face, I called out his name with just enough force to stop him in his tracks. "I have another class I have to get to," he said as he began to lose control realizing that this teacher would not tolerate such childishness, such mindlessness, such disgusting behavior. "Not now," I said, as I gave him an opportunity to explain himself. He had no back-up now. His friends were gone, and the students coming to my next class would just have to wait outside in the hall. He and I would thrash it out then and there. He had had no idea about the kind of teacher, person, woman I was. Through the years, I have found that anyone who had ever underestimated me as a person had paid for it dearly as they kicked themselves for their naive, incomplete ability to judge who I was. Most regretted their actions profoundly. This student was one of them, especially when I told him I was immediately going to call his parents and show them his work. He began to apologize profusely and sincerely, but I would never forget the look on his face when he realized the nature of this diminutive woman standing before him, of this teacher.

When I got to the lounge, I was fuming. Everyone could see it, could see my behavior which was so deviant from my normal self. When I calmed down, gathered my wits, and began to laugh, telling them the tale, they roared with me. For weeks after, they would always ask me what the topic was for the day. Yet they were all watching the student, waiting for him to move a millimeter out of line again. We teachers always marshalled our forces for one another whenever it was necessary.

And whenever it was necessary, I had to inform my principal of my pregnancies. "You're pregnant!" he would exclaim as I walked into his office, closing the door for privacy. "You're glowing!" he'd smile. I believe he thought I lived in a perpetual state of pregnancy, especially since our three children were five years apart. When I was the teacher-of-the-year finalist in 1984 and walked into his office to tell him, I closed the door. He said, "You're pregnant again!" I started laughing. "Not this time," I said, "but it's still good news." The students always hit me with looks of incredulity when they discovered my state of being with child. I remember that when I became pregnant with Alexis, and when I started wearing my maternity clothes, one of my favorite senior boys, unable to contain his curiosity any longer (it was obvious that he and two other young men were discussing the staggering notion of their teacher as a sexual being), asked me if I was wearing a new fashion or if I was pregnant. When I said "Yes" to the pregnancy, the whole class clapped. It was as though the teacher was for them, and the thought of sharing me with anyone else, especially a man, particularly a man who had been with me in the most intimate way, was almost like dealing with a being from another world. Their concept of "teacher" became enlarged because of it. It was okay to sit next to several senior girls who were very pregnant, yet it was harder to adjust to the teacher in her billowing dresses. Yet the students were always attentive and considerate during my years of teaching when I was carrying my children.

All children need nurturing, love, and attention. As a teacher, I strove to live that lesson of life as I presented the lessons of the day. It was always the more obvious questions that elicited my immediate attention, though, that made me snap to it, that kept the course of the day active and alive. For instance, every teacher who has ever faced a class of students has heard, "Why do we have to learn this?" whether "this" is the periodic chart of the elements, an axiom of geometry, or a usage rule in English. I believe that all teachers are more inclined to expend more energy, time, and thought explaining the "why learn" of the lesson rather than the content of the lesson itself. The answer to "why learn" is that we learn because we have to live. I have discovered that all experiences in the classroom, whether I have been teaching them or learning them, have been for a reason, a purpose, though, at the time, they may have seemed mundane and inconsequential. Teachers touch students every day, and those who do so positively, though entering their lives unexpectedly, are generally those forces, those unforgettable people, capable of changing lives for the better. We do not know at the time why we touch and are touched by others at particular points in our journeys, but everything is for a purpose. God's plan is worked out far in advance of our existences on the planet. It is in the interplay of all whom we meet and in our uses of free will that we determine our own particular outcomes.

I explained to my students that I was born to be an English teacher. They were confused by my statement and wanted to know why I was so positive in my knowledge of it. I pointed to

"Hingle's English" which I always kept on my bulletin board and showed them that if they unscrambled "English," they would come up with the possessive of my last name, "Hingle." They always loved that little story, the point of which one of my students, now a policeman, had shown me long ago. And I would always be a teacher, even if cancer took me out of the classroom, for I knew that I was leaving a positive, permanent influence on my students because I cared.

The scope of what I taught included instructional material, manners, listening techniques, skills relating to successful relationships with others, counseling, and keeping up with the gifted and talented. I explained, demonstrated, cajoled, encouraged, and demanded while exercising fairness. My areas of responsibility included the bookroom, yearbook, darkroom, newspaper, literary magazine, American literature, English literature, world literature, writing, grammar, and everything else in between. I learned so much myself that I felt that my teaching was simply an extension of where my own education had left off in the classroom: the only difference was that I was in front of the desk rather than behind it.

Because of my particular job description and talents as a teacher, I would often be invited to lecture or present my own interpretations of what being a teacher was all about, whether it was at a school board meeting or at a session for career education relating to teachers. I would sometimes begin my presentation, depending on my audience, by asking which particular qualities students wanted in a teacher. The answers ranged from a sense of fair play to a sense of humor, from knowledge of subject matter (confidence in the classroom with the material at hand) to knowledge of dealing with individual personalities and capabilities of students so that each attained his or her own self confidence from the presence of the teacher. Also desirable were the teacher's innate sense of knowing how to pace the class so that students acquired optimum performance levels without the tension and/or boredom which resulted from either too much pressure or too little concern, as well as a feeling on the teacher's part which said, "Yes, I push you, but I know that you are only human and that you have a level of toleration just like everyone else on the planet."

I recall so many students who would put themselves under incredible pressure to achieve, and they would become almost overwhelmed by the stresses from outside sources or forces on which they hadn't planned. For instance, students who had to work until 12 at night, who had to make their own clothes, who were pressured sexually, who had to pay for unexpectedly wrecking the family car, who had books and/or notebooks stolen, who came from alcoholic families, who came from divorced homes, invariably struggled with life rather than with school. Yet these students were often those who prevailed and endured through it all. These were not those students who had had everything given to them because parents could not give love or approval, nor were these students selfish and uncaring. Day after day, I saw young people maturing before my very eyes because of the exacting pressures of the world with which they struggled.

As so I was led to consider what kind of teacher I wanted to be, what I wanted to do to effect the best for my students and for myself. I recalled my best, most memorable teachers down the line, the encouragers, the ones with patience, those who took a special interest in each child whether that child lived in a house with marble floors or in a house with newspaper on the walls.

Two of the most outstanding teachers I have ever known were tragically touched by cancer in their lives. One had a daughter (a student of mine) who died from a brain tumor, and the other was a victim of Hodgkin's disease from about the time I was in his eighth-grade class until I became a teacher, the time of his death. These two men were brilliant, dedicated teachers who could have done anything they wanted in life, but they loved the classroom, the students, and the whole experience of teaching and learning. Always, when I recalled that expression, "Those who can, do, and those who can't, teach," I would do a slow burn which would be directed at the person who had so unfeelingly and flippantly coined that erroneous phrase, because some of the most alive, caring, effective persons I have ever known have been teachers, those who gave first, but who received greater gifts because of the reciprocation which can only be honestly given when the receiver is worthy of the gift.

I cleared $432 the first month that I taught school. I felt as if I were rich. I remember that I even had money left at the end of the month as I launched into what I though would be my life's work. And as the months passed quickly, I was even more excited about my paycheck because I knew that I was getting paid for something I was beginning to love. I was entering the world of "teacher" as I stood before the class in my mini-skirt and long hair (Could that have been in this lifetime? The year-books say "Yes."), and though I was entering Room 77 to replace an unforgettable, superb teacher who had been pro-moted, I felt that the world lay wide open for me, as well as for my students.

Being a teacher was an awesome feeling, one of anticipation and of optimism, and I never lost that feeling until cancer weakened me to a point of absolute weariness during my last year in the classroom, resulting in the joy of life being wrench-ed from me so ruthlessly that I could hardly deal with it. I was like the student whose lunch money was extorted, like the one who was a victim of prejudice, like the one who was wrongfully blamed for cheating. I needed professional intervention, but it would be long in coming. For more than a year, I would strug-gle alone with the grief of losing my work, a part of my identity, because of cancer. I stepped out of myself and watched a woman dying because of whom she could no longer be, be-cause of a person she no longer was, knowing that cancer could kill not only body but also soul.

One of the forces which helped me to survive my identity crisis was remembering what my students who had been per-sonally touched by cancer had taught me. The teacher became the learner, as the student became the teacher. The child indeed became the father of the (wo)man, as Wordsworth so appropriately offered.

I would always know when I had a student who had been through the loss of a parent to cancer, especially the young men. They or their close friends would generally refer to the loss in some way in order for me to know, and there would develop a tacit understanding, a bond between us, when I would become, in some degree, the mother image. They would always react to my presence in the classroom in a posi-tive way, even if they sat in the back to be with friends. I would always know that they were paying attention, wanting my approval, my nurturing.

Through the years, in-class writing exercises offered some of the students a chance to deal with expressing how cancer had affected their lives, and at the time, I never knew what a revelation it would be for me in my struggle later. Often, in the beginning of the school year, I would assign a paper entitled "An incident I would (or would not) want to relive." One of the most outstanding papers I ever received was from a student whose mother had died at M.D. Anderson of breast cancer. I was amazed that she could write of the loss, of the grief, in such a clear, moving manner. And yet years before I was diagnosed with cancer, I could never bring myself to read her paper aloud, yet the reading aloud of the excellent papers was an exercise which the students eagerly awaited as papers were returned. I talked to the class about the beauty and honesty of Bridget's writing, but it was one of the only times that I could not perform as a teacher. When she allowed her friends to read it, they knew why. My silence spoke louder than my words.

On the other hand, however, Brenda, 17, was my victory. Innominate strength, ineffable courage, she had survived cancer and was able to relate the experience eloquently, both orally and in writing. She expressed her struggling through the radiation therapy, resulting in weaknesses and in debilitation, yet she was one of the strongest young people I have ever known. She had had a wrenching sophomore year, but her year with me as a senior was a maturing experience for the entire class and for this teacher. The personification of joy, she seemed to cause me to hear "Ode to Joy" as I considered her participation in life. When she won the American Legion Award at graduation partly for courage in the face of adversity, I felt that she was absolutely deserving. Her fellow students truly admired and loved her.

When I knew I had cancer, I called her. It was one of the most strengthening experiences of our lives to discuss such a killing force which we would both survive. She confided that she had picked up the phone several times to try to make the connection with me, but she always held back, afraid that she would break down before her teacher. My reaching out was positive for both of us. And now, ten years after her encounter with cancer, she retains that radiance, that glow, that people who know the true meaning of the essence of living possess.

Just as life had always been a challenge, so was the activity, indeed, the activities, of the classroom. One of my favorite assignments (another teacher is responsible for the beauty of its originality, and I thank him for his sharing it with me) was having my students early in the school year make a list of the thirty most important things they wanted and/or had in their lives—those things that were meaningful and special to them—and to prioritize them in order of most important, that "I couldn't live without. . ." first on the list; however, only five could be things that could be purchased or bought. They were limited in the concept of material goods. The assignment always piqued their interest, leading them to discover insights into themselves which they never knew existed, and for me as a teacher, leading to all sorts of inexhaustible, enjoyable writing assignments ranging from definition papers to "identification" papers. For me as a person, as a woman, however, the assignment was also worthwhile. I began my list years ago, changing it occasionally, and then dramatically, as cancer entered the scene.

The "after cancer" experience caused me to realize that I had not once mentioned love (touch, sex, sharing—all kinds of love) and happiness on my list, and now they were on top, inseparable. My second one was life which was qualified by a sense of purpose and a sense of self expression. Again, cancer would be a major force in re-directing me to find my sense of purpose as I launched out into the world; I knew, however, that I did not want life if I did not have love and happiness. There was a tie for third with family, husband, children, and people (they make life full, interesting, and dear), along with prayer and God. I needed to know that a higher force or power was hearing, directing, and loving me so that I could know, love, and serve Him. Food was fifth, with *water* being the major consideration since I had hardly any saliva and knew where every water fountain in North America was. In addition, I could not omit gumbo (one has to be a Southerner to truly appreciate the real thing), chateaubriand, fried chicken, wine and cheese, and fresh fruit, much less chocolate.

Clothes came next, particularly casual, comfortable ones. I

still wear some I had when I first started teaching, but I also love my Reeboks and Liz Claiborne attire. I had to fit in health which granted serenity and included healing. Next were work, support, great teachers or sources of learning, commitment and persistence, challenges and goals, money (enough to satisfy, but not enough to bore or to destroy), literature, sight (and contact lenses—essential!), sunshine and air conditioning (okay, so I was cheating by pairing a few—it was not an easy assignment), spare time (privacy, leisure, relaxation), and I scratched out "lists" which was next. Following were growing things, the country, fall, my own special place in the world (Prairieville, Louisiana 70769), sleep (on old sheets, the comfort and peace of it), memories (pictures, a sense of the past), roses, antiques, my fireplaces blazing with oak logs, my bicycle (a newly-acquired treasure), my desk, music, and freedom. Each extended to other areas but it was "work" that now had my full attention.

Thomas Carlyle's expression of what "work" is, something which is characterized by a perennial nobleness and sacredness, held true for me in my teaching career. I thought I would teach forever. When I accepted the fact that I would never be able to use my voice again for any extended period of time, especially not as I had used it in the classroom, I felt like a doctor who knows he can never heal again, like a musician who can never hear the sweet strains of his compositions, like the artisan unable to complete his craft. The effect was similar to that of Conrad Aiken's Paul Hasleman experiencing growth in "Silent Snow, Secret Snow," that incredible short story where the 13-year-old cannot face the world which becomes grotesque and bizarre to him, resulting in his becoming a seed rather than a vibrant plant. I knew that I could not die as a rosebud, that I had to find some way to continue to blossom. But losing my work was not unlike experiencing a death blow.

I looked to the memorabilia, excellent papers, and letters I had kept, gifts and products of my students. One particular item was calling out to me, a poem that one of my most outstanding students had written over ten years ago, yet still a classic. I had never forgotten the beauty and the message of it, and I retrieved it, yellowed and worn, from my endless stacks of English files. It showed the beauty and necessity of calling a person a "friend," of the infinite joy and fulfillment of being called a friend, and I have remembered and been touched deeply when anyone, man or woman, has ever called me that. It is as follows:

To A Friend

The times are few in life
That foster lingering feeling:
Fortune has fastidious tastes
And flash fun is too appealing.

'Tis rare a constant light today
Directs tomorrow's path,
Seldom that this moment's treasure
Is later held as what one hath.

Life quickly rushes forth,
Fast, onward toward an unseen sea
Of having seen, of having been,
But never quite becoming "me."

However fast the time may go,
I have as my desire
That never may I grow so old
That of your company I tire,

That however far I chance to roam,
Need might draw us near,
That never may an evil bring
Between us shouting or a tear,

That never become I so proud
That I can't bend to you,
That ever will I stand beside you
When, perchance, you want me to.

Most of all I hope
You'll be, as now you are, a friend
To whom I may talk, a person
I honor—on whom I depend.

You're some of what I am
And some of what I'd like to be.
You blunder and you wonder, you,
Forever be a friend to me.

Travis Causey

The student, the writer, has now become my friend, my peer, and our relationship has grown. I thank him for the poem which uplifted me, which enhanced my life.

The highest rewards were these: having a student tell me that she prayed that I would be around to teach her younger brothers and sisters; having a grand student make a "5" (the highest score possible) on the Advanced Placement Exam in English Literature; convincing a 21-year-old man to stay in school and obtain his diploma (Yeah, Michael!); stopping long enough in the hall to listen to a Steve Martin joke told me by two of my favorite girls (and falling all over each other laughing), especially when I needed it; and bringing roses to Jamie in the hospital, one of my outstanding senior boys who could not go to Florida with the other seniors when he graduated because of physical problems which had caused death in others, but which only served to strengthen him. I learned so much from my students, and learning from others, no matter what our ages or positions, enlarges life.

Teachers generally measure time by nine months, holidays, summers, five or six hours of daily teaching, and checks (never enough) at the end of the month. I suggest that we teachers measure time by students' smiles, in our daily satisfaction as we overcome the hassle of paper shuffling to get to the heart of the teaching, in the "thank you's" from the kids who really matter. Those are the measurements that really stand for something; take it from this teacher whose swan song was never fully uttered satisfactorily. I loved my work for 14 years, I will always be a teacher, and I taught because it made me feel alive.

Chapter 6

Renunciation

"Renunciation — is a piercing Virtue —"
Emily Dickinson

During the first week in June, 1987, about a dozen women teachers, mostly those English teachers from my department at East Ascension, were gathered together at a table in a local restaurant, eagerly awaiting our orders. The occasion was one of my retirement parties, and we were all animatedly discussing such varied topics as "the end of school," students, our children, men, sex, summer plans, and funny things that had happened to us lately. When the food arrived, my friend Lillie looked over her items on her plate suspiciously. One thing I had always loved about Lillie was her keen sense of fair play. For instance, she had always complimented me on how I had fairly treated everyone in the English department for as long as she had known me, and now the element of fairness was surfacing again, only this time it centered on her seafood platter.

I could see a look of dissatisfaction in her eyes. "What's wrong, Lillie?" I asked. She explained that something seemed to be missing from her plate as she carefully compared the contents of hers with Audreye's. Sure enough, Lillie was right. Hers was lacking catfish. I had heard of being "short sheeted" and even "short changed," but never "short catfished." Well, I guess there was a time for everything. We all began such a clamor, as only women teachers can, that the waitress hurried out to see what was the matter. As Lillie was excitedly explaining her predicament, Vicki, another of my friends in the English department, quickly scanned the area, noting a superb piece of fried catfish under the table. We all screamed with laughter. It was turning into one of those fun parties, the memory of which has caused me absolute joy every time I recall it. The association is always "catfish."

Lillie got another piece of fish, and we continued our stories and laughter for about 2 more hours until I jumped up, recalling that my son had a baseball game at 4 p.m. It was 3:30, and this guest of honor hated to break up the party, but duty (there is always some kind of "duty" somewhere in the universe) called, and so I departed with tears in my eyes and with a smile on my face.

I was beginning to learn, though, that not all things that we wanted and didn't yet have could be so easily attained as Lillie's catfish. We all want things or persons that we long for, yearn for, and desire greatly, but do not yet have within our grasps. Usually, the striving for our objects of desire enlarges our lives, making them worthwhile and meaningful. We hope that as we break down the walls which separate us from what we wish, we are able to resolve satisfactorily the barriers responsible for the breach existing between us and our goals. We know that the child will always long for the ice cream cone, that the teenager will always desire the car of his own, that the housewife and/or career woman works toward a vacation from the demands of daily living, that the man yearns for the woman of his dreams. These acquisitions may or may not occur, depending on unseen forces and events.

There are some things we cannot have, though, and those things must be renounced, or given up. I did that with my teaching career, but not freely or completely until a year from the time I retired at age 36 because of cancer. It was an act which pierced my soul, and yet the "virtuous" aspect of it would not surface until much later. I did feel cheated at first, though.

At least when Edward gave up the throne of England, he received the women he loved, I reasoned. I felt, however, like an empty cup. I was gaining nothing in the renunciation because the element of choice was missing. I was wrong as I discovered later, though, but the difficulty of renouncing at that time would lie in the pain compounded with the suffering I had already experienced. Would the pleasure ever come?

Other "retirement" parties evoked memories which included newspaper articles about my accomplishments as an educator, cards and personal mementoes, photographs, food, roses, jewelry, and crystal. But it was in the interaction with those dear people who had given so much of themselves for me that I will always feel loved and remembered, from the official retirement party from the staff at East Ascension (the food was out of this world, and former colleagues with whom I taught and who had taught me attended, which was uplifting), to the retirement party from my sisters of Alpha Delta Kappa sorority for women teachers (my dear friend Judi Betts, with whom I had taught for years and who was now an internationally-known watercolorist, was there for me, my incentive for writing my book), to the retirement party from 20 of my special seniors who arranged everything themselves at a Baton Rouge restaurant—they picked me up, treated me, and toasted me.

The party with the students was unforgettable, though. I was so touched that these young men and women, in the summer of one of the turning points of their lives, took such a special interest in me that they stopped their own lives for a while in order to come together to be with me, their teacher. When we gathered in the restaurant, we were having fun. It was as though people couldn't believe that an adult could have so much fun being with young people; indeed, our table became the liveliest one in the place, centering on past memories and future plans—some had opted for college, marriage, military service, work, and play. Jeff made the toast, which was for a "full life" for everyone. Here was a young man who would go places, I thought. He was a born leader, poised and assured. I smiled my teacher smile. As we assembled outside before going to our cars, I stopped them all. I could not resist the urge to tell them how much they all meant to me, assuring them of my health and well being, and Sean said "How could we ever forget you, Mrs. Hingle? You will always be with us." And I know that I will.

Returning to school to visit, to step back into Room 77, was not easy. It was more a grief than a joy, more a chore than a delight. Though I was amused at the Vanna White posters which my dear friend had now placed in two strategic spots in "my" room, I could not help but recall the bulletin boards (the "Pleasure Dome" which had demonstrated the best of the writing; the "Wizard of Oz" which revealed the perils of the term paper; the "Man of La Mancha" which pointed out the stages of the life of man with literary quotations), posters, and art work that my students had created; James' rendition of Grendel was a wonder, pulling all the students into the story of Beowulf before I ever had to utter a word; Wayne's pictograph of the history of English literature was a masterpiece, a mini-story of what had passed before to result in what was happening now, but the treasures remained in our minds as the walls changed with the personality of the new teacher, with the times.

Once, Alexis the Outspoken caught me staring aimlessly out the window as I concentrated on my rose bed, and in her uncanny ability to read me, said, "You miss your students, don't you, Mom?" I answered, "Yes, but if I were at school with them, I'd be missing all the fun of being here with you!" and I picked her up and swung her around in one of our thrilling dances, enjoying her screams of delight and laughter.

Still, I had to contend with other reminders of being out of the classroom. The clerk behind the counter at the drugstore got sarcastic with me when I said I was a retired teacher. She said, "Well, I guess the kids got to be too much for you to handle." I looked her in the eye, and said, "Not at all. Unlike some people, I really love kids. I just happened to have gotten cancer." She was never smart-mouthed to me again after that. Another time, a wonderful salesperson told me that I must have been 14 when I retired, because I looked great! I smiled, and my cancer story unfolded for a few moments. She was deeply touched.

Being 36 and retired was like having all the money in the world with no desire to spend it, for in gaining retirement, I was left with a lacuna in my life, a missing part, an empty space. Most retirees have options or directions at least tentatively established, but because of the abruptive nature of my illness, I did not. I had my life, husband, children, family, friends, and home, but no creative outlet, no sense of purpose. One of my uncles told me there was a "niche" for me in the world, and I prayed I would find it soon. But right then, I felt as if I were in my own self-imposed hell, a nothingness, yet I had rejected the concept of nihilism years earlier. I remembered a professor saying years ago that his wife's concept of hell was satin sheets. Then I thought about the great "hells" that were manifested in literature.

John Milton's hell in *Paradise Lost* was the actual "hellfire and brimstone" concept, a place with the devil leering at you, plotting his chessboard with you as a favored pawn ready to effect his diabolical deeds; indeed, Milton's projected hell, however, was dark and foreboding, an extension of his own hell on earth where he would be forever blind. Dante's inferno was much more varied in its circles, however, with the nature of the sinners' sins dictating their own particular kinds of hell such as those confined to "existing" in human excrement because of their vile natures (the students in Advanced Placement English always loved *The Inferno* because of its ingenious punishments leading them to speculate on their own concepts of "crime," "punishment," "heaven," "hell.") Homer in *The Odyssey* presented the "land of the dead," where all souls met and relived past lives, usually in torment, an unresolved hell where despair and emptiness abounded. Mine was more like Homer's depiction, yet my identity did not even exist anymore, I felt.

There was a land of the dead on earth, I reasoned, but I would have to bring mine back to life. I would have to re-establish goals and objectives, beginning by slowly re-gaining that determination I had had as a child when I knew I would be valedictorian of my class, even if it took 12 years to accomplish; that persistence I had had as a teacher to maintain excellent standards for myself and for my students; that drive to work toward and develop my full potential as a wife, woman, and mother so that my family would absolutely benefit from my presence. The tools for rebuilding were there; I just needed to pick them up, but the job of reconstruction would not be easy.

I had had to let go of other things in my life which I had loved (mostly because of outside factors and forces over which I had no control), and I knew that all people renounce and rebuild constantly, yet the "security," the "locked in" quality of being a teacher was at stake because of the complacency (as well as satisfaction) which my job had afforded. I had to launch out again, knowing that if the boat stays on the shore too long, it will decay. It is only useful when it is in the water. At least I had to begin by getting my feet wet.

Poets dealt with renunciation, with turning points, every day, expressing the letting go of love, friends, creativity, or life in every poetic form from the sonnet to the elegy. It was Tennyson's "Ulysses" that engaged my attention as I began to consider renunciation and what it involved. In the poem, Ulysses has returned home after 20 years of struggling with every conceivable kind of force which barricaded him from his objects of desire, yet his determination to be re-united with the woman he loved and with his home finally effected his reunion. That was not enough, though, for in his acquistion, he knew that he had to relinquish the very objects of his desire, paradoxically, because what he desired most was an active, "alive" life. His phrase "How dull it is to pause, to make an end,/ To rust unburnished, not to shine in use!" kept echoing through my mind, reminding me that the only time our objects of desire are ever valuable is when they assure us of active, alive existences.

Our objects of desire must still challenge us after their acquisition, for if they don't, they stifle our growth. Ulysses knew that even after he gained Penelope, there was still something missing in his life, "some work of noble note," which remained elusive, calling to him. And so he renounced his life at home to set out again, for it is in a dynamic context that humanity lives; indeed, as "the slow moon climbs," so do our re-awakened goals climb, pulling us into the unknown, teaching us that " 'Tis not too late to seek a newer world," no matter where we are in our life's journey. Sometimes we feel that what we are giving up is almost too much to bear, yet in reality it is the magical nature of the "unknown" which may hold more attraction for us than the known. And that is what hoping and risking are all about, often leading to more satisfaction than we can ever imagine. We need to become a world filled with more people like Ulysses, more willing to take risks, as we launch our boats utilizing his as a model:

> Push off, and sitting well in order smite
> The sounding furrows; for my purpose holds
> To sail beyond the sunset, and the baths
> Of all the western stars, until I die.

I promise myself that I will not die until I experience all of what I want in life.

Support is essential in living. John Donne knew the meaning of living life surrounded by people who cared, expressed in his "No man is an island, entire of itself." Kids chatter on the telephone, friends and families plan weekends together, and man and woman constantly re-experience one another. Even Henry David Thoreau couldn't hack it in the woods alone for any extended length of time. Other people make life full.

I remember, during one of my trips back to M.D. Anderson for a check-up, when I learned the value of cancer support groups from another cancer patient. His name was Allen. I found myself sitting next to this young man who could be no older than 28 or so (I had taught students who were now approaching 34, and he seemed so young to me), who smiled at me. We struck up a conversation. His cancer had begun in his nose, and his profuse, uncontrolled nosebleeds had been the cause for his diagnosis. He was originally from a part of the world that still looked upon cancer as having the plague. It had been over a year, and he had not told his parents yet. I thought, "My God, you are going this alone. No man can get through this alone and retain his sanity."

But then he told me about Make Today Count, a cancer support group (even loved ones, including close family members and spouses regularly attend meetings) that exists to encourage and educate its members about the "life after" cancer experience. Even though I had gained tremendous support from family and friends, it was not the same as getting understanding from those who were undergoing the same thing that I was. Once, one of my doctors said to offer comfort, "I know how you feel, Pat," when I expressed my frustration because of neck fibrosis resulting from radiation therapy. "No, you don't!" I retaliated. And he couldn't have, nor could anyone else who had never been through the cancer experience, no matter how caring they wanted to be.

I remember the first time I met someone else who had a scar on her neck similar to mine, Orena, another head and neck patient, at a Baton Rouge Make Today Count meeting. We became instant friends as we saw each other's glass of water (our trademark), knowing that that moment of recognition was like finding the pot of gold at the end of the rainbow. We discussed typical feelings about our experience, things like having to bring our water with us to mass every Sunday in order to receive holy eucharist, the body of our Lord, Jesus Christ. I thought I was the only woman alive who had ever experienced that, but now I knew I was not alone.

The group is wonderful because it is so uplifting. Because of Make Today Count, I am able to discuss my frustrations, losses, feelings, strengths, and struggles with and about my particular cancer experience honestly and openly with people who have been through a similar experience. I expressed at one meeting that an $80 session of psychotherapy couldn't even begin to address the problems I had encountered because of cancer nearly so well as an hour of being with my soul mates in Make Today Count could. Make Today Count helps me to re-establish my identity as a woman who had cancer but who is now cured, as a person whose life has been enlarged and not diminished because of cancer. The group is a wonderfully positive force in my life.

As I gained Make Today Count, I lost my dad. He died October 31, 1986 (it was the worst Halloween that my children ever had), from congestive heart failure, a man who lived life as he wanted. He was a self-made man (building businesses, running the post office in Prairieville where he was postmaster for what seemed countless years, coaching baseball for 50 years, and teaching me about life), and I felt that the greatest gift he had ever given me was my introduction to books.

It began when I was in the second grade, and I was supposed to sing in the carnival ball, but I couldn't because I got the flu. He brought me my first comic books. I cherished them, reading them over and over as though I had just discovered the secret to the fountain of youth. They were all there, Dagwood and Blondie, Archie and Veronica, and the classics (I did not know then that they would lead to my insatiable love of literature, but he had given me the spark). Years later, when I had a poem to recite in a school play which began, "A book is like a magic land which opens up at your command," I knew my love affair with books would never end, a truth to which my husband will most readily attest as he one day stated to me, peering through the stacks of countless books in the house, "Patricia, don't you think 10 copies of *Les Misérables* is overdoing it a bit?"

My dad was a great teacher of mine, explaining life's lessons, things that couldn't be learned from books, however. I learned about people from him, about meeting them halfway as well as having them meet you halfway, about not being prejudiced because of the color of someone's skin or because of his religion or beliefs, about striving for what I wanted and working hard until I attained it. Though he is now gone from this earth, I still talk to him through prayer, visiting his grave, asking him to intervene to God so that I will be pointed in a positive direction in order to regain my zest for living, so that I can become fulfilled in my life's purpose. And I know that he hears me. And though he angered me at times and bewildered me at others, I loved him as I knew he loved me.

My children were very upset when my daddy died. Allyson mentioned often how she never forgot his laughter and funny stories, and Chip was the most upset because Pawpaw was to have been his baseball coach the next season. When he made some splendid plays at second base, though, he said, "Mom, I know that Pawpaw was smiling down at me from heaven." The love of the game goes on.

Alexis, however, was most memorable in her ability to recall Pawpaw. The day before he died in intensive care in the hospital, I broke a hospital rule. I sneaked her into his room where he was connected to endless tubes and machines, yet he recognized her immediately, lifting both arms to grasp her as his heart was failing him physically. Emotionally, though, his heart would be forever with her, fulfilled, as he smiled the saddest smile I ever saw, hardly being able to say her name. At that moment, I didn't give a damn about hospital rules or doctor's orders or medical cures, because I knew I was giving him the greatest comfort at that moment, his grandbaby.

And Alexis, in her inimitable way, would flash that unforgettable smile and would say, "I got to tell Pawpaw 'goodbye.' " My mom was with him in his death the next day, just as she had been with him all of her life, and they had been husband and wife for 44 years, never straying from the other. "He told me when I was 13 (he was 15) that he loved me alone and he always would," my beautiful mother told me. They married when they were in their early 20's and lived together through life's ups and downs.

Ups and downs. She let him go, not having a choice. In her renunciation, however, she gained a sense of self purpose and of independence as she began to grow in her ability to embrace life alone at the age of 65. I saw my mother blossom into a woman who was assertive, assured, and happy in her new identity. As I considered how she, with the help of God, had been catalytic in effecting change in her life which brought her back into the world of people when I was graduated from high school, I also saw how she was able to adapt again to a crisis in her life which would only serve to strengthen her. I learned from my mother, another great teacher, that courage can bring positive change as long as one is willing to take the risk. And I thanked God for two of the best teachers I ever had, my mother and father, role models whose different types of strengths would sustain me and encourage me to grow as a person, to continue to embrace life after cancer.

I renounced my father's life, too, but never his influence. For when I was born, he and my mother had lost four children, three through miscarriage and one who had lived three days. I was their hope, yet I was sickly and puny. I was their first child who would live, yet the pediatrician told my daddy that I was better off dead. The whole concept of doctor as healer left him then, and he never trusted another doctor again after that. Little did that doctor know what I meant to my parents, to those who would see to it that I lived and that I was loved. My dad's recounting of that story taught me that doctors are simply men and women underneath their magical white coats, highly-trained professionals, but no different from anyone else in the world, and that those few who truly deserve admiration are the real healers, for the concept of healing is entrusted by God to those who are worthy of it. Because of life which my parents gave me through the gift of God, I have loved and been loved, given birth to three beautiful children without compromising myself because of the absolute love of a wonderful man, taught and learned, and through it all, I experienced the joy of living. The doctor was wrong about this child of life.

In the renunciation of job and of father and of identity (partially, at least), I still gained things and people through my cancer experience. I had begun to understand the importance of self health because of the dedication and concern of my wonderful doctors who had entered my life; of the "true" friends, old and new, which I loved; of the importance of "family" as a bonding force beyond belief. My students would sometimes moan and groan throughout the literary presentations in the classroom, not so much because they could not understand the material but because often they could not relate to it. "Wait!" I would say. "In time, you will understand the grief of a child and a parent dying, as in the case of Cordelia and Lear; of the joy of watching your beloved disrobe as Porphyro is captivated by the physical beauty of Madeline; of the pleasure of being 'tangled' in the hair and 'fettered' to the eye of your love as Lovelace describes his unforgettable experience with his Althea; of the pain of losing someone you love because of death, as in the case of Romeo and Juliet. All of what we study today, you will realize in due time," I would say. And it has happened and will continue to happen to me.

Anyone whose life is always balanced is never really living, for he is simply going through the motions of existing, afraid to travel a certain highway or finding fault or judging those around him mercilessly, yet never really understanding what living is all about. He believes he never made mistakes, that he is beyond reproach, that he is perfect. He has never lived.

The virtue of renouncing is in the benefits we gain later on down the line from the renunciation. There are always greater things to gain, offering higher plateaus to reach. Ulysses said it best:

> Though much is taken, much abides; and though
> We are not now that strength which in old days

Moved earth and heaven, that which we are, we are—
One equal temper of heroic hearts,
Made weak by time and fate, but strong in will
To strive, to seek, to find, and not to yield.

I will never yield to cancer. Though much has been taken from me, I will center my attention now on what "abides," on the virtues, on the benefits, and build on them. I may be weakened, but I am alive, whole, stronger in more ways than I know, and more determined than ever to fight the good fight as God guides me down the right paths. I will never renounce Him nor my faith in myself to be fulfilled.

Chapter 7

Consummation

"I am my beloved's and his desire is toward me."
Solomon's Song, 7:10

My husband, Walter, and I were far removed from the security of the halls of my school, from those halls we had initially paced, as we began together to face the reality of the possibility of my having cancer; indeed, now our attention was riveted on one another in those unfamiliar halls of M.D. Anderson Hospital where we were suddenly faced with the ineffable presence of cancer. We wanted to touch one another, to hold on to some semblance of sanity at least through an embrace, but we were denied the intimacy, the solace, of loving one another even for a moment because of the covert rule of the hospital and, indeed, of all hospitals, which was "Do not show any emotion as an individual or especially to anyone you love in these halls."

Instead, we felt as if we were walking through an endless array of fun-house mirrors, each in its own unique way distorting and destroying what had taken us twelve years to build in our marriage, and I began to feel that the invader of my body was somehow going to invade my relationship with my husband, that the cells which were degenerate and merciless and devouring to those surrounding healthy ones would extend themselves into a deadly, unseen force which would threaten the foundation of our existence as man and woman.

However, as we stood alone together, I felt his love for me take control of it all. He could not speak, though, for fear of breaking. Instead, he turned away from me for a moment, and he walked over to another man with whom he had spoken earlier, another man whose wife had just been diagnosed as a cancer patient. The two men spoke in Spanish, quietly and briefly (I found this unusual, for my husband was never a quiet talker nor did he ever finish a conversation quickly), and when my husband returned to my side, I asked him, " What did you say to him?" rather sharply, for I was frustrated because of his momentary walking away which was not so much an abandonment of me at it was an inability to deal with a pressing problem concerning the two of us.

" 'My wife is my life' is what I told him," he said. And then he repeated it so softly to me that I could hardly hear him. And I knew that my man, my former Marine, my rock, my lover, my stronghold, my strength, my husband, my friend, was being consumed, just as I was, by cancer. It was starting to eat him alive.

As soon as we were afforded some privacy in one of the rooms at Station 52, we touched one another's faces. He said, "You are too beautiful, too good, for this to happen to you." He began to wish aloud that the cancer had befallen him rather than me, to rationalize that he had worked at times in industry where known carcinogenic areas were publicly acknowledged, to question why I was the one who would have to undergo the first-hand suffering. Throughout the ordeal, though, he would stand by me and love me, through the self pity; the sleepless nights; the torments of the radiation therapy; the cursing; though all of the stages of the cancer process, including denial, rationalization, anger, acceptance, and healing.

The "through sickness and health" phrase of the marriage vows would be tested to its greatest limit because of cancer, yet my husband would remain undaunted in his devotion, caring, and love for me. In my experiences of knowing other cancer patients, I discovered many whose spouses could not handle the stress of the illness on the marriage, and impenetrable walls would be established because of cancer. My husband was not one of those spouses.

I was awestruck that my husband desired me sexually when I looked and felt the worst I ever had in my entire life. He had a way about him, a quality that erased the scar on my neck, the criss-crossed radiation markings on my face, the inferno in my throat, so that we could enjoy one another sexually without being threatened, intimidated, or limited in our lovemaking which had a basis long-established as sacred, exclusive, and mutually satisfying during our marriage. I remember his telling me later that I was "all women" to him, and in his comment I realized that he was paying me the greatest compliment of all, that he was telling me that I provided the variety of loving which was the potential of all women to give to men, yet it was all-inherent in me, in my personality, in my being. I was his beloved, his alone, his forever.

Since I was a teacher of English literature, I was fairly familiar with love poetry by women to their men; indeed, there was very little positive poetry that dealt with honest, meaningful, full, lasting, truly loving relationships between men and women in the world. Instead, a greater proportion of the poetry dealt with "love" that was thwarted, transient, tormented, unfulfilled, and out of reach.

I zeroed in on Elizabeth Barrett Browning's sonnet to Robert written during their courtship, a sonnet describing how she wanted to be loved by him, as she explained her understanding of the reason why his love for her was so rare, so precious. In her "Sonnet 14," she states that if he must love her, then it should be because of love alone, "for love's sake only," and for no other reason. The implication is that the lover must be pleased and happy in his love for his woman, not allowing the advice or demands of someone else, or of the conventions of the time, to dictate his priorities for love, whether they include religious preference, flight from another woman, financial pressures, or any other unacceptable force.

Unencumberance of love is an essential criterion for loving, and Mrs. Browning goes on to point out that love may become pretentious, incapable of growth, and stagnant because of pre-conceived conditions imposed on the loving initially, as pointed out in her lines where she states that she (as well as I) rejects the concept of a man loving a woman for a particular quality, such as "her smile—her look—her way/Of speaking gently—for a trick of thought/That falls in well with mine" or for sympathy or pity. Rather, she believes the woman should be loved for her entire being, or as my husband deftly stated, "There is nothing about you that I do not love. I love everything about you." Mrs. Browning goes on to state that if she (and all women) is loved for the sake of love, then the love will be lasting and eternal. It must be unconditional. I am loved in that way.

"Nothing will ever alter my love for you," my husband would tell me often and sincerely. And because of his statement, I sought to understand the force and the power of his love for me, and I looked to the moment of our first meeting.

We met at work, after his badgering my supervisor (a neighbor of his) to introduce us. He admitted that he had had his eye on me, but after the introduction, he asked me for dates three times before I finally accepted. It wasn't that I didn't like him or didn't find him attractive (indeed, he was the most handsome man I had ever met), but I was dating several other men at the time and he would ask me for a date when I already had one. Finally he said, "Break it," when I told him about another date. I did. I always loved how he persistently pursued me, never letting up as we made our first connection.

We set up ground rules as we started dating, beginning with the understanding that I would cut his hair if he took me to an expensive restaurant, as he explained that he didn't have enough money for both—he really was a risk-taker—I had never cut anyone's hair before, as I told him, but it would be an adventure, fun for both of us; we continued with the agreement that sex would wait because we both wanted the relationship to grow, to get somewhere, before we made a serious sexual commitment.

He admitted that he knew he loved me months before he ever touched me in a sexual manner. We had given ourselves that precious gift of time which allows friendship to grow into love, and yet many people do not allow themselves even brief intervals in order to get to know one another. We both wanted what we had to grow. His mother told me that she remembered his walking into walls and staring into space as he could not get me out of his head nor heart for any specified period of time. And so after several more months together, he proposed, and I accepted.

He knelt before me as he asked me to be his wife. We had both forsaken all others from that first date, that first kiss, and when he gave me my engagement ring, he said that that was the only one he would ever purchase. We were married June 1, 1974.

The honeymoon was short and sweet, mainly because we had little money and less time. I had just begun teaching and he was still in college, trying to complete his degree because he had joined the United States Marine Corps during the Vietnam years which had interrupted his college career. We were planning to go to summer school together that summer. But even though the honeymoon was brief, it was most memorable because of a particular lakeside restaurant we visited with a piano, piano player, and dance floor on the lower level all to ourselves. We danced through one night with our own private live music, all of "our" songs.

And then we settled down to living life as a married couple. We had never before lived together, so the adjustment to apartment life centered around chores like putting out garbage, washing clothes, cooking, and paying bills. We finally moved into our home in the country a year later, our home where we live together today.

We had unrealistic expectations of ourselves, of one another, of the marriage, as a great many people do. As the early years passed and the children began to arrive, I had to admit that spontaneity of living and expression of my feelings were almost non-existent in the marriage. My husband seemed angry and critical about almost everything, and he was exacting, demanding perfection with every step I seemed to make. It seemed the more I continued to give, the more sarcastic and caustic he became so that I began to feel that I could never please him. I did not know what the problem was as I grew more manipulative and controlling, and we would both verbally abuse one another more and more as time went by. I walked on eggs all the time. Children and work became escapes from the marriage, yet I wasn't even aware of what was happening. It seemed that for years I prayed that my marriage would be strengthened, changed, improved. Yet I did not know what to do. It became more and more difficult to enjoy sex with a man who had so initially loved me, yet now was putting me down as he seemed to wear a perpetual frown. The marriage was beginning to crumble slowly, and I could not figure out why. It was cancer that turned it around full circle and began to save it, yet it would get much worse before it got better.

As a devout Roman Catholic, I took my religious marriage vows seriously, never believing in divorce, always thinking that my marriage would survive anything because of the strength of our love. In a dream before the cancer was diagnosed, I saw myself stand before God and ask Him to help us. And then I saw cancer, and then, life. I did not tell my husband about the dream until we were months into marriage counseling, until I knew he could accept anything I said without judging or berating or condemning me. I waited until I knew that he was finally listening to me and considering my feelings about living.

When I was diagnosed with cancer and when I finished my radiation therapy in June of 1986, I promised God that if He let me live a year, my marriage would either change or end, because it was the greatest stress of my life, contributing to my illness, causing me to hate myself and my husband. I was increasingly sharp with our children. My only respite had become my job, and that was now gone, and I knew why. God was causing me to face the problems within the marriage and to do something about them. All I knew was that I could not fight with my husband anymore. Unless it stopped, I knew that I would die. The battle with cancer was a prelude to the battle within and about the marriage.

No one outside our home knew of the marital problems, and my husband never felt that there was anything wrong because I was always there, always dependable, always loving. But things were about to change dramatically.

Cancer gave me the courage to fight for life, and it also gave me the courage to stand up to my husband in order to tell him about the serious problems in our marriage. It had been impossible to do before because I knew he would never listen. But now my life, my existence, my quality of living was on the line, and for the first time, I became selfish. I wanted a loving man to love back. If he couldn't be that way with me, I didn't want him. I deserved to love and to be loved in a worthwhile manner because I existed as a human being. I didn't want to feel that I had to be Mother Earth, the Delphic Oracle, or Sigmund Freud in order to have a healthy relationship. I simply wanted to be me, to be relaxed, to please myself, to love myself, and to be loved by a worthy partner. The time for playing games was over.

I put myself into psychotherapy at the suggestion of Dr. Ed Vinci, the internal medicine specialist, because of the difficulty of coping with cancer. He believed that I needed outside help and suggested Dr. Christine Angelloz, a Baton Rouge psychologist, whose card I carried around for months before I summoned the courage to see her June 26, 1987, a year after my radiation therapy had ended. Many events occurred that day, a date which I will remember for the rest of my life, because for the first time in my existence, I was honest with myself and with those around me. When I saw Christine for the first time, I explained to her that I had come for help in dealing with cancer, but more importantly, because of the deteriorating condition of my marriage. And so the story began to unfold.

I confronted Walter that night about the state of our marriage. He turned and walked away. I did not follow him to bed. I slept on the couch for the first time that I could remember. I knew that many women remained in loveless, hopeless marriages because of so many fears which included financial woes, husband's anger, loneliness, and children's welfare, but I knew that I could no longer live a lie. I wanted truth in my life, and even though I longed for a partner who could truly love me for myself so that I could return love, I also knew that the possibility of any other relationship was out of the question unless I resolved the problems in this marriage.

When my husband saw that he no longer could raise his voice to me or coerce me or blame me or belittle me in order to get his way, he knew we were in serious trouble. For the first time since I had known him, I saw him afraid, more fearful of losing me than when I had had my cancer diagnosed.

It was about that time that Mother and I began to attend Al-Anon meetings in order to try to understand the behavior of one of my family members who had become a drinker and whose behavior was becoming harmful to his and to others' health. As I attended my first meeting, listening to others in the group describe the behavior of their loved ones who had been overtaken by alcohol, I suddenly realized that the behavior they were describing was identical to my husband's, except that he did not drink, and neither did I.

As I confronted my psychologist with the information, she and I began to discuss the behavior of adults whose parents had been alcoholics (my husband's dad and my dad had both been alcoholics) and how the behavior of the parents always affects the children even though they are non-drinkers. It was a major revelation, a keen insight into the unacceptable and unexplainable behavior that we were both evidencing as mature adults. In the past three years, psychologists have begun to deal with the fact that children who grow up in alcoholic homes have tremendous problems adjusting to married life, and many marriages end in divorce, yet many can be saved through professional counseling as I was now getting.

Still, we had so many wounds that would take time to heal. I felt like Tennyson's Aurora who, in her eagerness to gain Tithonus, settled for the gift of immortality for him without obtaining the gift of eternal youth. Her desire for immediate gratification was thwarted because of her lust which overpowered her common sense in gaining her desired object—she found herself trapped in a world almost impossible to bear as she witnessed her beloved age mercilessly as she grew more beautiful and more desirable. I had, in my desire for relief from the strains of the marriage, acted in a manner which caused me even greater stress and distress than the state of the marriage itself, as I, in desperation, had filed for a legal separation and divorce from my husband. My psychologist, however, kept assuring me that I still loved my husband underneath my hurt, and when our daughter Alexis came to me and said, "Please let Daddy love you, he loves you so much," I listened. Never had I seen such a small child so serious about anything in life. I dropped the legal proceedings and began to re-consider my feelings and also to consider those of my husband. I had always been a person who had viewed life in terms of black and white, yet I learned from cancer that alternatives existed in the world if we allowed ourselves the guidance from God to accept them. I called my husband, and we were re-united.

I began to understand that he had never been aware of the rift in the marriage, that he had never intentionally meant to hurt me, and I truly felt that he and I had enough love for one another to begin again, to start anew, to reconcile, and to resurrect a love like no other couple had ever had. I realized that my expectations of him had been unbending and perfectionistic, and that all men need understanding and love and comfort and security from the women they love. I dedicated myself to these positive qualities, to these sacred qualities, as I knew that his greatest fault was in his loving me too much. As long as he realized that I, as well as he, needed to grow in the marriage, I felt that we could endure it all together. So I let him love me, and I loved him.

Through it all, we remained faithful to one another, knowing that fidelity was one of the foundations of true love, knowing that neither of us had ever strayed before, nor were we likely to in the course of our love. My husband remained in counseling in the darkest hours of his life, never losing faith in God, and I knew that there were few men alive who had the fortitude, character, and integrity to do what he had done.

William Shakespeare expressed it best in his sonnet beginning "Let me not to the marriage of true minds/Admit impediments. Love is not love/Which alters when it alteration finds,/Or bends with the remover to remove./ O, no! it is an ever—fixed mark,/That looks on tempests and is never shaken." Centuries later, the psychoanalyst Erich Fromm in his *Art of Loving* reiterated Shakespeare's definition of love as unshakeable, but he went further as he stressed the importance of complete disclosure and depth of commitment:

> There is only one proof for the presence of love:
> the depth of the relationship, and the aliveness
> and strength in each person concerned; this is the
> fruit by which love is recognized.

* * *

> To love somebody is not just a strong feeling—it is a
> decision, it is a judgment, it is a promise. If love
> were only a feeling, there would be no basis for the
> promise to love each other forever.

And so in our failures and in our successes, my husband and I loved and will continue to love, for we have faith in one another and in God. We have a deep and abiding relationship based now on mutual respect which leads to freedom in our loving one another, and in our lives. We want a strong family structure, a strong relationship between ourselves. I want my daughters to be loved by a man like their dad, my son to be a loving man to a woman like his dad is to me.

Looking back, I relive many of our joys together. When he bought me my engagement ring, he spent his only $1000 that he had on the ring, all for me. He has never held anything back from me. I remember wading in cool streams with him during our honeymoon, of experiencing sexuality with him that was so grand that we wondered how anybody could ever have what we had as we totally gave ourselves to one another, of seeing his joy as he held each of our children in his arms for the first time, of flying with him as he piloted the plane with me alongside him, of participating in life with him as he loved his woman and children beside him.

I could never have revealed so much about our lives a year ago; indeed, I needed to know now that what I said about our marriage in writing was understood by him, not necessarily wanting his approval but telling him that I had to be honest with myself and with the world, and when he read my words, he admitted his hurt, but he also stressed to me that if I felt it had to be told, then to do it for myself, assuring me that the marriage would be ever-strong and unchanged by my story. He is the only man I have ever told how much I admire, respect, and love, due in part to his reaction to my self-expression. He is finally allowing me that gift of freely expressing myself without fear of recrimination or derision or denunciation. All women want that.

And so I know that we have real love, a love that Robert Frost describes in his "Birches" as one which must be experienced on earth, for "Earth's the right place for love." I want my miles to go before I sleep, my time on earth with my husband. Also, Elizabeth Barrett Browning, in her "Sonnet 22," expresses her desire to love her beloved on earth rather than in heaven because of the intrusive nature of the angels which she believes would serve only to distract the "deep, dear silence" of the lovers. She opts to "stay rather on earth, Beloved," because she states that mere men cannot invade the lovers' place "to stand and love in for a day."

Yet it is the poet and writer John Donne in his exquisite "A Valediction, Forbidding Mourning" who, when writing to his wife, states the concept of the necessity of absolute freedom in marriage which, paradoxically, binds the lovers beautifully in their loving, no matter how far, physically, one lover may be from the other, revealed in his unforgettable conceit, "Our two souls therefore, which are one, /Though I must go, endure not yet /A breach, but an expansion, /Like gold to airy thinness beat." So it is the malleability, the flexibility of the union, of the gold, to be shaped, extended, or changed, that permits a dynamic, lasting, growing relationship. A precious metal that neither time, nor space, nor other outside force can ever dim, but which emerges perpetually bright, polished by the shine of life, is that one soul, therefore.

Women live according to moon phases. Obviously, our menstrual cycles, governed by the rotation of the earth as it moves through space, change our personalities and bodies periodically. As the moon changes its features and shape, however, a change occurs in all women, in our adaptability to men, to our relationships, and to living. We are never balanced. Indeed, we must be renewed in our lovemaking, in our need for fulfillment as beings designated "womankind," in our identities as human beings. Richard Lovelace, the seventeenth-century English cavalier poet, expressed in his "To Althea, from Prison" his definition of freedom when he said, "If I have freedom in my love and in my soul am free, /Then angels alone that soar above enjoy such liberty." He has touched the essence of what men, and women, want from relationships with each other.

Shakespeare summed up the necessity of making mistakes in living in one of his sonnets, of the concept of imperfection found in the quality of human existence (by the very nature of our existence, we are imperfect beings, which is all right). And he discloses that it is now time to understand that ours is a world where things are not perfect. At the same time he encourages, indeed, allows, members of his audience to forgive themselves as they forgive others in their unrealistic expectations of life:

No more be grieved at that which thou hast done:
Roses have thorns, and silver fountains mud,
Clouds and eclipses stain both moon and sun,
And loathsome canker lives in sweetest bud.

So I will continue to nurture my roses as well as their thorns, to let my moon pass through its various phases, and most importantly, to understand that my cancer experience does not have to destroy or blight the "sweetest bud," my life, but to let cancer remain an imperfection which will give me strength as it will become overshadowed by my love for myself, by my husband's love for me and my love for him, and by the love of my God for us all.

Chapter 8

Regeneration

"Sweet is the rose, but grows upon a briar; . . .
So every sweet with sour is tempered still,
That maketh it be coveted the more:
For easy things, that may be got at will,
Most sorts of men do set but little store.
Why then should I account of little pain,
That endless pleasure shall unto me gain!"
                    Edmund Spenser, from "Sonnet 26"

I was now examining my rose bed on this cold January day, knowing that I would soon cut back the canes, eliminating those that had died so that new growth could occur; I would till and fertilize the soil, anticipating the beginning of the warmth of the spring; I would eradicate the ant hills and pesky insects, knowing that roses need all the help they can get to flourish, knowing that they are beyond compare when they do. The hope of a new year was with me again. The dynamics of the rose bed represented life in all its stages, from infancy to fruition to decay to dormancy to regeneration. It was all there in my mini world of gardening, representing the inevitability of change which always marked a dynamic life.

I recalled the changes in my life over the past two years, centering now on regeneration. It is now two years to the day that I went to Dr. Fourrier with the lump in my neck, the cancer that would not end, but change, my life. An important lesson that I learned from cancer is that it doesn't have to be deadly, perhaps only catalytic, if it is reported and treated early in its manifestation, as most other problems in life should be addressed. The human will can heal more than any medicine can. More importantly, though, is the fact that cancer caused me to take a hard look at myself, my marriage, and my life, giving me courage to change the things that mattered to me, the things that I loved. There are alternatives to every problem in life if we step back and examine situations objectively.

Life is always marked by paradoxes. The poets have often stated that the phoenix must die in order to rise from the ashes; indeed, life teaches that man must experience hate in order to know love, must fall to rise, must struggle to free himself, must give to receive, and must die to old ways of living to live a full life, yet his potential is limited by himself alone—no one else can truly develop a human being, for he must do that for himself. Sometimes, others simply point the way.

My husband was one who helped point the way for me in my recovery and healing. When I retired, Walter wanted to give me something wonderful to cheer me, to show his love for me, yet he could not decide on the gift until he watched me stop my chores long enough one night to catch a report on the magnificence of the Broadway play, *Les Misérables*, an adaptation of the novel which I had taught several years in my Advanced Placement English class. I burst into tears when I heard of the wonder of it, of the beauty of it, knowing that the reality of never being able to teach the story again was inescapable. He held me, letting me release my tears and sobs, and as he tilted my chin, looking at me with love in his eyes, he said, "We're going to see it. You deserve it. It will be my gift to you." And so we went.

The splendor of it was surpassed only by my knowledge that I had somehow gained even more satisfaction from the teaching of the story, from the bringing it alive in the classroom to my students who would never have the opportunity to view its operatic grandeur, yet they would always know of the story of Jean, so beautifully portrayed by Colm Wilkinson, an actor whose performance will remain with me for the rest of my life, touching my very soul.

It was hard to believe that a year from the operating table found me in New York City with my husband, enjoying several Broadway plays. Though his favorite was *Cats*, it was *Starlight*

Express that granted me absolute delight, especially the song where Poppa explains that each person is responsible for effecting his own energy, drive, determination, and eventual happiness. He sang of every individual having the potential of his own power to change his life, and he sang with the most convincingly powerful voice I had ever heard. I will never forget the song, the experience of *Starlight*. And that trip with my husband was one of the most enjoyable ones of my life. He said, "We'll do whatever you want to do!" Carte blanche in New York City was like discovering sunken treasure. I dragged the man all over the place, loving every minute of it. We experienced a great spontaneity of life together on that trip. I was beginning to feel some normalcy creeping back into my life, some wellness, thanks to his love.

Another wonderful event of the year was the wedding of one of my brothers, an occurrence which reaffirmed the normalcy of living. I was asked to read the selections he and his new wife had chosen, and I was especially touched by the definition of "love" from I Corinthians 13: 1-13, but especially verses 4-7 which state that "Love is patient, love is kind. Love is not jealous, it does not put on airs, it is not snobbish. Love is never rude, it is not self-seeking, it is not prone to anger; neither does it brood over injuries. Love does not rejoice in what is wrong but rejoices with the truth. There is no limit to love's forbearance, to its trust, its hope, its power to endure." I was familiar with the selection; indeed, my husband and I had selected the same one to be read at our wedding, and I would be asked to read it again at another wedding. How true it was, I realized. For my husband and I had both renounced the anger and injury of living, embracing truth and trust in our relationship. For we knew that love was the center of living, the foundation which had to exist before balance could ever really be considered, but the building of the secure foundation had not been easy.

It is easier to ignore major problems in our lives, especially because we do not want to "rock the boat" of our daily existences. We believe that any change will bring imbalance, rendering us dizzy and out of control. We do not realize, though, that often we are already out of balance and we need a bit of "boat rocking" to set us on the right path in our journeys. Erich Fromm, in his *To Have or to Be?*, dealt with the concept of the difficulty of the human will to effect a positive change, even when it comes down to a "life and death" matter:

> Yet another explanation for the deadening of our
> survival instinct is that the changes in living
> that would be required are so drastic that people
> prefer the future catastrophe to the sacrifice
> they would have to make now.

* * *

> This is also the kind of behavior that occurs
> in people who will risk dying rather than undergo
> an examination that could lead to the diagnosis of a
> grave illness requiring major surgery.

It all comes down to sacrifice, to strength. It would have been easier for me to ignore my lump in my neck, not going to the doctor when I did; to ignore the problems in my marriage and continue on a collision course with disaster, yet the driving force that caused me to effect change for myself, to get a diagnosis for my health and for my marriage and to act on them, was love. I loved myself and my husband enough to rock the boat.

When I told my dad I had cancer, he had an easy solution. "Get it out now," he said. I felt he was the only person around me who knew that I would continue to live. There was no question in his mind. He had taught me to be active so I could remain alive. I learned how to get help from others, from utlizing psychotherapy, to putting my body in the hands of my doctors, to calling upon Christ to carry me when I fell, to allowing my husband to love me. Instead of continuing to climb walls, I began to break them down. I told a technician who marvelled at my courage during one of my bone scans that I knew that if I had only one healthy cell left in my body, God would use it to regenerate health for me. At that moment, I never feared cancer again.

In fact, I know that there is a natural cure for cancer today. That cure is love. I believe that cancer is caused by hate, fear, sadness, loneliness, depression, anxiety, insecurity, torment, and anger. Love can conquer cancer, but it is not an easy conquest. It must come from inside ourselves as we allow others to help us, to love us. A deep and abiding faith in God is essential, for He never stops hearing us and answering our prayers.

I wanted to re-address some of the earlier conflicts in my life as I looked back over the past two years of my cancer experience. Balance is never certain nor always acceptable. It is better that it remain elusive, for it keeps us on our toes, reminding us never to take life and its possibilities for granted. I will live on the brink every day with cancer for the rest of my life. It will be a gentle reminder that a little unsteadiness goes a long way, that sometimes water spills out of the cup, but the action is one of fulfillment rather than imbalance; that the empty cup is always balanced yet always unfilled.

I also learned and promised myself that I will tear down all walls which do not suit my purposes so that love in all forms will be constantly entering my life as I allow it to enter. When any barrier appears to loom up, I will address it and deal with it, whether it relates to job, marriage, children, or self. I will effect the following for myself: accept the problems of my family of origin, especially those associated with alcoholism, and deal with them so that my immediate family will be happy and healthy; "go for" my life's desires as I continue to re-establish my self esteem which is the only way I will ever be truly happy; welcome unplanned forces in my life, especially new friends who add to the joy of spontaneous living; not limit myself in any way; continue to say "NO" knowing that I will no longer be a caretaker but a caregiver, expecting others who really care for me to meet me halfway in any kind of commitment; never allow anyone to walk on me again as I assert myself, not living or dying for anyone else's approval, but only mine. I know that the only way I can let my pitcher fill to the brim again and again is to allow myself to be refreshed, and so I will please myself as I become selfish, putting myself and my needs at the forefront more and more.

I believe that every cancer patient who has ever lived has had to face a serious problem in his life before the cancer was diagnosed. The cancer was perhaps an unplanned force which gave two options—live a full life or die—it must be decided now. I opted for life. I have learned that being too "nice" and too "pleasing" to others in not conducive to self sufficiency or to growth, because others tend to take advantage more and more of one who has a pleasing nature. I renounce that old self in favor of this new one who will please herself.

Today people want everything *now*. If they don't get it, they are angry, jealous, and sick. The concepts of delayed gratification, monogamy, and happiness are alien to most people because of their attitudes towards what they desire. In my reading of novels and self-help books, I notice that God is missing from almost every one, which is unfortunate. People who learn that giving up is essential in order to gain have learned one of the great lessons of the world.

My children are some of the best givers that I know. Alexis, for instance is constantly drawing and gluing and coloring pictures of "her house" with her family, all with smiles, and she gives them to me and to her dad. She beams when she gives. Normalcy around our home it being re-established, yet it is a better normalcy with no fighting, with everything out in the open. Alexis intended to give me a rabbit's foot (purple) for Christmas. She wheedled $2 out of me for it. When she got it, though, she loved it so much that she decided to keep it, but declared that she would share it with me. She likes to get close to me and touch my face with it, then touch hers. It's our special closeness that she had devised, a special solution to her problem of dealing with renunciation. She found a way for both of us to keep it.

Alexis also has a special barrette with a man in the moon smiling on it, and Allyson has a sticker with a cat curled up in the crescent of the moon, smiling. She will not trade it for anything, for I brought it to her when I returned from one of my trips from M.D. Anderson. Allyson is my sun/moon girl, my child whose beauty is enhanced by the faintest or by the brightest force of light, my child who glows like Lord Byron's cousin as the night light of the moon envelops her; my child who comes alive like Keats' Madeline as the moonlight shines through stained glass as it casts its colors, kaleidoscopic, on her; my child who shines like Frost's girls whose long hair is "thrown" "before them" to dry in the sun. She sends out her rays to all around her. I hope for her to glow eternally.

When I found out about my cancer, and when my friends found out, one very dear one wrote a poem to me the day before my surgery. It is as follows:

Yesterday . . . . . .
   Just at that mystical moment
   When day touched night
   Far back in the farthest corner
     of the heavens
   I saw the first star of night

So dim and distant was its light
   That I had to strain to see it

But suddenly as I stared into the sky
   The night darkened
And the light from that small little star
   Lit up that dark, distant corner

And there again like a child
   I stood
   Watching that little star

And in a hushed voice
   I breathed a wish
   On that first bright star
And that wish, my dear friend
   Was wished for you

More like a prayer
   Than a wish it was
   Though to a child
   They are both the same

With a childlike faith
   I bowed my head
   And closed my eyes

And asked the good Father of all
   To be with you in the days and weeks to come
   To be with your doctors when His healing they do
   To keep you safe
   To kiss all your hurts away
And to bring you home safely
   To your three little ones
And to the one with whom your life
   You chose to share

And though this prayer-like wish
   Is simple, yet so sincere it is
   That I know our Heavenly Father
   Has heard each word
   And will hold you close
   And still your fears
   And will make you strong
   And well again

For your goodness has not gone unnoticed
By the One who cares for us all.

Having wished this prayer
    I lifted my head
    And opened my eyes
    To see before me
    A heaven lit with a million stars

And again I am reminded
    That so quick is the work of our Lord
    That our troubles He soothes
    Sometimes before we have time to ask

And as I look into this heaven of light
    No doubt have I
    That just as quickly as day
    Turns into night

This time of illness
    Will speed quickly by

And in years to come
    Will be as dim and distant
    As that faint first star of night.

As always your friend,
Cassie

And indeed He has heard your prayer, my friend. It has given me great comfort in the darkest days, and my life has been enriched because of you, my friend, and what you mean to me. Your prayer has helped in my healing. The illness is dimming, and I am recovering, and I am healing because of the love of people like you, my dear, unselfish, loving friend.

My home is my haven now, my man and my family my joy. As my husband and I completed our sessions together in group therapy, we were asked to render a story of our lives in any manner we chose on paper. Mine took the form of an open book with the pages being the years of my life. The book was opened to pages 37 and 38 (and I wasn't even paying attention to the rules of pagination establishing uneven pages to the right), the critical point in my life, not where cancer had entered my life, but where it had turned it around. I will be 38 in a few days, and for the first time that I know of, I am content. I depicted "Pat" before the cancer experience and "Pat" after it, a woman who was more stable, more self-assured, and much happier. One of my dear friends, Kerry, said it was wonderful to see my beautiful smile again, for she had missed that most about me during my illness.

There is a story of the emergence of the first true rose recorded in a Scottish ballad, "Bonny Barbara Allan," which relates how a young man, Sir John Graeme, fell in love with Barbara Allan, how he inadvertently slighted her which resulted in his being ultimately rejected, and how he died of a broken heart, never making the only connection of his life which really mattered. She died shortly thereafter, also of a broken heart, and they were buried side by side, a rose growing from his heart, a brier from hers. In their deathly intermingling, our rose of today supposedly evolves.

The story is simple, beautiful, yet sad. The tale reveals the thwarting of real love because of an inability to express true feelings which results in sorrow, in pain, in lost love. The literary lesson is clear, though. The emergence of the rose, though bittersweet, becomes an important symbol for those of us who live, for those of us who are able to act now. For the rose is the catalyst, the power, for realizing our objects of desire. We must simply reach for it. It is there waiting for us.

Spenser's "Sonnet 26" sums up the paradoxes of life shown in "Sweet is the rose, but grows upon a briar," and his example of the value of the complex nature of the rose is further explained when he points out that easily-acquired objects are really of little value to most men. "Go for the rose" is his message, for a few scratches, thorns, and bruises are better than nothing at all. In his closing couplet, he sums up one of life's great lessons, explaining that pain must be experienced in order to experience pleasure, that the pleasure/pain paradox is a part of living which men who call themselves "alive" must undergo. The experience will strengthen, the experience will foster hope.

I had come a long way from utter hopelessness to self fulfillment (Indeed, during one of my sessions in psychotherapy, Christine wrote down for me as I expressed it, "You didn't care about living even though you had fought desperately to live."), knowing that "alive" was the central word in my life now. I know that as men thirst for their women, so must the women continue to fill themselves through themselves for those they love, including self. Just as I know my roses will have a banner year this year, I also know that I am blossoming in my being as my cup fills, as my moon becomes fuller and fuller. And it is all because cancer, that unplanned force, saved my life.

Continuation

May 11, 1988

My roses are coming slowly, strongly, surely. This morning, as every morning, I am in the rose bed nurturing the blossoms, touching every bush, removing foliage crinkled by over-spraying, and then standing back in wonder, admiring the power, the force and beauty of each plant, of the green abounding in profusion.

My neighbor hails me across our yards, and he comes over to chat, attracted by the beauty of two of my floribundas, telling me how much he admires their splendor as he leaves for work every day. I reply that I will give him cuttings for his trellis when the time is right, at that preparation time of dormancy which allows the bushes, eventually, to reach their optimum capacity to flourish. Though he is anxious, he understands and agrees. He continues to talk about his late mother's roses, of their beauty. I return to my work, my therapy, and I cut five blossoms, carry them inside the house, place them in a crystal vase on my desk which has been strategically placed so that I have the most wondrous perspective of my rose bed as I write, and contemplate how far my roses have come this growing season.

In the beginning of the year, my husband and I weeded the garden with a vengeance, children pitching in as they gathered two acres of spent leaves and dumped them into the bed after weeds were discarded. The bushes were cut back and fertil-ized, yet the first setback came in the force of an army of worms which seemed to manifest themselves the moment my first buds appeared. We wrestled with the creatures and won, but many buds were damaged. Still, my mother received first blooms for her April 17th birthday, though not as many as I would like to have given her. For me, as a prelude to Mother's Day, husband and children weeded and fertilized the bed again, and today, the evidence of the coming of splendid blossoms is unmistakable.

There are perspectives which exist beyond my rose garden, I realize, as I gaze across my yard, across the road, through the woods, to the world. The great things in life come incremental-ly, gaining a refinement in the process. My husband and I, for example, are refining our home, our family, our relationship, every day. My front porch is a great starting place. Two wrens, mates, used to sleep in the niches of the porch, sometimes together in a space so tiny I wondered how a spider could fling a cobweb across it. Certain nights my husband would say, "It's a one-birder night," or "It's a two-birder night," depending on the activities of the birds or on our own time of retiring. Then a cat came, surreptitiously, like my cancer. She upset the entire existence of the wrens who had by then built a nest in one of my porch ferns and were now nourishing their family. Overnight, they disappeared. It has been a year or so, and today I saw the wren on my swing, tentative, testing the territory. He was unsure. We all are. We all want to establish our niches, our comfortable places in the world. For some, it is easy. Others have had places and positions foisted on them by parents or by circumstance, and at points in their lives they realize that they are pleasing all but themselves. Change is possible. I am working on re-securing my niche in the world. I pray that my husband and children find theirs as they act on their instincts. The journey implies imbalance, imbalance implies challenge, challenge implies risk, and risk implies courage.

My husband gave me, long ago, a message with an etched rose inside it, "More than yesterday, less than tomorrow." An expression of his love for me, it has also become a way of living for all of us, a way of looking at new horizons. We planted two new trees together this year, he built a woodrack for us, and he and our son put up a basketball goal. The tree house, dog yard, and garage need work, but we're getting there. By degrees. By increments.

All of our children were conceived in this home, in this place where the plumbing sometimes creaks, where Momma sometimes burns the roux (an essential paste for cooking certain Southern dishes), where the dog sometimes muddies the porch, and where kids sometimes get sick. This home has also become a retreat, a shelter, a comfort, a place of wellness, a spot of security in an insecure world, for we have built something wonderful here that was not here before we were.

My former students contact me here, leaving notes, calls, letters, gifts. They visit, coming from nearby or from as far away as England. They know where their teacher is. I believe I will always be here, for there is a quiet strength here. My husband and I have talked so long into the night so many times about us, our family, our existence, our identity, that I feel a connection with the depths of the planet based on this spot of earth which family inhabits. Here, my husband and I have gained a second sense in our relationship which results in unspoken acts between us, a sense of mutuality which pervades our deepest human relationship as two people who live, as two people who love. We have also learned that it is all right to step back from life's crises and to re-marshal forces, as long as we do it together. We give each other space, time, and distance. But we give. And we understand. And we know that we are not perfect. We can live with that knowledge. And we are working at our marriage every day. For we are refining our lives.

Favorite Family Photos

My brother, Joe, and myself
with our beloved dog.

Walter with a beloved friend.

New York City, May, 1987.

Our first photo together.

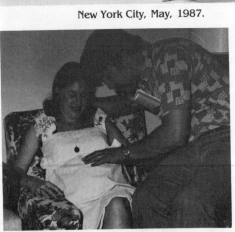

Anticipating our first child.

Kerry O'Casey, Walter, and "T."

One of my favorite pictures
of Walter with the children.

Christmas, 1985.
Alexis (end) found
posing a lot of fun.

1988 rose bed.

Walter George Hingle, Jr.
"Chipper"
June 21, 1977

HEUREUSE FETE DES MERES

MAMAN, JE T'AIME CHIPPER

My Mother's Day card   May 8, 1988
In his own way, Chip gave me roses.

Chip's first deer,
December 23, 1987.

Chip wearing karate shirt.

Chip and Dad at our family baseball park.

First day home from hospital, June, 1977.

Vacation in Houston, 1978.

Allyson Joy Hingle
"Allyce"
May 23, 1979

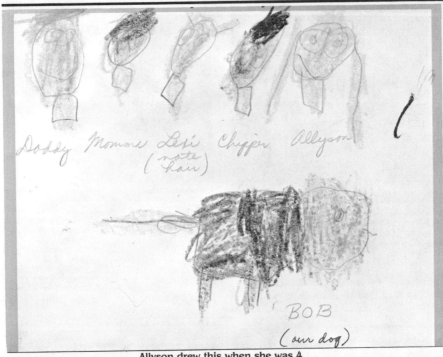

Daddy   Momma   Lesi   Chipper   Allyson
(note hair)

BOB
(our dog)

Allyson drew this when she was 4.

Disneyworld, 1987.

Allyson always had the greatest pigtails.

Allyson was a calm baby.

Swinging, 1987.

With Chip in woods near home.

My Mom and my daughters.

Alexis Judith Hingle
"Lexi"
June 11, 1982

Alexis' favorite animal

Disneyworld, 1987.

Christmas, 1987.

Christmas Eve at midnight mass, 1987.

Walter and
Alexis were
always on the
same wave length.

Disneyworld, 1987.

Home Plates of Ascension, Inc.
P. O. Box 323
Prairieville, Louisiana 70769
(504) 644-7844

Please send:

_____ copies of **A Coming of Roses** @ _____ $8.95

add $2.00 per book postage and handling _____

add 7% tax within B. R. _____

add 4% tax within La. _____

Total Enclosed $ _____

Ship to:

Name _____

Address _____

City & State _____

Zip _____